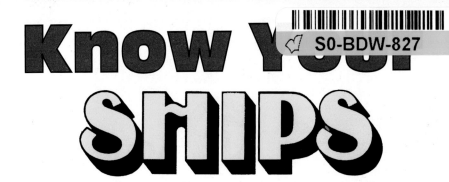

## Guide to Boats & Boatwatching
## Great Lakes & St. Lawrence Seaway

© 2003 – Updated Annually

ISBN: **1-891849-06-9**
ISSN: 0190-5562

# Marine Publishing Co. Inc.

**P.O. Box 68, Sault Ste. Marie, MI 49783**
**(734) 668-4734** – phone & fax

# www.knowyourships.com

**Editor & Publisher**
Roger LeLievre

**Researchers**
Jody Aho, Philip A. Clayton, Matt Miner, Gerry Oudekirk,
Neil Schultheiss, Wade P. Streeter, Franz VonRiedel (tugs),
John Vournakis and George Wharton

**Founder**
Thomas Manse, 1915-1994

**Front cover: Kinsman Independent** passes
under the Blue Water Bridge in 1995. *(Marc Dease)*
**Back cover: Teakglen** upbound in the St. Clair River Oct. 5, 2002,
during her first and only trip under that name. *(Jim Hoffman)*

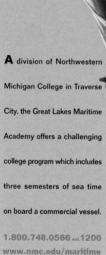

# CONTENTS / '03

**Wilfred Sykes, upbound on Lake Michigan.** *(Roger LeLievre)*

**Philip R. Clarke, as seen from the Sarnia shore.** *(George Wharton)*

Kinsman Independent loads Buffalo-bound grain at the Harvest States Elevator No. 2 in Superior in May 1999.
*(Glenn Blaszkiewicz)*

# KINSMAN INDEPENDENT

By Jody Aho

**Vessel of the Year**

**W**hen the 1952-built steamer **Kinsman Independent** steamed into Buffalo harbor on Dec. 16, 2002, for probably the last time, an era ended.

The vessel was the last straight-decker (non-self-unloader) in service on under the U.S. flag on the Great Lakes and the last engaged in the grain trade to Buffalo, which, before the opening of the present St. Lawrence Seaway, was once a thriving grain trans-shipment center to points east. Future cargos to the General Mills elevator in that port will be carried on self-unloaders. The KI's passing also means the end of the Buffalo "grain-scoopers," longshoremen employed to help unload the once-huge grain-carrying fleet.

Her name is particularly fitting. Many of the largest Great Lakes fleets of the 20th century were formed to serve the specific needs of a single company, such as U.S. Steel, National Steel and Bethlehem Steel. But there were also outside fleets whose interests almost always involved landing contracts with a variety of steel companies. ▶

**Kinsman Independent** started, and appears to be ending her career with independent operations, the kind that have all but disappeared from the Great Lakes.

In 1952, with Great Lakes shipyards busy during the Korean conflict, a facility not usually involved in constructing ore boats – Defoe Shipbuilding Co. of Bay City, Mich., – was awarded a contract from Pioneer Steamship Co., which was managed by the Hutchinson family, for a new vessel, largely based on the "super" class of vessel (**Leon Fraser** and others) built for Pittsburgh Steamship Co. in 1942, but to slightly larger dimensions and with some mechanical and design enhancements.

## The vessel was not destined to set any size or capacity records ...

Hull 422, launched as **Charles L. Hutchinson**, became the flagship of the Pioneer Steamship Co. The vessel was not destined to set any size or capacity records – at 642-feet 3-inches long, she was not even in the top 10 longest lakers when she entered service on Sept. 24, 1952. The **Hutchinson**'s engine had some history behind it: Built by Bethlehem Steel in 1941, it was originally installed in a saltwater vessel, the **Alcoa Prospector**, which was sunk during World War II by enemy action but recovered for scrap. The engine was still suitable for use and was installed in the **Hutchinson**. Never a speedster, the steam turbine powerplant was capable of pushing the vessel at just over 14 miles per hour loaded.

Although similar, the **Hutchinson** had some advantages over the "supers" of a decade earlier. For one, she burned oil. The **Hutchinson** also offered better cubic dimen- ▶

**The Indy takes on one of her last cargos. Grain trimmers work to make sure the cargo is level.** *(Glenn Blaszkiewicz)*

**Ernest R. Breech, at the Soo Locks in the early 1960s (below).** *(Thomas Manse)*

**Breech under the Ford flag in 1987.** *(Roger LeLievre)*

**Charles L. Hutchinson (above) shortly after she was built.** *(Thomas Manse)*

sions in her cargo holds, making her well-suited for coal and grain cargoes when compared to vessels of similar size. This cargo hold design would come into play in extending the vessel's career many years later. More visible to casual observers were the outward features of the **Hutchinson**. The vessel incorporated an enclosed after deckhouse, with cabins built out to the outer hull at the spar deck level, and an additional superstructure on the boat deck level. The after mast was built into the forward side of the stack, a streamlined feature that was a Great Lakes first (not even the prototypical **Wilfred Sykes** of 1949 had this feature) and was subsequently used in the **Edward L. Ryerson** of 1960 and many of the Canadian straight-deckers in the 1960s. The short, streamlined stack, together with a spacious pilothouse forward, gave the vessel a contemporary, one-of-a-kind look that has remained a favorite of boatwatchers. Interestingly, the classic "counter" stern common to most Great Lakes ships built before World War II was retained in the **Hutchinson** at a time when a modified cruiser stern similar to what was used on the **Sykes** was gaining popularity in new ship design on the Lakes. The forward end also included four guest rooms, a lounge, small galley and dining room.

During her first several years, **Charles L. Hutchinson** was a regular visitor to Duluth, loading iron ore for a variety of lower Great Lakes ports. Her status as the largest vessel in any of Hutchinson's fleets (the family also operated the Buckeye Steamship Co.) was eclipsed in July 1961 when the **Pioneer Challenger** joined the Pioneer Steamship Co. Still, the Hutchinson continued in her same role.  ▶

In 1962, the Pioneer Steamship Co. division folded. Most of its vessels were aging, smaller carriers that could not find new homes with other owners and were scrapped shortly after the end of the 1961 season. Some of the fleet's larger vessels were luckier. The new **Pioneer Challenger** went to the Columbia Transportation Div. of Oglebay Norton Co. and was renamed **Middletown**, a name she carries today. The **Charles L. Hutchinson** was bought by the Ford Motor Co. over the winter of 1961-'62 and renamed **Ernest R. Breech**, after a former chairman of the Ford Motor Co. board of directors.

> As the nation entered a recession in the early 1980s, demand for Ford automobiles – at least the larger automobiles popular through most of the 1970s – waned, so the company looked for alternative business for its boats.

With the change in ownership came a change in trade routes. While Duluth and Superior remained frequent loading ports, the Ford Motor Co.'s steel mill on the Rouge River in Dearborn became the usual destination for the **Breech**. The vessel would also make some shorter runs, carrying iron ore from Escanaba or Marquette to the mill, and would also occasionally carry coal. The same general pattern prevailed over the next two decades.

As the nation entered a recession in the early 1980s, demand for Ford automobiles – at least the larger automobiles popular through most of the 1970s – waned, so the company looked for alternative business for its boats. The **Breech**'s sister ship from Defoe Shipbuilding – the **Richard M. Marshall** (which went through two ownership changes earlier in its career and joined the **Breech** in the Ford fleet in 1966 as **John Dykstra**) was engaged in some unusual runs in the early 1980s, including carrying iron ore to Hamilton, Ont., a rare venture for any U.S. laker. The **Breech** had some better options available thanks to her large cubic dimensions that made her suitable for the grain trade. During the early 1980s she carried grain from Duluth and Superior to Buffalo on an increasingly frequent basis. As a non-self-unloader, the long turn-around time at the Rouge River steel mill was becoming a liability, so Ford started looking for ways to turn the iron ore duties over to the more efficient self-unloaders. By the fall of 1984, Ford had purchased the steamers **Walter A. Sterling** and **Edward B. Greene** from Cleveland-Cliffs Steamship Co., which had fallen on hard times in the shipping business earlier in the decade. This move put Ford's largest boat, the **William Clay Ford**, out of service immediately. Her size and speed were competitive, but since she lacked self-unloading gear, her unloading time was too great to be cost effective. **William Clay Ford** and fleetmate **John Dykstra** were sold for scrap in 1986. The **Breech** was saved and would settle into her new role in the grain trade.

Not long after, and even with two newly purchased self-unloaders, it become apparent to Ford that it might be better off leaving the Great Lakes shipping industry entirely, hiring other companies to carry its raw materials. Ford certainly didn't anticipate long-term benefit from remaining in the grain trade. At the same time, one of the oldest independent operators on the Great Lakes – George Steinbrenner's Kinsman Lines – was looking to update its fleet. It only seemed natural that she would make a better fit there, as her days of primarily carrying iron ore were over. As a relative youngster at age 35, the vessel still had many solid years of service ahead. The rumor mill about a possible sale was active in 1987, and early in 1988 the sale was confirmed. The **Breech** would ▶

become the new **Kinsman Independent**, and an older vessel of the same name would be sold overseas for scrap.

During the early summer of 1988, the new **Kinsman Independent** received the red hull of Kinsman Lines, returning her color scheme to the one she carried in her Hutchinson days. The vessel sailed on its maiden voyage for Kinsman in late June, settling quickly into her typical Duluth-Superior to Buffalo run. The vessel would make occasional departures from this routine, most notably visiting Thunder Bay to load. The most serious accident to befall the vessel during her career took place on one of those Thunder Bay runs on Nov. 24, 1990. While the normal route from eastern Lake Superior into Thunder Bay involves going around the eastern side of 44-mile long Isle Royale, the **Kinsman Independent** wound up miles off course and ran hard aground off the middle of Isle Royale in darkness early that cold November Saturday morning. The damage ran into the millions, and the vessel had to be towed into Thunder Bay for repair. While it was rumored that her career might be over, **Independent** was repaired over the winter of 1990-'91 and resumed service.

During the 1990s, the grain trade for U.S. straight-deckers continued its decline. Interlake Steamship Co.'s **J. L. Mauthe** was laid up on July 5, 1993, after spending most of the previous decade on a similar grain run. Even Kinsman's business declined sufficiently so that by the end of the 1995 season, the fleet's other vessel, the **Kinsman Enterprise**, became excess capacity (she was towed away for scrap in 2002). With further declines in business, the **Kinsman Independent** soon found herself with summers off, sailing only during the spring and fall grain rushes. Gone were the days where an occasional iron ore load might keep her busy during slow times in the grain business.

Fueling the rumor that **Kinsman Independent**'s days were numbered was news that the grain elevator in Buffalo, where the **Independent** docked, was due to be fitted with a hopper to receive grain from self-unloaders, making the labor-intensive unloading process used by the **Kinsman Independent** obsolete. The hopper was installed and successfully used during the 2002 season.

**Kinsman Independent** tied at Buffalo with a storage cargo during the winter of 2002-'03, with no word yet as to what her future holds.

**Kinsman Independent in winter lay-up at Buffalo.**
*(Brian Wroblewski)*

**Kinsman Independent inbound at Duluth.** *(Cy Woodard)*

## Fleets & Vessels

The 1983-built, ocean-lakes bulk carriers **Fraser** and **MacKenzie** were bought by Canada Steamship Lines from FedNav Ltd. and renamed **Spruceglen** and **Birchglen** in late 2002. The pair were built for the well-known Misener fleet, which went out of business in 1991.

N.M. Paterson & Sons left the shipping business in 2002, selling its three operating vessels to Canada Steamship Lines. **Paterson** was renamed **Pineglen**, **Cartierdoc** was renamed **Cedarglen** and **Mantadoc** was rechristened **Teakglen**.

Canada Steamship Lines' **Atlantic Huron**, built in 1984, was widened by 3 feet during the winter of 2002-'03 at Port Weller Drydocks. Her new breadth is 78 feet. A similar job was performed last winter on ULS Group's **Canadian Century**, which returned to service in 2002 under the name **John D. Leitch**.

**John D. Leitch on christening day.**
*(Jimmy Sprunt)*

**Bluewing** and **Greenwing**, the first two of a planned six vessels built in China for Great Lakes-saltwater service, made their first trips in 2002. Both are operated by Canfornav, Montreal. Look for the other new vessels to pass our way in 2003.

FedNav Ltd.'s newest two bulk carriers, **Federal Elbe** and **Federal Leda**, are expected to make their first trips to the Great Lakes this season.

▶ **Bluewing on her maiden voyage to Lake Superior.** *(Roger LeLievre)*

**Pineglen is the former Paterson.** *(Roger LeLievre)*

**Quedoc scrap tow leaves Thunder Bay in 2002.** *(Rob Farrow)*

# Scrapyard

The demolition of surplus vessels picked up the pace in 2002 with torches beginning their work on **Vandoc** (N.M. Paterson & Sons) at Sault Ste. Marie; **Algogulf** (Algoma Central) and **Comeaudoc** (N.M. Paterson & Sons) at Port Colborne; and **Canadian Voyager** (ULS

Group), **Manitoulin** (Canada Steamship Lines) and **Algoriver** (Algoma Central) at overseas ports. In line for scrapping in 2003 are **Quedoc** (N.M. Paterson & Sons), **Kinsman Enterprise** (Great Lakes Associates), and **Canadian Venture** (ULS Group). And, although they all sailed in 2002, **Canadian Provider**, **Algosound**, **Kinsman Independent**, **Canadian Mariner**, **Oakglen** and **Mapleglen** may all be nearing the end of the line. ▶

**Comeaudoc, upbound in the St. Marys River in 1972.** *(Thomas Manse)*

**Algoriver in December 1998. She's now being scrapped in Turkey.** *(Roger LeLievre)*

Algogulf, in tow of the tug Progress, heads through the Welland Canal for the last time May 26, 2002. *(Roger LeLievre, top)*

Three days later, tugs help Kinsman Enterprise to the scrapyard. *(Brad Jollife, left)*

The Enterprise is moored next to the partially-demolished forebody of the Louis R. Desmarais at Port Colborne, Ont. *(Roger LeLievre, below)*

# Casualties

The **Canadian Prospector** and the saltwater visitor **Stellanova** hit almost head-on last Oct. 12 near the Cote St. Catherine Lock in the St. Lawrence Seaway, sending both vessels to shipyards for repairs. ... **Algowood** missed a turn in morning fog at Sault Ste. Marie on April 15, 2002 and fetched up on the rocks at Mission Point, a popular place for boatwatchers. She returned to service later in the season.

**Blunted bow of the Canadian Prospector shortly after its 2002 collision.** *(Jimmy Sprunt)*

# Lay-up Log

**Joseph H. Frantz** spent 2002 tied up at Toledo, as did **Richard Reiss** at Erie. ... **Edward L. Ryerson** continued its lay-up at Sturgeon Bay, but proved quite popular to visitors during two open houses in 2002. ... **John Sherwin**'s near-record sidelineing – now in its 22nd year – continued at Superior, with fleetmate **Elton Hoyt 2nd**, laid up the past two seasons, tied next door for company. ... **Algoisle** and **Seaway Queen** remain idle at Toronto, **Algontario** is still benched at Thunder Bay and **Canadian Ranger** is now being used for grain storage at Trois-Rivières, Quebec. ... **Teakglen**, which made only one powered trip in 2002 under that name, is providing similar service at Goderich with **Willowglen**, although **Teakglen** could see future operation if conditions warrant. ... No longer active but in use in a storage capacity for powdered cement are **J.B. Ford** (Superior), **E.M. Ford** (Saginaw), **Lewis G. Harriman** and **S.T. Crapo** (Green Bay) and **CTC #1** (South Chicago). ... The carferry **Spartan** remains in idleness at Ludington, with the abandoned ferry **Arthur K. Atkinso**n tied up alongside. ... The ferry **Viking** left its long-term lay-up at Erie at the end of 2002, bound for a new job as a pulpwood barge. ... **L.E. Block** is still rusting away at an Escanaba dock.

**Visitors tour the idle steamer Edward L. Ryerson at Sturgeon Bay in 2002.** *(Roger LeLievre)*

**Hybrid vessel Canadian Transfer in the Saginaw River.** *(Ryan Kenny)*

# MARINE MILESTONES

**5 Years
1998** / **Canadian Transfer** enters service for Upper Lakes Group. Using the bow section of **Hamilton Transfer** (ex-**Crispin Oglebay**) and the stern section of the **Canadian Explorer**, this unique vessel has one of the more involved stories of conversion, reconstruction and lengthening of any in Great Lakes history. ... Enerchem Transport, Inc., which entered the tanker business after acquiring the former Halco, Inc. tankers in 1987, ceases operations as its remaining vessels are sold to Algoma Tankers. Continuing the pattern of the last two decades, the popular **Edward L. Ryerson** enters another long-term lay up at the end of the season. She has not sailed since.

**10 Years
1993** / The **Irvin L. Clymer**, the last coal-burner that sailed for USS. Great Lakes Fleet, is sold for scrap after three years of inactivity. ... Regulatory changes affecting all of the major lock systems in the Great Lakes are announced. March 25 through Jan. 15 is established as the permanent operating season for the Soo Locks. The maximum allowable draft through the Welland Canal and St. Lawrence Seaway locks is increased to 26' 3", a change of three inches over the previous limit.

**Halifax was launched 40 years ago this year.** *(A.F. Sagon-King)*

**20 Years / 1983**

The continued downturn in the steel industry ends the careers of several more Great Lakes vessels. **George M. Humphrey** sails for the last time, while the **John Hulst** and **Horace Johnson** are on their way to the scrapyard after an extended lay up. Things look a bit more optimistic on the Canadian side of the Lakes, as several new lakers enter service. **John B. Aird** joins the Algoma Central fleet in June. Several other vessels built for dual Lakes and ocean service also debut for Canadian fleets this year, including **Canadian Ambassador** (now **Ambassador**), **Canada Marquis** (the new **Birchglen**), **Selkirk Settler** (now **Spruceglen**) and **Saskatchewan Pioneer** (now **Lady Hamilton**).

**25 Years / 1978**

**Harry L. Allen** burns in a Jan. 21-22 fire in Duluth that also consumes the Capitol No. 4 grain elevator. The 68-year old vessel is damaged so badly that she is sold for scrap later that year. ... Partially replacing capacity lost from the **Edmund Fitzgerald** sinking three years earlier, Columbia Transportation Div. of Oglebay Norton Co. acquires the **Ernest T. Weir** from National Steel, soon renaming her **Courtney Burton**. The **Weir** becomes excess capacity in the National Steel fleet when the company's first and only 1,000-footer, **George A. Stinson**, enters service in October.

**40 Years / 1963**

The year is one of the busiest of the St. Lawrence Seaway era for Canadian shipbuilders. Canada Steamship Lines adds three new maximum size (730 foot long by 75 foot wide) straight-deckers, **Murray Bay** (**Canadian Provider**), **Black Bay** (**Canadian Voyager**) and **Baie St. Paul** (**Canadian Pathfinder**, but never sailed under this name), while the Papachristidis and Halco fleets also order new construction in the **Newbrunswicker** (now **Canadian Mariner**) and **Quebecois** and **Frankcliffe Hall** (now **Halifax**), respectively. Mohawk Navigation Co.'s new **Silver Isle** (now **Algoisle**) looks unlike most Great Lakes vessels, with all cabins aft and a distinctive two-tone paint scheme. ▶

**Ernest T. Weir passes Edmund Fitzgerald at Sault Ste. Marie in 1973.** *(Thomas Manse)*
**Inset: Silver Isle was the first modern laker to have all cabins aft.** *(Eric Treece)*

While U.S. fleets are slow to embrace commerce through the new St. Lawrence Seaway system, the Pittsburgh Steamship Div. of U.S. Steel is in its second year of sending its larger vessels to St. Lawrence River ports. **Arthur M. Anderson**, **Cason J. Callaway** and **Philip R. Clarke** participate in the fall grain rush, carrying grain from Toledo and bringing ore back from St. Lawrence River locations. The trio's lengthening in the mid-1970s would prevent any such future Seaway ventures.

Scotiadoc sank 60 years ago after a collision on Lake Superior.
*(Thomas Manse Collection)*

### 50 Years / 1953

Tragedy strikes twice in six weeks in northern Lake Superior. The **Henry Steinbrenner** sinks in a May 11 storm with 17 of her 31 crewmembers. On June 20, the N. M. Paterson & Sons vessel **Scotiadoc** sinks after colliding with the Canada Steamship Lines' **Burlington** in dense fog. ... Shipyards on the U.S. side of the Lakes enjoy a second consecutive busy year. The last four members of the "AAA"-class (**J. L. Mauthe**, **Reserve**, **Armco** and **William Clay Ford**) enter service between April 2 and Aug. 4. Some of the other new additions include **Richard M. Marshall**, **John J. Boland** (now **Saginaw**) and **McKee Sons**, converted from a C-4 ship.

### 60 Years / 1943

The 16 vessels of the "Maritime"-class, built to increase tonnage hauled during World War II, enter service. Seven of the 16 are still with us in some capacity. **Mississagi** and **Cuyahoga** are the former **George A. Sloan** and **J. Burton Ayers**, respectively. The bow of the **Canadian Transfer** began life as the **J.H. Hillman, Jr**. The **Richard Reiss** operated steadily through the 2001 season and sat out the 2002 season. **Willowglen** is the former **Lehigh** and is in grain storage use at Goderich. The hull of **Sewell Avery** is a dock face near the Algoma Steel plant in Sault Ste. Marie, Ont. Finally, the **C.T.C. No. 1**, formerly **Frank Purnell**, later **Steelton** and then **Pioneer**, is used for cement storage in South Chicago. – *Jody Aho*

**Birthday boat Armco turns 50 in 2003.** *(Neil Schultheiss)*

# Vessel Index

**Algoport along the St. Lawrence Seaway.**
*(Alain Gindroz)*

| Vessel Name / Fleet Number | Vessel Name / Fleet Number | Vessel Name / Fleet Number |
|---|---|---|
| Barker, Kaye E. ...........................I-6 | Bremon ...................................IB-1 | Caribou Isle ............................C-4 |
| Barry J. ...................................K-9 | Brenda L. ................................F-6 | Caribou ..................................M-8 |
| Basse-Cote ...........................L-10 | Bristol Bay .............................U-3 | Carl M. .................................M-17 |
| Bavaria ..................................IB-5 | Brochu ....................................F-3 | Carlee Emily............................K-4 |
| Bay Pride ................................T-8 | Buccaneer .....................IW-1, W-1 | Carleton, George N. ..............G-17 |
| Bayfield .................................M-3 | Buckeye ..................................O-3 | Carol Ann ...............................K-9 |
| Bayfield ...............................MU-3 | Buckley ...................................K-8 | Carolina Borealis ..................C-18 |
| Bayship ...................................B-5 | Buckthorn ...............................U-3 | Carroll C. I. ..........................M-14 |
| BBC America .........................IB-5 | Buffalo ..................................A-10 | Cartier, Jacques....................C-23 |
| BBC Brazil .............................IB-5 | Bunyan, Paul ..........................U-2 | Cashin...................................II-1 |
| BBC Canada ..........................IB-5 | Burns Harbor...........................B-9 | Cast Performance ..................IC-1 |
| BBC Chile ..............................IB-5 | Burro .....................................M-7 | Cast Power.............................IC-1 |
| BBC Denmark ........................IB-5 | Burton, Courtney ....................O-3 | Cast Progress .........................IC-1 |
| BBC Finland ..........................IB-5 | Busch, Gregory J......................B-21 | Catharina-C ...........................IC-3 |
| BBC Holland ..........................IB-5 | Busse, Fred A. .......................D-12 | Catherine-Legardeur ..............S-17 |
| BBC Iceland ..........................IB-5 | | Cavalier Grand Fleuve.............C-21 |
| BBC Japan .............................IB-5 | **C** | Cavalier Maxim......................C-21 |
| BBC Norway ..........................IB-5 | | Cavalier Royal.......................C-21 |
| BBC Scotland ........................IB-5 | C. West Pete ..........................B-1 | CEC Blue.................................IG-3 |
| Beaver D. ..............................M-14 | C.T.C. No. 1 .............................H-3 | CEC Faith................................IG-3 |
| Beaver Islander .......................B-7 | C.T.M.A. Vacancier ...................L-9 | CEC Fantasy ...........................IG-3 |
| Beaver State...........................L-4 | Cabot ....................................IC-9 | CEC Force...............................IG-3 |
| Beaver.........................A-14, U-6 | Cadillac ................................S-27 | CEC Future .............................IG-3 |
| Beeghly, Charles M. ...............I-6 | California ..............................G-21 | CEC Hunter ............................IG-3 |
| Bee-Jay ..................................G-5 | Callaway, Cason J...................G-20 | CEC Light ...............................IG-3 |
| Beluga Obsession ..................IB-3 | Callie M.................................M-10 | CEC Vision .............................IG-3 |
| Beluga Performer ..................IB-3 | Calumet .................................L-15 | Cedar.....................................ID-3 |
| Bergon...................................IB-1 | Canadian Argosy ..................M-17 | Cedarglen ...............................C-3 |
| Bernier, J.E. ...........................C-4 | Canadian Empress ..................S-23 | Celebrezze, Anthony J.............C-16 |
| Betsiamites ..........................L-10 | Canadian Enterprise.........U-13, S-6 | Celene....................................IE-3 |
| Betty D ................................D-16 | Canadian Leader ............U-13, S-6 | Cemba....................................D-4 |
| Bide-A-Wee ..........................S-19 | Canadian Mariner ..........U-13, S-6 | CGB-12000 .............................U-3 |
| Bigane, Jos. F. ......................B-10 | Canadian Miner ............U-13, S-6 | CGB-12001 .............................U-3 |
| Billmaier, D.L. .......................U-2 | Canadian Navigator .......U-13, S-6 | Challenge ..............................G-25 |
| Birchglen ...............................C-3 | Canadian Olympic ..........U-13, S-6 | Champion.....................C-8, D-16 |
| Biscayne Bay ..........................U-3 | Canadian Progress...........U-13, S-6 | Chanda Naree ........................IP-5 |
| Bittern ...................................C-4 | Canadian Prospector .......U-13, S-6 | Channel Cat ..........................M-20 |
| Black, Martha L.......................C-4 | Canadian Provider ..........U-13, S-6 | Charlevoix...............................C-9 |
| Block, Joseph L. ......................C-7 | Canadian Ranger ............U-13, S-6 | Charlie E. ................................I-7 |
| Block, L.E. ..............................B-3 | Canadian Sailor..............E-14 | Chebucto ................................C-4 |
| Blough, Roger .......................G-20 | Canadian Transfer ..........U-13, S-6 | Cheraw...................................U-2 |
| Blue Dog ...............................S-15 | Canadian Transport.........U-13, S-6 | Cherokee .....................B-2, L-4 |
| Blue Heron V..........................B-15 | Canadian Venture .....................I-7 | Chiangi Hope ..........................IS-9 |
| Blue Heron ............................U-10 | Canadian..............................M-17 | Chicago II................................C-10 |
| Bluewater...............................U-5 | Canmar Courage .....................IC-1 | Chicago's First Lady ...............M-19 |
| Bluewing ...............................IC-2 | Canmar Fortune ....................IC-1 | Chicago's Little Lady..............M-19 |
| BMI-105 ..................................B-3 | Canmar Glory ........................IC-1 | Chi-Cheemaun........................O-8 |
| Boatman No. 3 .....................M-14 | Canmar Honour ......................IC-1 | Chief Shingwauk ....................L-14 |
| Boatman No. 4 .....................M-14 | Canmar Pride .........................IC-1 | Chief Wawatam .....................P-15 |
| Boatman No. 6 .....................M-14 | Canmar Triumph ....................IC-1 | Chinook................................M-20 |
| Bogdan..................................IN-2 | Canmar Valour .......................IC-1 | Chios Charity .........................IH-3 |
| Bogun, Ivan ...........................IM-4 | Canmar Venture ....................IC-1 | Chios Harmony.......................IH-3 |
| Boland, John J. ......................A-10 | Canmar Victory ......................IC-1 | Chios Pride.............................IH-3 |
| Bonnie B. III .........................M-14 | Cantankerous ........................E-13 | Chios Sailor............................IH-3 |
| Bounty....................................V-1 | Cap Streeter .........................S-15 | Chios Sky ...............................IH-3 |
| Bowes, Bobby .......................D-6 | Cape Hurd...............................C-4 | Chippewa .............................A-14 |
| Boyd, David ..........................G-26 | Cape Roger .............................C-4 | Chippewa ...............................G-9 |
| Boyer, Willis B. ....................MU-22 | Capetan Michalis ...................IU-1 | Chris Ann...............................H-12 |
| Bramble .................................U-3 | Capricorn ..............................IB-1 | Cicero ...................................IC-9 |
| Brandon E. ............................C-19 | Capt. Shepler .......................S-12 | Cinnamon ..............................IC-2 |
| Bray, James M. .......................U-2 | Captain George ......................F-7 | City of Algonac .......................D-1 |
| Bremer Flagge ......................IB-5 | Carey, Emmet J.......................O-7 | City of Milwaukee ...............MU-27 |
| | Caribbean Trader ...................IT-7 | |

# TUGS

**McKeil Marine tug Salvor (above). Alice A. on the drydock at Hamilton in 2002 (right).** *(Both photos: Jeff Cameron)*

**North Carolina breaks ice at Duluth.** *(Glenn Blaszkiewicz)*

**John A. Perry returns from a towing job at Indiana Harbor.** *(Roger LeLievre)*

| Vessel Name / Fleet Number | Vessel Name / Fleet Number | Vessel Name / Fleet Number |
|---|---|---|
| Fairchild ...................................U-2 | Federal Hudson...........................IF-2 | Federal Yoshino..........................IF-6 |
| Fairlane .....................................IJ-5 | Federal Hunter ...........................IF-2 | Federal Yukon ............................IF-2 |
| Fairlift ........................................IJ-5 | Federal Kivalina..........................IF-2 | Felicity.........................................S-12 |
| Fairload......................................IJ-5 | Federal Leda ................................II-3 | Ferbec..........................................C-3 |
| Fairmast.....................................IJ-5 | Federal Maas ...............................IF-2 | Fir...................................................U-3 |
| Faith ...........................................D-15 | Federal Oshima ..........................IF-2 | Flinders, Captain Matthew .....M-11 |
| Falcon, G.W. ..............................L-4 | Federal Polaris ............................IV-3 | Flinterborg..................................IF-3 |
| Famille DuFour II.......................F-1 | Federal Progress ........................IF-2 | Flinterdam...................................IF-3 |
| Famille DuFour ..........................F-1 | Federal Rhine ..............................IF-2 | Flinterdijk....................................IF-3 |
| Federal Agno..............................IW-3 | Federal Rideau.............................IF-2 | Flinterduin ..................................IF-3 |
| Federal Asahi .............................IT-9 | Federal Saguenay.......................IF-2 | Flintereems.................................IF-3 |
| Federal Baffin ............................IF-2 | Federal Schelde..........................IF-2 | Flinterhaven...............................IF-3 |
| Federal Bergen...........................IM-1 | Federal Shimanto ......................IF-6 | Flinterland..................................IF-3 |
| Federal Elbe ...............................II-3 | Federal St. Laurent ....................IF-2 | Flintermaas.................................IF-3 |
| Federal Ems ...............................IA-10 | Federal Venture ..........................IF-2 | Flintermar...................................IF-3 |
| Federal Franklin ........................IF-2 | Federal Welland .........................IF-2 | Flintersky....................................IF-3 |
| Federal Fuji.................................IV-3 | Federal Weser .............................IA-10 | Flinterspirit.................................IF-3 |
| | | Flinterstar ...................................IF-3 |
| | | Flinterzee....................................IF-3 |
| | | Flinterzijl.....................................IF-3 |
| | | Flo-Mac........................................M-14 |
| | | Florida ..........................................G-21 |
| | | Ford, E.M. ....................................I-4 |
| | | Ford, J.B.......................................L-2 |
| | | Forest City ...................................G-28 |
| | | Forney...........................................U-2 |
| | | Fort Dearborn ............................C-12 |
| | | Fort Saint-Jean II.......................C-25 |
| | | Fortuna.........................................IO-3 |
| | | Fourth Coast...............................D-5 |
| | | Fox, Terry .....................................C-4 |
| | | Frantz, Joseph H. .......................O-3 |
| | | Fraser ...........................................MU-14 |
| | | Fraser, Simon..............................C-4 |

**Charles M. Beeghly blows her steam whistle.**

**Buffalo navigates the Rouge River at Detroit.** *(Both photos: Wade P. Streeter)*

Arthur M. Anderson at ACME Steel in S. Chicago Aug. 30, 2002. *(Gary Clark)*

**Saltwater vessel Volmeborg in Lake St. Clair.** *(Gene W. Peterson)*

Algocape upbound with ore from Sept-Iles in the St. Lawrence Seaway. *(Marc Vander Meulen)*

| Vessel Name / Fleet Number | Vessel Name / Fleet Number | Vessel Name / Fleet Number |
|---|---|---|
| Sandviken .......................IV-3 | Shirley Irene ....................K-4 | Stahl, Roger ....................G-2 |
| Santiago .........................IB-5 | Shirley Joy .......................L-4 | Star of Chicago .............S-15 |
| Sarah No. 1 ......................T-2 | Shoreline II.....................S-15 | Star of Saugatuck.........S-28 |
| Saturn.............................A-6 | Showboat Mardi Gras .....H-8 | State of Michigan..........G-23 |
| Sault au Cochon............M-14 | Showboat Royal Grace ...M-11 | STC 2004 .......................B-11 |
| Sauniere ..........................A-6 | Sideracrux ......................IS-8 | Ste. Claire ...................MU-30 |
| Savard, Felix-Antoine .....S-17 | Siderpollux.....................IS-8 | Steelhead .....................M-20 |
| Savard, Joseph................S-17 | Silversides ...................MU-11 | Stefania I .......................IF-5 |
| Sawmill Explorer .............S-2 | Simcoe ............................C-4 | Stella Borealis...............C-18 |
| Scan Arctic....................IS-2 | Simonsen .......................U-2 | Stellamare.....................IJ-5 |
| Scan Atlantic.................IS-2 | Simpson, Miss Kim .........T-12 | Stellanova .....................IJ-5 |
| Scan Bothnia.................IS-2 | Singelgracht ................IS-12 | Stellaprima ...................IJ-5 |
| Scan Finlandia ..............IS-2 | Sioux.............................L-4 | Still Watch.....................T-4 |
| Scan Germania ..............IS-2 | Sirri..............................IF-4 | Stinson, George A........A-10 |
| Scan Hansa ...................IS-2 | Siscowet .......................U-4 | Stokmarnes....................II-1 |
| Scan Oceanic ................IS-2 | Skagen ..........................IR-1 | Stolt Accord .................IS-13 |
| Scan Pacific...................IS-2 | Skyline Princess............M-19 | Stolt Alliance................IS-13 |
| Scan Partner .................IS-2 | Skyline Queen...............M-19 | Stolt Aspiration.............IS-13 |
| Scan Polaris ..................IS-2 | Slotergracht ................IS-12 | Stolt Kent .....................IS-13 |
| Scandrett, Fred ............T-11 | Sluisgracht ...................IS-12 | Stolt Taurus ..................IS-13 |
| Scheldegracht ..............IS-12 | Smallwood, Jos. & Clara...M-8 | Stolt Titan ....................IS-13 |
| Schippersgracht ...........IS-12 | Smith, Dean R...............M-10 | Stormont ......................M-14 |
| Schlaeger, Victor L. ......C-11 | Smith, F.C.G....................C-4 | Straits Express..............A-14 |
| Schwartz, H.J.................U-2 | Smith, H.A......................H-9 | Straits of Mackinac II .......A-14 |
| Scow 50.........................A-11 | Smith, L.L. Jr..................U-12 | Strange Attractor............IO-1 |
| Sea Bear ........................S-5 | Snoekgracht ...............IS-12 | Strekalovskiy, Mikhail ......IM-4 |
| Sea Castle ......................I-7 | Solymar ........................IH-4 | Strelkov, Petr ................IN-5 |
| Sea Chief........................B-3 | Soo River Belle ..............N-9 | Sturgeon .......................U-4 |
| Sea Colt .........................S-5 | Sora ..............................C-4 | Sugar Islander ...............E-2 |
| Sea Eagle II ...................B-14 | Sotka ............................IF-4 | Sule, Gustav ..................IE-5 |
| Sea Eagle .......................S-5 | Soulanges .....................C-14 | Sullivan, Denis ..............P-6 |
| Sea Fox II.......................S-4 | South Bass ....................M-22 | Sullivans (The)..............MU-2 |
| Sea Queen II ................A-13 | South Carolina..............G-21 | Sundew .........................U-3 |
| Sea-Born .......................S-1 | South Channel ..............C-8 | Sunliner .......................W-4 |
| Seaflight 1 ...................G-14 | South Shore ..................S-15 | Sunny Blossom ..............IL-1 |
| Seaflight II ...................G-14 | South Trader ..................IT-7 | Superior .......................G-21 |
| Seaguardian II...............IT-3 | Southdown Challenger ......H-3 | Suriot IV........................C-25 |
| Seahound ......................N-1 | Southdown Conquest........H-3 | Susan E. .........................H-3 |
| Sealink ..........................IT-3 | Spaarnegracht ..............IS-12 | Susan L. .........................S-7 |
| Sealuck ..........................IT-3 | Spar Garnet ..................IS-11 | Susan Michelle...............D-2 |
| Seaway Queen ........U-13, S-6 | Spar Jade .......................IS-11 | Susanin, Ivan .................IM-4 |
| Segwun .........................M-27 | Spar Opal ......................IS-11 | Sverdlov, Jakov ..............IP-7 |
| Selvick, Bonnie G. ...........T-1 | Spar Ruby ......................IS-11 | Swallow .........................IB-1 |
| Selvick, Carla Anne ..........S-7 | Spartan ..........................L-3 | Swan .............................IB-1 |
| Selvick, John M................C-2 | Speer, Edgar B. ...............G-20 | Swing............................IB-1 |
| Selvick, Kimberly.............D-12 | Spence, John .................M-14 | Sykes, Wilfred.................C-7 |
| Selvick, Sharon M............S-7 | Spencer, Sarah ..............G-27 | Sylvia ...........................IC-14 |
| Selvick, William C. ..........S-7 | Spiegelgracht ..............IS-12 | |
| Seneca ..........................Z-1 | Spirit Trader ...................IT-7 | **T** |
| Serindipity Princess ......P-3 | Spray ............................C-4 | |
| Seven Sisters ...............H-11 | Spring Laker ..................IS-7 | Tandem .........................C-21 |
| Sevilla Wave .................IT-1 | Spruceglen ....................C-3 | Tavi..............................IF-4 |
| Shamrock ......................J-5 | Spuds ...........................R-5 | Tawas Bay .....................U-2 |
| Shannon 66-5 ...............T-5 | Spuigracht ...................IS-12 | Taxideftis ......................IS-1 |
| Shannon.......................G-2 | Spume ...........................C-4 | Teakglen .......................C-3 |
| Shark.............................C-4 | St. Clair ................A-10, M-14 | Tecam Sea .....................IE-2 |
| Sharon Jon....................S-16 | St. John, J.S. ....................O-3 | Techno Venture .............M-14 |
| Sheila P.........................P-15 | St. Laurent, Louis.............C-4 | Tecumseh II ...................P-15 |
| Shelia Ann....................IC-15 | St. Mary's Cement ...........B-13 | Teleost ..........................C-4 |
| Sherwin, John.................I-6 | St. Mary's Cement II..........B-14 | Templeman, Wilfred ........C-4 |
| Shipka ..........................IN-2 | St. Mary's Cement III.........B-14 | Tennessee .....................G-21 |
| Shipsands......................T-12 | Stadacona ....................IC-15 | Terry S. ..........................N-1 |
| | | Texas ...........................G-21 |

# GREAT LAKES GLOSSARY

**AAA CLASS** – Vessel design popular on the Great Lakes in the early 1950s. Arthur M. Anderson is one example.

**AFT** – Toward the back, or stern, of a ship.

**AHEAD** – Forward.

**AMIDSHIPS** – The middle point of a vessel, referring to either length or width.

**ARTICULATED TUG-BARGE (ATB)** – Tug-barge combination. The two vessels are mechanically linked in one axis, but with the tug free to move, or articulate, on another axis. Jacklyn M / Integrity is one example.

**BACKHAUL** – The practice of carrying a revenue-producing cargo (rather than ballast) on a return trip from hauling a primary cargo.

**BARGE** – Vessel with no engine, either pushed or pulled by a tug.

**BEAM** – The width of a vessel measured at the widest point.

**BILGE** – Lowest part of a hold or compartment, generally where the rounded side of a ship curves from the keel to the vertical sides.

**BOW** – Front of a vessel.

**BOWTHRUSTER** – Propeller mounted transversely in a vessel's bow under the waterline to assist in moving sideways. A sternthruster may also be installed.

**BRIDGE** – The platform above the main deck from which a ship is steered / navigated. Also: PILOTHOUSE or WHEELHOUSE.

**BULKHEAD** – Wall or partition that separates rooms, holds or tanks within a ship's hull.

**BULWARK** – The part of the ship that extends fore and aft above the main deck to form a rail.

**DATUM** – Level of water in a given area, determined by an average over time.

**DEADWEIGHT TONNAGE** – The actual carrying capacity of a vessel, equal to the difference between the light displacement tonnage and the heavy displacement tonnage, expressed in long tons (2,240 pounds or 1,016.1 kg).

**DISPLACEMENT TONNAGE** – The actual weight of the vessel and everything aboard her, measured in long tons. The displacement is equal to the weight of the water displaced by the vessel. Displacement tonnage may be qualified as light, indicating the weight of the vessel without cargo, fuels, stores; or heavy, indicating the weight of the vessel loaded with cargo, fuel and stores.

**DRAFT** – The depth of water a ship needs to float. Also the distance from keel to waterline.

**FIT-OUT** – The process of preparing a vessel for service after a period of inactivity.

**FIVE-YEAR INSPECTION** – U.S. Coast Guard survey, conducted in a drydock every five years, of a vessel's hull, machinery and other components.

**FLATBACK** – Lakes' slang for a non self-unloader.

**FOOTER** – Lakes' slang for 1,000-foot vessel.

**FORECASTLE** – (FOHK s'l) Area at the forward part of the ship and beneath the main cabins, often used for crew's quarters or storage.

**FOREPEAK** – The space below the forecastle.

**FORWARD** – Toward the front, or bow, of a ship.

**FREEBOARD** – The distance from the waterline to the main deck.

**GROSS TONNAGE** – The internal space of a vessel, measured in units of 100 cubic feet (2.83 cubic meters) = a gross ton.

**HATCH** – An opening in the deck through which cargo is lowered or raised. A hatch is closed by securing a hatch cover over it.

**HULL** – The body of a ship, not including its superstructure, masts or machinery.

**INTEGRATED TUG-BARGE (ITB)** – Tug-barge combination in which the tug is rigidly mated to the barge. Presque Isle is one example.

**IRON DECKHAND** – Mechanical device that runs on rails on a vessel's main deck and is used to remove and replace hatch covers.

**JONES ACT** – U.S. cabotage law that mandates cargos moved between American ports to be carried by U.S.-flagged, U.S.-built and U.S.-crewed vessels.

**KEEL** – A ship's steel backbone. It runs along the lowest part of the hull.

**LAID UP** – Out of service.

**MARITIME CLASS** – Style of lake vessel built during World War II as part of the nation's war effort. Richard Reiss is one example.

**NET REGISTERED TONNAGE** – The internal capacity of a vessel available for carrying cargo. It does not include the space occupied by boilers, engines, shaft alleys, chain lockers, officers' and crew's quarters. Net registered tonnage is usually referred to as registered tonnage or net tonnage and is used to figure taxes, tolls and port charges.

**RIVER-CLASS SELF-UNLOADER** – Group of vessels built in the 1970s to service smaller ports and negotiate narrow rivers such as Cleveland's Cuyahoga. David Z. Norton is one example.

**SELF-UNLOADER** – Vessel able to discharge its own cargo using a system of conveyor belts and a moveable boom.

**SLAG** – By-product of the steelmaking process which is later ground and used for paving roads.

**STEM** – The extreme forward end of the bow.

**STEMWINDER** – Vessel with all cabins aft.

**STERN** – The back of the ship.

**STRAIGHT-DECKER** – A non-self-unloading vessel. Edward L. Ryerson is one example.

**TACONITE** – Processed, pelletized iron ore. Easy to load and unload, this is the primary method of shipping ore on the Great Lakes and St. Lawrence Seaway. Also: PELLETS

**TRACTOR TUG** – Highly maneuverable tug propelled by either a Z-drive or cycloidal system rather than the traditional screw propeller.

# Great Lakes & Seaway Fleets

**Paul H. Townsend arrives at Muskegon.** *(David Swain)*

# GREAT LAKES / SEAWAY FLEETS

Listed after each vessel in order are: Type of Vessel, Year Built, Type of Engine, Maximum Cargo Capacity (at mid-summer draft in long tons) or Gross Tonnage* (tanker capacities are listed in barrels), Overall Length, Breadth and Depth (from the top of the keel to the top of the upper deck beam) or Draft*. The figures given are as accurate as possible and are given for informational purposes only. Vessels and owners are listed alphabetically as per American Bureau of Shipping and Lloyd's Register of Shipping format. Former names of vessels and years of operation under former names appear beneath the vessel's name. A number in brackets following a vessel's name indicates how many vessles, including the one listed, have carried that name.

## KEY TO TYPE OF VESSEL

| | | |
|---|---|---|
| **2B**..........................................Brigantine | **DR**......................................................Dredge | **ITB** ..................Integrated Tug/Barge |
| **2S**......................2 Masted Schooner | **DS**.......................................Spud Barge | **PA**...........................Passenger Vessel |
| **3S**......................3 Masted Schooner | **DV**................................Drilling Vessel | **PB** .........................................Pilot Boat |
| **4S**......................4 Masted Schooner | **DW**..................................................Scow | **PF** ...........................Passenger Ferry |
| **AC**.................................Auto Carrier | **ES**..............................Excursion Ship | **PK** .........................Package Freighter |
| **AT**..............................Articulated Tug | **EV** .......................Env. Response Ship | **RR** ................................Roll On/Roll Off |
| **ATB**...............Articulated Tug/Barge | **FB**.....................................................Fire Boat | **RT** ...........................Refueling Tanker |
| **BB**...............................................Bum Boat | **FD**.........................Floating Dry Dock | **RV** ...........................Research Vessel |
| **BC** ......................................Bulk Carrier | **FT**...........................................Fishing Tug | **SB** ...........................................Supply Boat |
| **BK** ......................Bulk Carrier/Tanker | **GA**.....................Gambling Casino | **SC**.....................................Sand Carrier |
| **BT**.....................................Buoy Tender | **GC**.................................General Cargo | **SR** ...........................Search & Rescue |
| **CC** .............................Cement Carrier | **GL**.............................................Gate Lifter | **SU** ...............................Self-unloader |
| **CF**...................................................Car Ferry | **GR**.........................Grocery Launch | **SV**...................................Survey Vessel |
| **CO**...............................Container Vessel | **GU** .....................Grain Self Unloader | **TB** .................................................Tug Boat |
| **CS**...................................Crane Ship | **HL** ...........................Heavy Lift Vessel | **TF** .....................................Train Ferry |
| **DB**...................................Deck Barge | **HY** .............................................Hydrofoil | **TK**.........................................Tanket |
| **DD**...................................Destroyer | **IB**.......................................Ice Breaker | **TT**...........................Tractor Tug Boat |
| **DH** ...............................Hopper Barge | **IT**.................................Integrated Tug | **TV**...............................Training Vessel |

## KEY TO PROPULSION

| | |
|---|---|
| **B**............................................................Barge | **S** ..............................Steam - Skinner "Unaflow" Engine |
| **D**..........................................................Diesel | **T**..................................Steam - Turbine Engine |
| **Q**.....................Steam - Quad Exp. Compound Engine | **U**.............Steam - Uniflow Engine - "Skinner" Design |
| **R**...................Steam - Triple Exp. Compound Engine | **W** ......................................Sailing Vessel (Wind) |

| Fleet #. | Fleet Name<br>Vessel Name | Type of<br>Vessel | Year<br>Built | Type of<br>Engine | Cargo Cap.<br>or Gross* | Overall<br>Length | Breadth | Depth or<br>Draft* |
|---|---|---|---|---|---|---|---|---|
| **A-1** | **A & L MARINE, INC., ST. JOSEPH, MI** | | | | | | | |
| | Margaret M. | TB | 1956 | D | 167* | 89' 06" | 24' 00" | 10' 00" |
| | *(Shuttler '56 - '60, Margaret M. Hannah '60 - '84)* | | | | | | | |
| **A-2** | **A .B. M. MARINE, THUNDER BAY, ON** | | | | | | | |
| | McAllister 132 | DB | 1954 | B | 7,000 | 343' 00" | 63' 00" | 19' 00" |
| | *(Powell No. 1 '54 - '61, Alberni Carrier '61 - '77, Genmar 132 '77 - '79)* | | | | | | | |
| | Radium Yellowknife | TB | 1948 | D | 235* | 120' 00" | 28' 00" | 6' 06" |
| | W. N. Twolan | TB | 1962 | D | 299* | 106' 00" | 29' 05" | 15' 00" |
| | Fleet also includes the 150' derrick barges Radium 603, Radium 604, Radium 607, Radium 610, Radium 611, Radium 617, Radium 623, Radium 625 and Radium 631) | | | | | | | |
| **A-3** | **ACHESON VENTURES LLC, PORT HURON, MI** | | | | | | | |
| | Highlander Sea | ES/2S | 1927 | W | 140* | 154' 00" | 25' 06" | 14' 00" |
| **A-4** | **ACME MARINE SERVICE, DULUTH, MN** | | | | | | | |
| | Dona | GR | 1929 | D | 10* | 35' 00" | 9' 00" | 4' 06" |
| | Marine Trader | BB | 1939 | D | 60* | 65' 00" | 15' 00" | 7' 06" |
| | Oatka | TB | 1934 | D | 10* | 40' 00" | 10' 00" | 4' 06" |

| Fleet #. | Fleet Name / Vessel Name | Type of Vessel | Year Built | Type of Engine | Cargo Cap. or Gross* | Overall Length | Breadth | Depth or Draft* |
|---|---|---|---|---|---|---|---|---|
| **A-5** | **ALCAN ALUMINUM LTD., PORT ALFRED, QC** | | | | | | | |
| | Alexis-Simard | TT | 1980 | D | 286* | 92' 00" | 34' 00" | 13' 07" |
| | Grande Baie | TT | 1972 | D | 194* | 86' 06" | 30' 00" | 12' 00" |
| **A-6** | **ALGOMA CENTRAL CORP., SAULT STE. MARIE, ON** | | | | | | | |

*ALGOMA CENTRAL MARINE GROUP, ST. CATHARINES, ON - DIV. OF ALGOMA CENTRAL CORP.*
\* *INDICATES VESSELS OPERATED BY SEAWAY MARINE TRANSPORT, ST. CATHARINES, ON*
*A PARTNERSHIP BETWEEN ALGOMA CENTRAL CORP. AND UPPER LAKES GROUP, INC.*

| | Vessel Name | Type of Vessel | Year Built | Type of Engine | Cargo Cap. or Gross* | Overall Length | Breadth | Depth or Draft* |
|---|---|---|---|---|---|---|---|---|
| | Agawa Canyon* | SU | 1970 | D | 23,400 | 647' 00" | 72' 00" | 40' 00" |
| | Algobay* | SU | 1978 | D | 34,900 | 730' 00" | 75' 10" | 46' 06" |
| | *(Algobay '78 - '94, Atlantic Trader '94 - '97)* | | | | | | | |
| | Algocape* {2} | BC | 1967 | D | 29,950 | 729' 09" | 75' 04" | 39' 08" |
| | *(Richelieu {3} '67 - '94)* | | | | | | | |
| | Algocen* {2} | BC | 1968 | D | 28,400 | 730' 00" | 75' 03" | 39' 08" |
| | Algoisle* | BC | 1963 | D | 26,700 | 730' 00" | 75' 05" | 39' 03" |
| | *(Silver Isle '63 - '94) (Last operated Dec. 21, 1999. Laid up at Toronto, ON.)* | | | | | | | |
| | Algolake* | SU | 1977 | D | 32,150 | 730' 00" | 75' 06" | 46' 06" |
| | Algomarine* | SU | 1968 | D | 27,000 | 729' 10" | 75' 04" | 39' 08" |
| | *(Lake Manitoba '68 - '87) (Converted to a self-unloader - '89)* | | | | | | | |
| | Algonorth* | BC | 1971 | D | 28,000 | 729' 11" | 75' 02" | 42' 11" |
| | *(Temple Bar '71 - '76, Lake Nipigon '76 - '84, Laketon {2} '84 - '86, Lake Nipigon '86 - '87)* | | | | | | | |
| | Algontario* | BC | 1960 | D | 29,100 | 730' 00" | 75' 09" | 40' 02" |
| | *([Fore Section] Cartiercliffe Hall '76 - '88, Winnipeg {2} '88 - '94; [Stern Section] Ruhr Ore '60 - '76)* | | | | | | | |
| | *(Last operated April 13, 1999 – 5 year survey expired July 1999. Laid up at Thunder Bay, ON.)* | | | | | | | |
| | Algoport* | SU | 1979 | D | 32,000 | 658' 00" | 75' 10" | 46' 06" |
| | Algorail* {2} | SU | 1968 | D | 23,750 | 640' 05" | 72' 03" | 40' 00" |
| | Algosoo* {2} | SU | 1974 | D | 31,300 | 730' 00" | 75' 05" | 44' 06" |
| | Algosound* | BC | 1965 | T | 27,700 | 730' 00" | 75' 06" | 39' 00" |
| | *(Don-De-Dieu '65 - '67, V. W. Scully '67 - '87)* | | | | | | | |
| | Algosteel* {2} | SU | 1966 | D | 27,000 | 729' 11" | 75' 04" | 39' 08" |
| | *(A. S. Glossbrenner '66 - '87, Algogulf {1} '87 - '90)* | | | | | | | |
| | Algoville* | SU | 1967 | D | 31,250 | 730' 00" | 77' 11" | 39' 08" |
| | *(Senneville '67 - '94) (Widened by 3' - '96)* | | | | | | | |
| | Algoway* {2} | SU | 1972 | D | 24,000 | 650' 00" | 72' 00" | 40' 00" |
| | Algowood* | SU | 1981 | D | 31,750 | 740' 00" | 76' 01" | 46' 06" |
| | Capt. Henry Jackman* | SU | 1981 | D | 30,550 | 730' 00" | 76' 01" | 42' 00" |
| | *(Lake Wabush '81 - '87) (Converted to a self-unloader - '96)* | | | | | | | |
| | John B. Aird* | SU | 1983 | D | 31,300 | 730' 00" | 76' 01" | 46' 06" |
| | Peter R. Cresswell* | SU | 1982 | D | 31,700 | 730' 00" | 76' 01" | 42' 00" |
| | *(Algowest '82 - '01) (Converted to a self-unloader - '98)* | | | | | | | |

*SOCIETE QUEBECOISE D' EXPLORATION MINIERE, SAINTE-FOY, QC - CHARTERER*

| | | | | | | | | |
|---|---|---|---|---|---|---|---|---|
| | Sauniere | SU | 1970 | D | 23,900 | 642' 10" | 74' 10" | 42' 00" |
| | *(Bulknes '70 - '70, Brooknes '70 - '76, Algosea {1} '76 - '82)* | | | | | | | |
| | *(Converted to a self-unloader, lengthened 122' - '76)* | | | | | | | |

*ALGOMA TANKERS LTD., DARTMOUTH, NS - A DIVISION OF ALGOMA CENTRAL CORP.*

| | | | | | | | | |
|---|---|---|---|---|---|---|---|---|
| | Algocatalyst | TK | 1972 | D | 65,325 | 430' 05" | 62' 04" | 34' 05" |
| | *(Jon Ramsoy '72 - '74, Doan Transport '74 - '86, EnerChem Catalyst '86 - '99)* | | | | | | | |
| | Algoeast | TK | 1977 | D | 64,956 | 431' 05" | 65' 07" | 35' 05" |
| | *(Texaco Brave {2} '77 - '86, Le Brave '86 - '97, Imperial St. Lawrence {2} '97 - '97)* | | | | | | | |
| | *(Converted from single-hulled to double-hulled tanker, '00)* | | | | | | | |
| | Algofax | TK | 1969 | D | 120,452 | 485' 05" | 70' 02" | 33' 03" |
| | *(Imperial Bedford '69 - '97)* | | | | | | | |
| | Algonova | TK | 1969 | D | 54,241 | 400' 06" | 54' 02" | 26' 05" |
| | *(Texaco Chief {2} '69 - '87, A. G. Farquharson '87 - '98)* | | | | | | | |
| | Algosar | TK | 1974 | D | 104,333 | 435' 00" | 74' 00" | 32' 00" |
| | *(Imperial St. Clair '74 - '97)* | | | | | | | |

*CLEVELAND TANKERS (1991), INC., CLEVELAND, OH - CHARTERED BY ALGOMA TANKERS LTD.*

| | | | | | | | | |
|---|---|---|---|---|---|---|---|---|
| | Gemini | TK | 1978 | D | 75,298 | 432' 06" | 65' 00" | 29' 04" |
| | Saturn {4} | TK | 1974 | D | 47,030 | 384' 01" | 54' 06" | 25' 00" |

**St. Clair enters Lake Huron from her namesake river.** *(Marc Dease)*

| Fleet #. | Fleet Name / Vessel Name | Type of Vessel | Year Built | Type of Engine | Cargo Cap. or Gross* | Overall Length | Breadth | Depth or Draft* |
|---|---|---|---|---|---|---|---|---|
| **A-7** | **ALLIED SIGNAL, INC., DETROIT, MI** | | | | | | | |
| | Allied Chemical No. 12 | TK | 1969 | B | 1,545 | 200' 01" | 35' 01" | 8' 06"* |
| **A-8** | **ALLOUEZ MARINE SUPPLY, SUPERIOR, WI** | | | | | | | |
| | Allouez Marine | GR | 1948 | D | 9* | 35' 02" | 11' 02" | 3' 06" |
| **A-9** | **AMERICAN MARINE CONSTRUCTION, BENTON HARBOR, MI** | | | | | | | |
| | Alice E | TB | 1944 | T | 146* | 81' 01" | 24' 00" | 9' 10" |
| | AMC 100 | DB | 1979 | B | 2,273 | 200' 00" | 52' 00" | 14' 00" |
| | AMC 200 | DB | 1979 | B | 2,273 | 200' 00" | 36' 00" | 11' 08" |
| | AMC 300 | DB | 1977 | B | 1,048 | 180' 00" | 54' 00" | 12' 00" |
| | Defiance | TB | 1966 | D | 26* | 44' 08" | 18' 00" | 6' 00" |
| **A-10** | **AMERICAN STEAMSHIP CO., WILLIAMSVILLE, NY** | | | | | | | |
| | Adam E. Cornelius {4} | SU | 1973 | D | 28,200 | 680' 00" | 78' 00" | 42' 00" |
| | *(Roger M. Kyes '73 - '89)* | | | | | | | |
| | American Mariner | SU | 1980 | D | 37,200 | 730' 00" | 78' 00" | 45' 00" |
| | *(Laid down as Chicago {3})* | | | | | | | |
| | American Republic | SU | 1981 | D | 24,800 | 634' 10" | 68' 00" | 40' 00" |
| | Buffalo {3} | SU | 1978 | D | 23,800 | 634' 10" | 68' 00" | 40' 00" |
| | H. Lee White {2} | SU | 1974 | D | 35,200 | 704' 00" | 78' 00" | 45' 00" |
| | Indiana Harbor | SU | 1979 | D | 78,850 | 1,000' 00" | 105' 00" | 56' 00" |
| | John J. Boland {4} | SU | 1973 | D | 33,800 | 680' 00" | 78' 00" | 45' 00" |
| | *(Charles E. Wilson '73 - 2000)* | | | | | | | |
| | Sam Laud | SU | 1975 | D | 23,800 | 634' 10" | 68' 00" | 40' 00" |
| | St. Clair {3} | SU | 1976 | D | 44,000 | 770' 00" | 92' 00" | 52' 00" |
| | Walter J. McCarthy Jr. | SU | 1977 | D | 78,850 | 1,000' 00" | 105' 00" | 56' 00" |
| | *(Belle River '77 - '90)* | | | | | | | |
| | ***STINSON, INC., CLEVELAND, OH - VESSEL MANAGED BY AMERICAN STEAMSHIP CO.*** | | | | | | | |
| | George A. Stinson | SU | 1978 | D | 59,700 | 1,004' 00" | 105' 00" | 50' 00" |
| **A-11** | **ANDRIE, INC., MUSKEGON, MI** | | | | | | | |
| | A-390 | TK | 1982 | B | 39,000 | 310' 00" | 60' 00" | 19' 03" |
| | *(Canonie 40 '82 - '92)* | | | | | | | |
| | A-397 | TK | 1962 | B | 39,700 | 270' 00" | 60' 00" | 25' 00" |
| | *(Auntie Mame '62 - '91, Iron Mike '91 - '93)* | | | | | | | |
| | A-410 | TK | 1955 | B | 41,000 | 335' 00" | 54' 00" | 26' 06" |
| | *(Methane '55 - '63, B-6400 '63 - '71, Kelly '71 - '86, Canonie 50 '86 - '93)* | | | | | | | |
| | B-7 | DB | 1976 | B | 1,350 | 165' 00" | 42' 06" | 12' 00" |
| | B-16 | DB | 1976 | B | 1,350 | 165' 00" | 42' 06" | 12' 00" |
| | Barbara Andrie | TB | 1940 | D | 298* | 121' 10" | 29' 06" | 16' 00" |
| | *(Edmond J. Moran '40 - '76)* | | | | | | | |
| | Barbara Rita | TB | 1981 | D | 15* | 36' 00" | 14' 00" | 6' 00" |
| | Candice Andrie | CS | 1958 | B | 1,000 | 150' 00" | 52' 00" | 10' 00" |
| | *(Minnesota {2} '58 - ?)* | | | | | | | |
| | Clara Andrie | DR | 1930 | B | 1,000 | 110' 00" | 30' 00" | 6' 10" |
| | John Joseph | TB | 1993 | D | 15* | 40' 00" | 14' 00" | 5' 00" |
| | John Purves | TB | 1919 | D | 436* | 150' 00" | 27' 07" | 16' 00" |
| | *(Butterfield '19 - '42, U. S. Army Butterfield [LT-145] '42 - '45, Butterfield '45 - '57)* | | | | | | | |
| | Karen Andrie {2} | TB | 1965 | D | 433* | 120' 00" | 31' 06" | 16' 00" |
| | *(Sarah Hays '65 - '93)* | | | | | | | |
| | Mari Beth Andrie | TB | 1961 | D | 147* | 87' 00" | 24' 00" | 11' 06" |
| | *(Gladys Bea '61 - '73, American Viking '73 - '83)* | | | | | | | |
| | Meredith Andrie | DS | 1971 | B | 521* | 140' 00" | 50' 00" | 9' 00" |
| | *(Illinois '71-'02)* | | | | | | | |
| | Rebecca Lynn | TB | 1964 | D | 433* | 120' 00" | 31' 08" | 18' 09" |
| | *(Kathrine Clewis '64 - '96)* | | | | | | | |
| | Robert Purcell | TB | 1952 | D | 28* | 45' 00" | 12' 06" | 7' 09" |
| | Scow 50 | DB | 1977 | B | 2,100 | 180' 00" | 54' 00" | 12' 00" |
| | U-738 | DB | 1981 | B | 2,100 | 180' 00" | 54' 00" | 12' 00" |

| Fleet #. | Fleet Name / Vessel Name | Type of Vessel | Year Built | Type of Engine | Cargo Cap. or Gross* | Overall Length | Breadth | Depth or Draft* |
|---|---|---|---|---|---|---|---|---|
| | **LAFARGE CORP., MUSKEGON, MI - VESSELS MANAGED BY ANDRIE, INC.** | | | | | | | |
| | Integrity | CC | 1996 | B | 14,000 | 460' 00" | 70' 00" | 37' 00" |
| | Jacklyn M. | AT | 1976 | D | 198* | 140' 02" | 40' 01" | 22' 03" |
| | *(Andrew Martin '76 - '90, Robert L. Torres '90 - '94)* | | | | | | | |
| | **[ATB Jacklyn M. / Integrity OA dimensions together]** | | | | | 543' 00" | 70' 00" | 37' 00" |
| A-12 | **APEX OIL CO., GRANITE CITY, IL** | | | | | | | |
| | Apex Chicago | TK | 1981 | B | 35,000 | 288' 00" | 60' 00" | 19' 00" |
| A-13 | **APOSTLE ISLANDS CRUISE SERVICE, BAYFIELD, WI** | | | | | | | |
| | Eagle Island | ES | 1976 | D | 12* | 42' 00" | 14' 00" | 3' 06" |
| | *(Grampa Woo '93 - '96)* | | | | | | | |
| | Island Princess {2} | ES | 1973 | D | 63* | 65' 07" | 20' 05" | 7' 03" |
| | Sea Queen II | ES | 1971 | D | 12* | 42' 00" | 14' 00" | 2' 07" |
| | Zeeto | ES/3S | | W | 35* | 54' 00" | 16' 00" | |
| A-14 | **ARNOLD TRANSIT CO., MACKINAC ISLAND, MI** | | | | | | | |
| | Algomah | PF/PK | 1961 | D | 125 | 93' 00" | 31' 00" | 8' 00" |
| | Beaver | CF | 1952 | D | 87* | 64' 09" | 30' 02" | 8' 00" |
| | Chippewa {6} | PF/PK | 1962 | D | 125 | 93' 00" | 31' 00" | 8' 00" |
| | Corsair | CF | 1955 | D | 98* | 94' 06" | 33' 00" | 8' 06" |
| | Huron {5} | PF/PK | 1955 | D | 80 | 91' 06" | 25' 00" | 10' 01" |
| | Island Express | PC | 1988 | D | 90* | 82' 07" | 28' 06" | 8' 05" |
| | Mackinac Express | PC | 1987 | D | 90* | 82' 07" | 28' 06" | 8' 05" |
| | Mackinac Islander | CF | 1947 | D | 99* | 84' 00" | 30' 00" | 8' 03" |
| | *(Drummond Islander '47-'02)* | | | | | | | |
| | Ottawa {2} | PF/PK | 1959 | D | 125 | 93' 00" | 31' 00" | 8' 00" |
| | Straits Express | PC | 1995 | D | 99* | 101' 00" | 29' 11" | 6' 08" |
| | Straits of Mackinac II | PF/PK | 1969 | D | 89* | 89' 11" | 27' 00" | 8' 08" |
| A-15 | **ATLANTIC TOWING LTD., SAINT JOHN, NB** | | | | | | | |
| | ATL 2301 | DB | 1977 | B | 3,500 | 230' 00" | 60' 00" | 14' 00" |
| | ATL 2302 | DB | 1977 | B | 3,500 | 230' 00" | 60' 00" | 14' 00" |
| | ATL 2401 | DB | 1981 | B | 4,310 | 240' 00" | 70' 00" | 15' 00" |
| | ATL 2402 | DB | 1981 | B | 4,310 | 240' 00" | 70' 00" | 15' 00" |

**Canadian Mariner loads grain at Thunder Bay.** *(Gene Onchulenko)*

| Fleet #. | Fleet Name / Vessel Name | Type of Vessel | Year Built | Type of Engine | Cargo Cap. or Gross* | Overall Length | Breadth | Depth or Draft* |
|---|---|---|---|---|---|---|---|---|
| | Atlantic Beech | TB | 1983 | D | 294* | 104' 02" | 30' 03" | 13' 02" |
| | (Irving Beech '83 - '98) | | | | | | | |
| | Atlantic Birch | TB | 1967 | D | 827* | 162' 03" | 38' 02" | 19' 08" |
| | (Irving Birch '67 - '99) | | | | | | | |
| | Atlantic Eagle | TB | 1999 | D | 3,080* | 247' 06" | 59' 05" | 19' 10" |
| | Atlantic Elm | TB | 1980 | D | 427* | 116' 01" | 31' 06" | 18' 08" |
| | (Irving Elm '80 - '98) | | | | | | | |
| | Atlantic Hawk | TB | 2000 | D | 3,080* | 247' 06" | 59' 05" | 19' 10" |
| | Atlantic Hemlock | TT | 1996 | D | 290* | 101' 00" | 36' 06" | 12' 06" |
| | Atlantic Hickory | TB | 1973 | D | 886* | 153' 06" | 38' 10" | 22' 00" |
| | (Irving Miami '73 - '95) | | | | | | | |
| | Atlantic Kingfisher | TB | 2002 | D | 3,453* | 239' 08" | 59' 00" | 26' 02" |
| | Atlantic Larch | TT | 1999 | D | 392* | 101' 01" | 36' 07" | 17' 01" |
| | Atlantic Maple | TB | 1966 | D | 487* | 125' 08" | 32' 04" | 17' 06" |
| | (Irving Maple '66 - '98) | | | | | | | |
| | Atlantic Oak | TB | 2002 | D | 402* | 94' 04" | 36' 04" | 157' 00" |
| | Atlantic Osprey | TB | 2003 | D | Under Construction | | | |
| | Atlantic Pine | TB | 1976 | D | 159* | 70' 00" | 24' 00" | 7' 08" |
| | (Grampa Shorty '76 - '76, Irving Pine '76 - '98) | | | | | | | |
| | Atlantic Poplar | TB | 1965 | D | 195* | 96' 06" | 30' 00" | 14' 00" |
| | (Amherstburg '65 - '75, Irving Poplar '75 - '96) | | | | | | | |
| | Atlantic Spruce {2} | TT | 1998 | D | 290* | 101' 00" | 36' 06" | 17' 00" |
| | Atlantic Teak | TB | 1976 | D | 265* | 104' 00" | 30' 00" | 14' 03" |
| | (Essar '76 - '79, Irving Teak '79 - '96) | | | | | | | |
| | Atlantic Willow | TT | 1998 | D | 360* | 101' 00" | 36' 06" | 17' 00" |
| | Irving Dolphin | TK | 1964 | B | 1,441 | 200' 00" | 50' 00" | 13' 00" |
| | Irving Juniper | TB | 1961 | D | 247* | 110' 00" | 27' 02" | 13' 03" |
| | (Thorness '61 - '84, Irving Juniper '84 - '98, Atlantic Juniper '98 - '99) | | | | | | | |
| **B-1** | **B & L TUG SERVICE, THESSALON, ON** | | | | | | | |
| | C. West Pete | TB | 1958 | D | 29* | 65' 00" | 17' 05" | 6' 00" |
| | Jodi-Lynn | TB | 1979 | D | 16* | 58' 00" | 16' 05" | 5' 00" |
| **B-2** | **BARGE TRANSPORTATION, INC., DETROIT, MI** | | | | | | | |
| | Cherokee {2} | DB | 1943 | B | 1,200 | 155' 00" | 50' 00" | 13' 06" |
| **B-3** | **BASIC TOWING, INC., ESCANABA, MI** | | | | | | | |
| | BMI-105 | DB | 1999 | B | 1,500 | 200' 00" | 42' 06" | 10' 00" |
| | Danicia | TB | 1944 | D | 382* | 110' 02" | 27' 03" | 15' 07" |
| | (USCGC Chinook [WYT / WYTM-96] '44 - '86, Tracie B '86 - '98) | | | | | | | |
| | Erika Kobasic | TB | 1939 | D | 226* | 110' 00" | 26' 05" | 15' 01" |
| | (USCGC Arundel [WYT / WYTM-90] '39 - '84, Karen Andrie {1} '84 - '90) | | | | | | | |
| | Escort | TB | 1969 | D | 26* | 50' 00" | 13' 00" | 7' 00" |
| | Krystal | TB | 1954 | D | | 45' 00" | 13' 00" | 7' 00" |
| | (Thunder Bay '54-'02) | | | | | | | |
| | L. E. Block | BC | 1927 | T | 15,900 | 621' 00" | 64' 00" | 33' 00" |
| | (Last operated Oct. 31, 1981; Laid up at Escanaba, MI.) | | | | | | | |
| | Sea Chief | TB | 1952 | D | 390* | 107' 00" | 26' 06" | 14' 10" |
| | (U. S. Army LT-1944 '52 - '62, USCOE Washington '62 - 2000) | | | | | | | |
| **B-4** | **BAY CITY BOAT LINE, LLC, BAY CITY, MI** | | | | | | | |
| | Islander {1} | ES | 1946 | D | 39* | 53' 04" | 21' 00" | 5' 05" |
| | Princess Wenonah | ES | 1954 | D | 96* | 64' 09" | 32' 09" | 9' 09" |
| | (William M. Miller '54 - '98) | | | | | | | |
| | West Shore {2} | ES | 1947 | D | 94* | 64' 10" | 30' 00" | 9' 03" |
| **B-5** | **BAY SHIPBUILDING CO., STURGEON BAY, WI** | | | | | | | |
| | Bayship | TB | 1943 | D | 19* | 45' 00" | 12' 06" | 6' 00" |
| **B-6** | **BAYSAIL, BAY CITY, MI** | | | | | | | |
| | Appledore | 2S/ES | 1989 | W | | 85' 00" | 19' 00" | 9' 00"* |

| Fleet #. | Fleet Name / Vessel Name | Type of Vessel | Year Built | Type of Engine | Cargo Cap. or Gross* | Overall Length | Breadth | Depth or Draft* |
|---|---|---|---|---|---|---|---|---|
| **B-7** | **BEAVER ISLAND BOAT CO., CHARLEVOIX, MI** | | | | | | | |
| | Beaver Islander | PF/CF | 1963 | D | 95* | 96' 03" | 27' 05" | 9' 09" |
| | Emerald Isle {2} | PF/CF | 1997 | D | 95* | 130' 00" | 38' 08" | 12' 00" |
| **B-8** | **BEST OF ALL TOURS, ERIE, PA** | | | | | | | |
| | Lady Kate {2} | ES | 1952 | D | 11* | 65' 00" | 16' 06" | 4' 00" |
| | *(G. A. Boeckling II '52 - ?, Cedar Point III ? - '89, Island Trader '89 - '97)* | | | | | | | |
| **B-9** | **BETHLEHEM STEEL CORP. - BURNS HARBOR DIVISION, CHESTERTON, IN** | | | | | | | |
| | Burns Harbor {2} | SU | 1980 | D | 78,850 | 1,000' 00" | 105' 00" | 56' 00" |
| | Stewart J. Cort | SU | 1972 | D | 58,000 | 1,000' 00" | 105' 00" | 49' 00" |
| **B-10** | **BIGANE VESSEL FUELING CO. OF CHICAGO, CHICAGO, IL** | | | | | | | |
| | Jos. F. Bigane | RT | 1973 | D | 7,500 | 140' 00" | 40' 00" | 14' 00" |
| **B-11** | **BILLINGTON CONTRACTING, INC., DULUTH, MN** | | | | | | | |
| | Coleman | CS | 1923 | B | 502* | 153' 06" | 40' 06" | 10' 06" |
| | Houghton | TB | 1944 | D | 21* | 45' 00" | 13' 00" | 6' 00" |
| | Panama | DS | 1942 | B | | 210' 01" | 44' 01" | 10' 01" |
| **B-12** | **BLACK CREEK CONSTRUCTION CO., NANTICOKE, ON** | | | | | | | |
| | H.H. Misner | TB | 1946 | D | 28* | 66' 09" | 16' 04" | 4' 05" |
| **B-13** | **BLUE CIRCLE CEMENT CO., DETROIT, MI** | | | | | | | |
| | Lewis G. Harriman | CC | 1923 | R | 5,500 | 350' 00" | 55' 00" | 28' 00" |
| | *(John W. Boardman '23 - '65)* | | | | | | | |
| | *(Last operated April 20, 1980) (In use as a cement storage vessel at Green Bay, WI.)* | | | | | | | |
| | St. Mary's Cement | CC | 1986 | B | 9,400 | 360' 00" | 60' 00" | 23' 03" |
| **B-14** | **BLUE CIRCLE CEMENT CO., TORONTO, ON** | | | | | | | |
| | Sea Eagle II | TBA | 1979 | D | 560* | 132' 00" | 35' 00" | 19' 00" |
| | *(Sea Eagle '79 - '81, Canmar Sea Eagle '81 - '91)* | | | | | | | |
| | St. Mary's Cement II | CC | 1978 | B | 19,513 | 496' 06" | 76' 00" | 35' 00" |
| | *(Velasco '78 - '81, Canmar Shuttle '81 - '90)* | | | | | | | |
| | St. Mary's Cement III | CC | 1980 | B | 4,800 | 335' 00" | 76' 08" | 17' 09" |
| | *(Bigorange XVI '80 - '84, Says '84 - '85, Al-Sayb-7 '85 - '86, Clarkson Carrier '86 - '94)* | | | | | | | |
| | *(Last operated Sept. 1, '00; In use as a cement storage barge at Green Bay, WI.)* | | | | | | | |
| | ***GREAT LAKES INT. TOWING & SALVAGE CO., INC. - CHARTERED BY BLUE CIRCLE CEMENT CO.*** | | | | | | | |
| | Petite Forte | TB | 1969 | D | 368* | 127' 00" | 32' 00" | 14' 06" |
| | *(E. Bronson Ingram '69 - '72, Jarmac 42 '72 - '73, Scotsman '73 - '81, Al Battal '81 - '86)* | | | | | | | |
| **B-15** | **BLUE HERON CO., TOBERMORY, ON** | | | | | | | |
| | Blue Heron V | ES | 1983 | D | 24* | 54' 06" | 17' 05" | 7' 02" |
| | Great Blue Heron | ES | 1994 | D | 112* | 79' 00" | 22' 00" | 6' 05" |
| **B-16** | **BLUE WATER EXCURSIONS, INC., FORT GRATIOT, MI** | | | | | | | |
| | Huron Lady II | ES | 1993 | D | 82* | 65' 00" | 19' 00" | 10' 00" |
| | *(Lady Lumina '93 - '99)* | | | | | | | |
| **B-17** | **BLUE WATER FERRY LTD., SOMBRA, ON** | | | | | | | |
| | Daldean | CF | 1951 | D | 145* | 75' 00" | 35' 00" | 7' 00" |
| | Ontamich | CF | 1939 | D | 55* | 65' 00" | 28' 10" | 8' 06" |
| | *(Harsens Island '39 - '73)* | | | | | | | |
| **B-18** | **BUFFALO CHARTERS, INC. / NIAGARA CLIPPER, INC., BUFFALO, NY** | | | | | | | |
| | Miss Buffalo | ES | 1964 | D | 88* | 64' 10" | 23' 05" | 7' 04" |
| | *(Miss Muskoka {1} '64 - '69, Miss Niagara '69 - '72)* | | | | | | | |
| | Miss Buffalo II | ES | 1972 | D | 88* | 86' 00" | 24' 00" | 6' 00" |
| | Niagara Clipper | ES | 1983 | D | 65* | 112' 00" | 29' 00" | 6' 06"* |
| **B-19** | **BUFFALO INDUSTRIAL DIVING, BUFFALO, NY** | | | | | | | |
| | West Wind | TB | 1941 | D | 54* | 60' 04" | 17' 01" | 7' 07" |
| | Joanne | TB | 1935 | D | 18* | 42' 06" | 11' 09" | 6' 09" |
| | *(Paul L. Luedtke '35-'02)* | | | | | | | |

**Middletown works up speed Sept. 1, 2002, in the St. Marys River.** *(Roger LeLievre)*

# MIDDLETOWN

**M**iddletown, celebrating her 60th birthday this year, is truly a one-of-a-kind laker. Built as the World War II tanker **USS Neshanic** at Sparrows Point, Md., the vessel entered service in April 1943. She was involved in several close encounters with enemy submarines and air attacks on the Atlantic and Pacific oceans, and on June 18, 1944, she was hit with a bomb from a Japanese plane while refueling a destroyer. Her war service battle decorations included a star for Gilbert Islands, a star for action at the Marshall Islands, another star for raids on Palau, Yup and Truk, one star for the Marianas operation (Saipan and Guam), one star for the Okinawa Gunto Operation, one star for Third Fleet Operations against Japan, one star for Tinian, and one star for Hollandia Operations.

**Vessel Spotlight**

After World War II, the tanker saw service for Gulf Oil Corp. as **Gulfoil**, until a fiery collision in 1958 with the tanker **S.E. Graham** at Newport, R.I., almost ended her career. Though considered unrepairable as a tanker, **Gulfoil** was bought by Maryland Shipbuilding which in turn, sold the hull to Pioneer Shipping Co., Cleveland, in 1960 for conversion to a lake bulk carrier. A mid-section was built in Rotterdam, The Netherlands, and towed to Baltimore to be attached to the bow and stern of the burned tanker. The new 730-foot lake boat, christened **Pioneer Challenger**, sailed from Baltimore for the St. Lawrence Seaway July 1, 1961. Oglebay Norton & Co. (Columbia Transportation Div.), Cleveland, acquired the vessel in 1962 and renamed her **Middletown**.

Bay Shipbuilding Co. converted the **Middletown** to a self-unloader in 1982. She survived another fire when, on Sept. 15, 1986, methane gas exploded in her boiler room causing injuries to some of the crew.

**Middletown** continues to sail actively for the Oglebay Norton fleet. Her cargoes include iron ore pellets, coal and stone products. On her bridge wings she proudly carries the battle stars awarded during World War II. – *George Wharton*

| Fleet #. | Fleet Name / Vessel Name | Type of Vessel | Year Built | Type of Engine | Cargo Cap. or Gross* | Overall Length | Breadth | Depth or Draft* |
|---|---|---|---|---|---|---|---|---|
| **B-20** | **BUFFALO PUBLIC WORKS DEPT., BUFFALO, NY** | | | | | | | |
| | Edward M. Cotter | FB | 1900 | D | 208* | 118' 00" | 24' 00" | 11' 06" |
| | *(W. S. Grattan 1900 - '53, Firefighter '53 - '54)* | | | | | | | |
| **B-21** | **BUSCH MARINE, INC., CARROLLTON, MI** | | | | | | | |
| | Gregory J. Busch | TB | 1919 | D | 299* | 151' 00" | 28' 00" | 16' 09" |
| | *(Humaconna '19 - '77)* | | | | | | | |
| | STC 2004 | DB | 1986 | B | 2,364 | 240' 00" | 50' 00" | 9' 05" |
| **C-1** | **C. A. CROSBIE SHIPPING LTD., ST. JOHN'S, NF** | | | | | | | |
| | Lady Franklin | GC | 1970 | D | 3,627 | 339' 04" | 51' 10" | 27' 11" |
| | *(Baltic Valiant '70 - '81)* | | | | | | | |
| **C-2** | **CALUMET RIVER FLEETING, INC., CHICAGO, IL** | | | | | | | |
| | Des Plaines | TB | 1956 | D | 175* | 98' 00" | 28' 00" | 8' 04"* |
| | John M. Perry | TB | 1954 | D | 76* | 66' 00" | 19' 00" | 9' 00" |
| | *(Sanita '54 - '77, Soo Chief '77 - '81, Susan M. Selvick '81 - '96, Nathan S. '96-'02)* | | | | | | | |
| | John M. Selvick | TB | 1898 | D | 256* | 118' 00" | 24' 00" | 12' 07" |
| | *(Illinois {1} 1898 - '41, John Roen III '41 - '74)* | | | | | | | |
| | Jimmy Wray | TB | 1954 | D | 95* | 72' 00" | 22' 00" | 7' 00"* |
| | *(Sea Wolf '54 - 2001)* | | | | | | | |
| | Tommy B. | TB | 1962 | D | 43* | 45' 00" | 11' 10" | 4' 11"* |
| | Trinity | TB | 1939 | D | 51* | 45' 00" | 12' 10" | 5' 07"* |
| **C-3** | **CANADA STEAMSHIP LINES, INC., MONTREAL, QC** | | | | | | | |
| | Atlantic Erie | SU | 1985 | D | 38,200 | 736' 07" | 75' 10" | 50' 00" |
| | *(Hon. Paul Martin '85 - '88)* | | | | | | | |
| | Atlantic Huron {2} | SU | 1984 | D | 34,600 | 736' 07" | 78' 01" | 46' 06" |
| | *(Prairie Harvest '84 - '89, Atlantic Huron {2} '89 - '94, Melvin H. Baker II {2} '94 - '97)* | | | | | | | |
| | *(Converted to a self-unloader, '89; widened by 3' – '03)* | | | | | | | |
| | Birchglen {2} | BC | 1983 | D | 35,315 | 730' 01" | 75' 09" | 48' 00" |
| | *(Canada Marquis '83 - '91, Federal Richelieu '91 - '91, Federal MacKenzie '91 - '01, MacKenzie '01 - '02)* | | | | | | | |
| | Cedarglen {2} | BC | 1959 | D | 29,100 | 730' 00" | 75' 09" | 40' 02" |
| | *(Ems Ore '59 - '76, Montcliffe Hall '76 - '88, Cartierdoc '88 - '02)* | | | | | | | |
| | CSL Laurentien | SU | 1977 | D | 34,938 | 739' 10" | 78' 01" | 48' 05" |
| | *(Stern section: Louis R. Desmarais '77 - '01) (Rebuilt with new forebody, '01)* | | | | | | | |
| | CSL Niagara | SU | 1972 | D | 34,938 | 739' 10" | 78' 01" | 48' 05" |
| | *(Stern section: J. W. McGiffin '72 - '99) (Rebuilt with a new forebody, '99)* | | | | | | | |
| | CSL Tadoussac | SU | 1969 | D | 29,700 | 730' 00" | 78' 00" | 42' 00" |
| | *(Tadoussac {2} '69 - '01) (Rebuilt with new midbody, widened by 3' - '01)* | | | | | | | |
| | Ferbec | BC | 1966 | D | 56,887 | 732' 06" | 104' 02" | 57' 09" |
| | *(Fugaku Maru '65 - '77)* | | | | | | | |
| | Frontenac {5} | SU | 1968 | D | 27,500 | 729' 07" | 75' 03" | 39' 08" |
| | *(Converted to a self-unloader, '73)* | | | | | | | |
| | Halifax | SU | 1963 | T | 30,100 | 730' 02" | 75' 00" | 39' 03" |
| | *(Frankcliffe Hall {2} '63 - '88; (Converted to a self-unloader, deepened 6' - '80)* | | | | | | | |
| | Jean Parisien | SU | 1977 | D | 33,000 | 730' 00" | 75' 00" | 46' 06" |
| | Mapleglen {2} | BC | 1960 | T | 26,100 | 714' 11" | 75' 00" | 37' 09" |
| | *(Carol Lake '60 - '87, Algocape {1} '87 - '94)* | | | | | | | |
| | Nanticoke | SU | 1980 | D | 35,100 | 729' 10" | 75' 08" | 46' 06" |
| | Oakglen {2} | BC | 1954 | T | 22,950 | 714' 06" | 70' 03" | 37' 03" |
| | *(T. R. McLagan '54 - '90)* | | | | | | | |
| | Pineglen {2} | BC | 1985 | D | 32,600 | 736' 07" | 75' 10" | 42' 00" |
| | *(Paterson '85 - '02)* | | | | | | | |
| | Rt. Hon. Paul J. Martin | SU | 1973 | D | 34,938 | 739' 10" | 78' 01" | 48' 05" |
| | *(Stern section: H. M. Griffith '73 - '00) (Rebuilt with a new forebody, '00)* | | | | | | | |
| | Spruceglen {2} | BC | 1983 | D | 35,315 | 730' 01" | 75' 09" | 48' 00" |
| | *(Selkirk Settler '83 - '91, Federal St. Louis '91 - '91, Federal Fraser {2} '91 - 2001, Fraser '01 - '02)* | | | | | | | |
| | Teakglen | BC | 1967 | D | 17,650 | 607' 10" | 62' 00" | 36' 00" |
| | *(Mantadoc '67 - '02) (In use as a grain storage vessel at Goderich, ON.)* | | | | | | | |

| Fleet #. | Fleet Name / Vessel Name | Type of Vessel | Year Built | Type of Engine | Cargo Cap. or Gross* | Overall Length | Breadth | Depth or Draft* |
|---|---|---|---|---|---|---|---|---|
| | **LAFARGE CANADA, INC., MONTREAL, QC - MANAGED BY CANADA STEAMSHIP LINES, INC.** | | | | | | | |
| | English River | CC | 1961 | D | 7,450 | 404' 03" | 60' 00" | 36' 06" |
| | *(Converted to a self-unloading cement carrier, '74)* | | | | | | | |
| **C-4** | **CANADIAN COAST GUARD, OTTAWA, ON** | | | | | | | |
| | **CENTRAL AND ARCTIC REGION, SARNIA, ON** | | | | | | | |
| | Advent | RV | 1972 | D | 72* | 77' 01" | 18' 05" | 5' 03"* |
| | Bittern | SR | 1982 | D | 21* | 40' 08" | 13' 06" | 4' 04" |
| | Cape Hurd | SR | 1982 | D | 55* | 70' 10" | 18' 00" | 8' 09" |
| | *(CG 126 '82 - '85)* | | | | | | | |
| | Caribou Isle | BT | 1985 | D | 92* | 75' 06" | 19' 08" | 7' 04" |
| | Cove Isle | BT | 1980 | D | 92* | 65' 07" | 19' 08" | 7' 04" |
| | Griffon | IB | 1970 | E | 2,212* | 234' 00" | 49' 00" | 21' 06" |
| | Gull Isle | BT | 1980 | D | 80* | 65' 07" | 19' 08" | 7' 04" |
| | Limnos | RV | 1968 | D | 460* | 147' 00" | 32' 00" | 12' 00" |
| | Louis M. Lauzier | RV | 1976 | D | 322* | 125' 00" | 27' 01" | 11' 06" |
| | *(Cape Harrison '76 - '83)* | | | | | | | |
| | Samuel Risley | IB | 1985 | D | 1,988* | 228' 09" | 47' 01" | 21' 09" |
| | Shark | RV | 1971 | D | 30* | 52' 06" | 14' 09" | 7' 03" |
| | Simcoe | BT | 1962 | E | 961* | 179' 01" | 38' 00" | 15' 06" |
| | Sora | SR | 1982 | D | 21* | 41' 00" | 14' 01" | 4' 04" |
| | Spray | SR | 1994 | D | 42* | 51' 09" | 17' 00" | 8' 02" |
| | Spume | SR | 1994 | D | 42* | 51' 09" | 17' 00" | 8' 02" |
| | Tobermory | SR | 1973 | D | 17* | 44' 01" | 12' 06" | 6' 07" |
| | Westfort | SR | 1973 | D | 22* | 44' 01" | 12' 08" | 5' 11" |
| | **LAURENTIAN REGION, QUEBEC, QC** | | | | | | | |
| | Des Groseilliers | IB | 1983 | E | 5,910* | 322' 07" | 64' 00" | 35' 06" |
| | F. C. G. Smith | SV | 1985 | D | 439* | 114' 02" | 45' 11" | 11' 02" |
| | Frederick G. Creed | SV | 1988 | D | 151* | 66' 11" | 32' 00" | 11' 10" |
| | George R. Pearkes | IB | 1986 | E | 3,809 | 272' 04" | 53' 02" | 25' 02" |
| | Ile Des Barques | BT | 1985 | D | 92* | 75' 06" | 19' 08" | 7' 04" |
| | Ile Saint-Ours | BT | 1986 | D | 92* | 75' 06" | 19' 08" | 7' 04" |
| | Isle Rouge | SR | 1980 | D | 57* | 70' 10" | 18' 01" | 8' 09" |
| | Louisbourg | RV | 1977 | D | 295* | 124' 00" | 26' 11" | 11' 06" |
| | Martha L. Black | IB | 1986 | E | 3,818* | 272' 04" | 53' 02" | 25' 02" |
| | Pierre Radisson | IB | 1978 | E | 5,910* | 322' 00" | 62' 10" | 35' 06" |
| | Tracy | BT | 1968 | D | 963* | 181' 01" | 38' 00" | 16' 00" |
| | Waban-Aki | AV | 1987 | D | 48* | 80' 05" | 36' 00" | 26' 10" |
| | **MARITIMES REGION, DARTMOUTH, NS** | | | | | | | |
| | Alfred Needler | RV | 1982 | D | 959* | 165' 09" | 36' 09" | 22' 01" |
| | Chebucto | RV | 1966 | D | 751* | 179' 02" | 30' 10" | 27' 02" |
| | Cygnus | RV | 1982 | D | 1,211* | 205' 01" | 40' 00" | 15' 05" |
| | Earl Grey | IB | 1986 | D | 1,971* | 230' 00" | 46' 02" | 22' 01" |
| | Edward Cornwallis | IB | 1986 | D | 3,727* | 272' 04" | 53' 02" | 24' 06" |
| | Hudson | RV | 1963 | D | 3,740* | 296' 07" | 50' 06" | 32' 10" |
| | Louis S. St-Laurent | IB | 1969 | D | 10,908* | 392' 06" | 80' 00" | 53' 06" |
| | Matthew | RV | 1990 | D | 857* | 165' 00" | 34' 05" | 16' 05" |
| | Parizeau | RV | 1967 | D | 1,328* | 211' 07" | 40' 00" | 21' 00" |
| | Provo Wallis | BT | 1969 | D | 1,313* | 209' 03" | 42' 08" | 16' 07" |
| | Simon Fraser | BT | 1960 | D | 1,353* | 204' 06" | 42' 00" | 18' 03" |
| | Sir William Alexander | ID | 1906 | D | 3,550* | 272' 06" | 45' 00" | 17' 06" |
| | Terry Fox | IB | 1983 | D | 4,234* | 288' 09" | 58' 06" | 29' 08" |
| | Tupper | BT | 1959 | D | 1,353* | 204' 06" | 42' 00" | 18' 03" |
| | **NEWFOUNDLAND REGION, ST. JOHN'S, NF** | | | | | | | |
| | Ann Harvey | IB | 1987 | D | 3,854* | 272' 04" | 53' 02" | 25' 10" |
| | Cape Roger | RV | 1977 | D | 1,255* | 205' 01" | 35' 05" | 22' 00" |
| | Henry Larsen | IB | 1988 | D | 6,172* | 327' 05" | 64' 08" | 35' 09" |
| | J. E. Bernier | IB | 1967 | D | 2,457* | 231' 04" | 49' 00" | 16' 00" |

| | Leonard J. Cowley | RV | 1984 | D | 2,243* | 236' 03" | 46' 07" | 24' 03" |
| | Sir Humphrey Gilbert | IB | 1959 | D | 2,152* | 237' 10" | 48' 02" | 21' 01" |
| | Sir Wilfred Grenfall | SR | 1987 | D | 2,404* | 224' 08" | 49' 03" | 22' 06" |
| | Teleost | RV | 1988 | D | 2,337* | 206' 08" | 46' 07" | 29' 02" |
| | *(Atlantic Champion '88 - '95)* | | | | | | | |
| | Wilfred Templeman | RV | 1981 | D | 925* | 166' 00" | 36' 09" | 22' 01" |
| **C-5** | **CARY McMANUS, DULUTH, MN** | | | | | | | |
| | Duluth | DR | 1962 | B | 401* | 106' 00" | 36' 00" | 8' 04" |
| **C-6** | **CELEST BAY TIMBER & MARINE, DULUTH, MN** | | | | | | | |
| | Essayons | TB | 1908 | R | 117* | 85' 06" | 21' 02" | 11' 09" |
| **C-7** | **CENTRAL MARINE LOGISTICS, INC., HIGHLAND, IN** | | | | | | | |
| | Edward L. Ryerson | BC | 1960 | T | 27,500 | 730' 00" | 75' 00" | 39' 00" |
| | *(Last operated Dec. 12, 1998 – 5 year survey expired Dec. 2001; Laid up in Sturgeon Bay, WI.)* | | | | | | | |
| | Joseph L. Block | SU | 1976 | D | 37,200 | 728' 00" | 78' 00" | 45' 00" |
| | Wilfred Sykes | SU | 1949 | T | 21,500 | 678' 00" | 70' 00" | 37' 00" |
| | *(Converted to a self-unloader, '75)* | | | | | | | |
| **C-8** | **CHAMPION'S AUTO FERRY, INC., ALGONAC, MI** | | | | | | | |
| | Champion {1} | CF | 1941 | D | 65* | 65' 00" | 29' 00" | 8' 06" |
| | Middle Channel | CF | 1997 | D | 97* | 79' 00" | 31' 00" | 8' 03" |
| | North Channel | CF | 1967 | D | 67* | 75' 00" | 30' 00" | 8' 00" |
| | South Channel | CF | 1973 | D | 94* | 79' 00" | 31' 00" | 8' 03" |
| **C-9** | **CHARLEVOIX COUNTY ROAD COMMISSION, BOYNE CITY, MI** | | | | | | | |
| | Charlevoix {1} | CF | 1926 | D | 43* | 50' 00" | 32' 00" | 3' 09" |
| **C-10** | **CHICAGO CRUISES, INC., CHICAGO, IL** | | | | | | | |
| | Chicago II | ES | 1983 | D | 42* | 123' 03" | 28' 06" | 7' 00" |
| | *(Star of Sandford '83 - '86, Star of Charlevoix {1} '86 - '87, Star of Toronto '87 - '87, Star of Chicago II '87 - '94)* | | | | | | | |
| **C-11** | **CHICAGO FIRE DEPT., CHICAGO, IL** | | | | | | | |
| | Victor L. Schlaeger | FB | 1949 | D | 350* | 92' 06" | 24' 00" | 11' 00" |
| **C-12** | **CHICAGO FROM THE LAKE LTD., CHICAGO, IL** | | | | | | | |
| | Fort Dearborn | ES | 1985 | D | 72* | 64' 10" | 22' 00" | 7' 04" |
| | Marquette {6} | ES | 1957 | D | 29* | 50' 07" | 15' 00" | 4' 00" |
| **C-13** | **CHICAGO WATER PUMPING STATION, CHICAGO, IL** | | | | | | | |
| | James J. Versluis | TB | 1957 | D | 126* | 83' 00" | 22' 00" | 11' 02" |
| **C-14** | **CIE PONTBRIAND, LTEE, SOREL, QC** | | | | | | | |
| | Soulanges | TB | 1905 | D | 72* | 77' 00" | 17' 00" | 8' 00" |
| | *(Dandy '05 - '39)* | | | | | | | |
| **C-15** | **CITY OF TORONTO PARKS & RECREATION DEPARTMENT, TORONTO, ON**<br>**ISLAND FERRY SERVICE** | | | | | | | |
| | Ongiara | PF | 1963 | D | 180* | 78' 00" | 36' 00" | 9' 09" |
| | P. & P. 1 | TB | 1984 | D | 14* | 37' 04" | 12' 04" | 3' 06" |
| | Sam McBride | PF | 1939 | D | 412* | 129' 00" | 34' 11" | 6' 00" |
| | Thomas Rennie | PF | 1950 | D | 419* | 129' 00" | 32' 11" | 6' 00" |
| | Trillium | PF | 1910 | R | 611* | 150' 00" | 30' 00" | 8' 04" |
| | William Inglis | PF | 1935 | D | 238* | 99' 00" | 24' 10" | 6' 00" |
| | *(Shamrock {2} '35 - '35)* | | | | | | | |
| **C-16** | **CLEVELAND FIRE DEPT., CLEVELAND, OH** | | | | | | | |
| | Anthony J. Celebrezze | FB | 1961 | D | | 66' 00" | 17' 00" | 5' 00" |
| **C-17** | **CLIFFORD TYNER, BARBEAU, MI** | | | | | | | |
| | Neebish Islander | CF | 1950 | D | 49* | 55' 00" | 20' 07" | 6' 00" |
| | *(Lillifred '50 - '56) (Last operated in 1995; Laid up at Neebish Island, MI.)* | | | | | | | |

**Oakglen upbound in the St. Marys River in 2002.** *(Roger LeLievre)*

# PAST & PRESENT

As bulk vessels go, they don't come much handsomer than the steamer **Oakglen**. A traditional-style straight-deck bulk carrier, the vessel was launched as **T.R. McLagan** at Midland, Ont., in 1953 for Canada Steamship Lines. She set a number of cargo records in her youth, including a corn record of 22,256 tons from Duluth to Montreal early in the Seaway era.

She was retired by CSL in 1984 and would probably have gone to the scrapyard along with many of her sisters at that time except for an angel in the form of P. & H. Shipping Ltd., which put her back to work in the grain trade under the name **Oakglen**. She stayed busy for P & H until 2001, when the firm decided to leave the vessel business. That year, the **Oakglen** "returned to her roots" when she and fleet mate **Mapleglen** were bought by Canada Steamship Lines, **Oakglen**'s original owner, which was expanding its grain-carrying business.

**T.R. McLagan on the St. Marys in 1971.** *(Roger LeLievre)*

Given her age, steam powerplant and small size, the **Oakglen** will probably not be around for many more seasons. Enjoy her while you can. – *Roger LeLievre*

| Fleet #. | Fleet Name<br>Vessel Name | Type of<br>Vessel | Year<br>Built | Type of<br>Engine | Cargo Cap.<br>or Gross* | Overall<br>Length | Breadth | Depth or<br>Draft* |
|---|---|---|---|---|---|---|---|---|
| **C-18** | **CLUB CANAMAC CRUISES, TORONTO, ON** | | | | | | | |
| | Aurora Borealis | ES | 1983 | D | 277* | 101' 00" | 24' 00" | 6' 00"* |
| | Carolina Borealis | ES | 1943 | D | 182* | 84' 06" | 20' 00" | 10' 04" |
| | *(HMCS Glenmont [W-27] '43 - '45, Glenmont '43-'02) (Rebuilt from a tug, '02)* | | | | | | | |
| | Jaguar II | ES | 1968 | D | 142* | 95' 03" | 20' 00" | 9' 00" |
| | *(Jaguar '68 - '86)* | | | | | | | |
| | Stella Borealis | ES | 1989 | D | 356* | 118 '00" | 26' 00" | 7' 00" |
| **C-19** | **CONTINENTAL MARINE, INC., LEMONT, IL** | | | | | | | |
| | Brandon E. | TB | 1945 | D | 19* | 42' 01" | 12' 10" | 5' 02"* |
| **C-20** | **COOPER MARINE LTD., SELKIRK, ON** | | | | | | | |
| | J. W. Cooper | PB | 19845 | D | 25* | 48' 00" | 14' 07" | 5' 00" |
| | Juleen I | PB | 1972 | D | 23* | 46' 00" | 14' 01" | 4' 05" |
| | Mrs. C | PB | 1990 | D | 28* | 50' 00" | 16' 00" | 5' 00" |
| **C-21** | **CROISIERES AML, INC., QUEBEC, QC** | | | | | | | |
| | Cavalier Grand Fleuve | ES | 1987 | D | 499* | 145' 00" | 30' 00" | 5' 06" |
| | Cavalier Maxim | ES | 1962 | D | 752* | 191' 02" | 42' 00" | 11' 07" |
| | *(Osborne Castle '62 - '78, Le Gobelet D' Argent '78 - '88, Gobelet D' Argent '88 - '89, Le Maxim '89 - '93)* | | | | | | | |
| | Cavalier Royal | ES | 1971 | D | 283* | 125' 00" | 24' 00" | 5' 00" |
| | Louis-Jolliet | ES | 1938 | R | 2,436* | 170' 01" | 70' 00" | 17' 00" |
| | Miss Olympia | ES | 1972 | D | 29* | 62' 08" | 14' 00" | 4' 08" |
| | Nouvelle-Orleans | ES | 1989 | D | 234* | 90' 00" | 25' 00" | 5' 03" |
| | Tandem | ES | 1991 | D | 102* | 66' 00" | 22' 00" | 2' 02" |
| | Transit | ES | 1992 | D | 102* | 66' 00" | 22' 00" | 2' 08" |
| **C-22** | **CROISIERES DES ILES DE SOREL, INC., SAINTE-ANNE-DE-SOREL, QC** | | | | | | | |
| | Le Survenant III | ES | 1974 | D | 105* | 65' 00" | 13' 00" | 5' 00" |
| **C-23** | **CROISIERES M/S JACQUES-CARTIER, TROIS-RIVIERES, QC** | | | | | | | |
| | Jacques Cartier | ES | 1924 | D | 441* | 135' 00" | 35' 00" | 10' 00" |
| | Le Draveur | ES | 1992 | D | 79* | 58' 07" | 22' 00" | 5' 24" |
| **C-24** | **CROISIERES MARJOLAINE, INC., CHICOUTIMI, QC** | | | | | | | |
| | Marjolaine II | ES | 1904 | D | 399* | 92' 00" | 27' 00" | 9' 00" |
| **C-25** | **CROISIERES RICHELIEU, INC., SAINT-JEAN-SUR-RICHELIEU, QC** | | | | | | | |
| | Fort Saint-Jean II | ES | 1967 | D | 109* | 62' 09" | 19' 10" | |
| | *(Miss Gananoque '67 - '77)* | | | | | | | |
| | Suroit IV | ES | 1973 | D | 64* | 58' 00" | 16' 00" | 10' 04" |
| | *(Miss Montreal '73 - '99)* | | | | | | | |
| **D-1** | **DALE T. DEAN – WALPOLE - ALGONAC FERRY LINE, PORT LAMBTON, ON** | | | | | | | |
| | City of Algonac | CF | 1990 | D | 92* | 80' 04" | 26' 01" | 6' 09" |
| | Walpole Islander | CF | 1986 | D | 71* | 74' 00" | 33' 00" | 7' 00" |
| **D-2** | **DAN MINOR & SONS, INC., PORT COLBORNE, ON** | | | | | | | |
| | Andrea Marie I | TB | 1963 | D | 87* | 75' 02" | 24' 07" | 7' 03" |
| | Susan Michelle | TB | 1995 | D | 89* | 79' 10" | 20' 11" | 6' 02" |
| | Welland | TB | 1954 | D | 94* | 86' 00" | 20' 00" | 8' 00" |
| **D-3** | **DAVID G. GARRICK, DULUTH, MN** | | | | | | | |
| | Mount McKay | TB | 1908 | D | 99* | 80' 00" | 21' 06" | 9' 00" |
| | *(Walter F. Mattick '08 - ' 19, Merchant '19 - '24, Marinette '24 - '47, Esther S. '47 - '66)* | | | | | | | |
| **D-4** | **DAVID MALLOCH, SCUDDER, ON** | | | | | | | |
| | Cemba | TK | 1960 | D | 151 | 50' 00" | 15' 06" | 7' 06" |
| **D-5** | **DAWES MARINE TUG & BARGE, INC., NORTH TONAWANDA, NY** | | | | | | | |
| | Fourth Coast | TB | 1957 | D | 17* | 40' 00" | 12' 06" | 4' 00" |
| | Sand Pebble | TB | 1969 | D | 30* | 48' 00" | 15' 00" | 8' 00" |
| | Tommy Ray | TB | 1954 | D | 19* | 45' 00" | 12' 05" | 6' 00" |

| Fleet #. | Fleet Name / Vessel Name | Type of Vessel | Year Built | Type of Engine | Cargo Cap. or Gross* | Overall Length | Breadth | Depth or Draft* |
|---|---|---|---|---|---|---|---|---|
| **D-6** | **DEAN CONSTRUCTION CO. LTD., BELLE RIVER, ON** | | | | | | | |
| | Americo Dean | TB | 1956 | D | 15* | 45' 00" | 15' 00" | 5' 00" |
| | Annie M. Dean | TB | 1981 | D | 58* | 50' 00" | 19' 00" | 5' 00" |
| | Bobby Bowes | TB | 1944 | D | 11* | 37' 04" | 10' 02" | 3' 06" |
| | Jubilee | DR | 1978 | D | 896* | 149' 09" | 56' 01" | 11' 01" |
| | Neptune III | TB | 1939 | D | 23* | 53' 10" | 15' 06" | 5' 00" |
| | Wayne Dean | TB | 1946 | D | 10* | 45' 00" | 13' 00" | 5' 00" |
| **D-7** | **DENNIS DOUGHERTY, SAULT STE. MARIE, MI** | | | | | | | |
| | Gerald D. Neville | TB | 1924 | D | 29* | 50' 00" | 13' 00" | 4' 06" |
| | (Tobermory '24 - '41, Champion {2} '41 - '81) | | | | | | | |
| **D-8** | **DETROIT CITY FIRE DEPT., DETROIT, MI** | | | | | | | |
| | Curtis Randolph | FB | 1979 | D | 85* | 77' 10" | 21' 06" | 9' 03" |
| **D-9** | **DIAMOND JACK'S RIVER TOURS, GROSSE ILE, MI** | | | | | | | |
| | Diamond Belle | ES | 1958 | D | 93* | 93' 06" | 25' 10" | 10' 01" |
| | (Mackinac Islander {2} '58 - '90, Sir Richard '90 - '91) | | | | | | | |
| | Diamond Jack | ES | 1955 | D | 82* | 72' 00" | 25' 00" | 8' 00" |
| | (Emerald Isle {1} '55 - '91) | | | | | | | |
| | Diamond Queen | ES | 1956 | D | 94* | 92' 00" | 25' 00" | 10' 00" |
| | (Mohawk '56 - '96) | | | | | | | |
| **D-10** | **DIRK SPLILLMAKER, EAST LANSING, MI** | | | | | | | |
| | Verendrye | RV | 1958 | D | 297* | 167' 06" | 34' 00" | 16' 07" |
| | (CCGS Verendrye '58 - '86, 500 '86 - '92) | | | | | | | |
| **D-11** | **DISSEN & JUHN CORP., MACEDON, NY** | | | | | | | |
| | Constructor | TB | 1950 | D | 14* | 39' 00" | 11' 00" | 5' 00" |
| | James W. Rickey | TB | 1935 | D | 24* | 46' 00" | 14' 00" | 7' 00" |
| **D-12** | **DOOR COUNTY CRUISES, LLC, STURGEON BAY, WI** | | | | | | | |
| | Fred A. Busse | ES | 1937 | D | 99* | 92' 00" | 22' 04" | 11' 00" |
| | Kimberly Selvick | TB | 1975 | D | 93* | 51' 10" | 28' 00" | 10' 00" |
| **D-13** | **DOW CHEMICAL CO., LUDINGTON, MI** | | | | | | | |
| | DC 710 | TK | 1969 | B | 25,500 | 260' 00" | 50' 00" | 9' 00" |
| **D-14** | **DUC d' ORLEANS CRUISE BOAT, CORUNNA, ON** | | | | | | | |
| | Duc d' Orleans | ES | 1943 | D | 112* | 112' 00" | 17' 10" | 6' 03" |
| | (HMCS ML-105 '43 - ?, HMCS Duc d' Orleans [ML-105] ? - '48) | | | | | | | |
| **D-15** | **DULUTH TIMBER CO., DULUTH, MN** | | | | | | | |
| | Faith | | 1906 | B | 705* | 120' 00" | 38' 00" | 10' 03" |
| **D-16** | **DUROCHER MARINE, DIVISION OF KOKOSING CONSTRUCTION CO., CHEBOYGAN, MI** | | | | | | | |
| | Betty D. | TB | 1953 | D | 14* | 40' 00" | 13' 00" | 6' 00" |
| | Champion {3} | TB | 1974 | D | 125* | 75' 00" | 24' 00" | 9' 06" |
| | General {2} | TB | 1954 | D | 119* | 71' 00" | 19' 06" | 9' 06" |
| | (U. S. Army ST-1999 '54 - '61, USCOE Au Sable '61 - '84, Challenger {3} '84 - '87) | | | | | | | |
| | Joe Van | TB | 1955 | D | 32* | 57' 09" | 16' 06" | 9' 00" |
| | Meagan Beth | TB | 1982 | D | 94* | 60' 00" | 22' 00" | 9' 00" |
| | Nancy Anne | TB | 1969 | D | 73* | 60' 00" | 20' 00" | 6' 00" |
| | Ray Durocher | TB | 1943 | D | 20* | 45' 06" | 12' 05" | 7' 06" |
| | Sam II | CS | 1959 | B | 700 | 90' 00" | 50' 00" | 7' 02" |
| **E-1** | **EASTERN CANADA TOWING LTD., HALIFAX, NS** | | | | | | | |
| | Point Chebucto | TT | 1993 | D | 412* | 110' 00" | 33' 00" | 17' 00" |
| | Pointe Aux Basques | TB | 1972 | D | 396* | 105' 00" | 33' 06" | 19' 06" |
| | Pointe Comeau | TT | 1976 | D | 391* | 104' 00" | 40' 00" | 19' 00" |
| | Pointe Sept-Iles | TB | 1980 | D | 424* | 105' 00" | 34' 06" | 19' 06" |
| | Point Halifax | TT | 1986 | D | 417* | 110' 00" | 36' 00" | 19' 00" |

| Fleet #. | Fleet Name / Vessel Name | Type of Vessel | Year Built | Type of Engine | Cargo Cap. or Gross* | Overall Length | Breadth | Depth or Draft* |
|---|---|---|---|---|---|---|---|---|
| | Point Valiant {2} | TT | 1998 | D | 302* | 80' 00" | 30' 01" | 14' 09" |
| | *(Launched as Ocean Jupiter {1})* | | | | | | | |
| | Point Vibert | TB | 1961 | D | 236* | 96' 03" | 28' 00" | 14' 06" |
| | *(Foundation Vibert '61 - '73)* | | | | | | | |
| | Point Vigour | TB | 1962 | D | 207* | 98' 05" | 26' 10" | 13' 05" |
| | *(Foundation Vigour '62 - '74)* | | | | | | | |
| | Point Vim | TB | 1962 | D | 207* | 98' 05" | 26' 10" | 13' 05" |
| | *(Foundation Vim '62 - '74)* | | | | | | | |
| **E-2** | **EASTERN UPPER PENINSULA TRANSIT AUTHORITY, SAULT STE. MARIE, MI** | | | | | | | |
| | Drummond Islander III | CF | 1989 | D | 96* | 108' 00" | 37' 00" | 12' 03" |
| | Drummond Islander IV | CF | 2000 | D | 377* | 148' 00" | 40' 00" | 12' 00" |
| | Neebish Islander II | CF | 1946 | D | 90* | 89' 00" | 29' 06" | 6' 09" |
| | *(Sugar Islander '46 - '95)* | | | | | | | |
| | Sugar Islander II | CF | 1995 | D | 223* | 114' 00" | 40' 00" | 10' 00" |
| **E-3** | **ECOMERTOURS NORD-SUD, INC., RIMOUSKI, QC** | | | | | | | |
| | Echo Des Mers | PA | 1966 | D | 887* | 169' 09" | 36' 05" | 16' 05" |
| | *(CCGS Nicolet '66 - '95, 650 '95 - '00)* | | | | | | | |
| **E-4** | **EDELWEISS CRUISE DINING, MILWAUKEE, WI** | | | | | | | |
| | Edelweiss I | ES | 1988 | D | 87* | 64' 08" | 18' 00" | 6' 00" |
| | Edelweiss II | ES | 1989 | D | 89* | 73' 08" | 20' 00" | 7' 00" |
| **E-5** | **EDGEWATER BOAT TOURS, SARNIA, ON** | | | | | | | |
| | Macassa Bay | ES | 1986 | D | 200* | 93' 07" | 29' 07" | 10' 04" |
| **E-6** | **EDWARD E. GILLEN CO., MILWAUKEE, WI** | | | | | | | |
| | Andrew J. | TB | 1950 | D | 25* | 47' 00" | 15' 07" | 8' 00" |
| | Edith J. | TB | 1962 | D | 19* | 45' 03" | 13' 00" | 8' 00" |
| | Edward E. Gillen III | TB | 1988 | D | 95* | 75' 00" | 26' 00" | 9' 06" |
| **E-7** | **EDWIN M. ERICKSON, BAYFIELD, WI** | | | | | | | |
| | Outer Island | PK | 1942 | D | 300 | 112' 00" | 32' 00" | 8' 06" |
| | *(USS LSM-? '42 - '46, Pluswood '46 - '53)* | | | | | | | |
| **E-8** | **EGAN MARINE CORP., LEMONT, IL** | | | | | | | |
| | Alice E. | TB | 1950 | D | 183* | 100' 00" | 26' 00" | 9' 00" |
| | *(L. L. Wright '50 - '55, Martin '55 - '74, Mary Ann '74 - '77, Judi C. '77 - '94)* | | | | | | | |
| | Daniel E. | TB | 1967 | D | 70* | 70' 00" | 18' 06" | 6' 08" |
| | *(Foster M. Ford '67 - '84)* | | | | | | | |
| | Denise E. | TB | 1912 | D | 138* | 80' 07" | 21' 06" | 10' 03" |
| | *(Caspian '12 - '48, Trojan '48 - '81, Cherokee {1} '81 - '93)* | | | | | | | |
| | Derek E. | TB | 1907 | D | 85* | 72' 06" | 20' 01" | 10' 06" |
| | *(John Kelderhouse '07 - '13, Sachem '13 - '90)* | | | | | | | |
| | Lisa E. | TB | 1963 | D | 75* | 65' 06" | 20' 00" | 8' 06" |
| | *(Dixie Scout '63 - '90)* | | | | | | | |
| | Robin E. | TB | 1889 | D | 123* | 84' 09" | 19' 00" | 9' 00" |
| | *(Asa W. Hughes 1889 - '13, Triton {1} '13 - '81, Navajo {2} '81 - '92)* | | | | | | | |
| **E-9** | **EMPIRE CRUISE LINES, U. S. A., ST. THOMAS, ON** | | | | | | | |
| | Marine Star | PA | 1945 | T | 12,773* | 520' 00" | 71' 06" | 43' 06" |
| | *(USNS Marine Star '45 - '55, Aquarama '55 - '94) (Last operated in 1962; Laid up at Lackawanna, NY.)* | | | | | | | |
| **E-10** | **EMPRESS OF CANADA ENTERPRISES LTD., TORONTO, ON** | | | | | | | |
| | Empress of Canada | ES | 1980 | D | 399* | 116' 00" | 28' 00" | 6' 06"* |
| | *(Island Queen V {2} '80 - '89)* | | | | | | | |
| **E-11** | **EMPRESS RIVER CASINO, JOLIET, IL** | | | | | | | |
| | Empress | GA | 1992 | D | 1,136* | 214' 00" | 66' 00" | 6' 07"* |
| | Empress II | GA | 1993 | D | 1,248* | 230' 00" | 67' 00" | 6' 08"* |
| | Empress III | GA | 1994 | D | 1,126* | 288' 00" | 76' 00" | 10' 07"* |

Stewart J. Cort (right) unloads into Sam Laud at Indiana Harbor Oct. 19, 2002. *(Gary Clark)*

| Fleet #. | Fleet Name / Vessel Name | Type of Vessel | Year Built | Type of Engine | Cargo Cap. or Gross* | Overall Length | Breadth | Depth or Draft* |
|---|---|---|---|---|---|---|---|---|
| **E- 12** | **ENTERPRISE 2000 CRUISE LINES LTD., TORONTO, ON** | | | | | | | |
| | Enterprise 2000 | ES | 1998 | D | 370* | 121' 06" | 35' 00" | 6' 00" |
| **E-13** | **ERIE INLANDS PETROLEUM, INC., PUT-IN-BAY, OH** | | | | | | | |
| | Cantankerous | TK | 1955 | D | 323 | 53' 00" | 14' 00" | 5' 00"* |
| **E-14** | **ERIE-WESTERN PENNSYLVANIA PORT AUTHORITY, ERIE, PA** | | | | | | | |
| | Canadian Sailor | ES | 2001 | D | 17* | 40' 00" | 12' 00" | 05' 03" |
| **E-15** | **ESCANABA & LAKE SUPERIOR RAILROAD CO., WELLS, MI** | | | | | | | |
| | Roanoke {2} | TF | 1930 | B | 30 rail cars | 381' 06" | 58' 03" | 22' 06" |
| | *(City of Flint 32 '30 - '70)* | | | | | | | |
| | Windsor {2} | TF | 1930 | B | 28 rail cars | 370' 05" | 65' 00" | 21' 06" |
| | *(Above two last operated May 1, 1994; Both laid up at Toledo, OH.)* | | | | | | | |
| | Pere Marquette 10 | TF | 1945 | B | 27 rail cars | 400' 00" | 53' 00" | 22' 00" |
| | *(Last operated Oct. 7, 1994; Laid up at Port Huron, MI.)* | | | | | | | |
| **F-1** | **FAMILLE DUFOUR CROISIERES, SAINTE-ANNE-DE-BEAUPRE, QC** | | | | | | | |
| | Famille DuFour | ES | 1992 | D | 451* | 132' 00" | 29' 00" | 11' 00" |
| | Famille DuFour II | PF | 1995 | D | 465* | 127' 06" | 34' 09" | 10' 06" |
| **F-2** | **FAUST CORP., DETROIT, MI** | | | | | | | |
| | Comorant | TB | 1991 | D | 10* | 25' 02" | 14' 00" | 4' 06" |
| | Linnhurst | TB | 1930 | D | 11* | 37' 06" | 10' 06" | 4' 08" |
| **F-3** | **FEDERAL TERMINALS LTD., PORT CARTIER, QC** | | | | | | | |
| | Brochu | TT | 1973 | D | 390* | 100' 00" | 36' 00" | 14' 06" |
| | Vachon | TT | 1973 | D | 390* | 100' 00" | 36' 00" | 14' 06" |
| **F-4** | **FERRISS MARINE CONTRACTING CORP., DETROIT, MI** | | | | | | | |
| | Magnetic | TB | 1925 | D | 30* | 55' 00" | 14' 00" | 6' 06" |
| | *(Col. J.D. Graham '24-'65, Nicholson 65-'83)* | | | | | | | |
| | Norma B. | TB | 1940 | D | 14* | 43' 00" | 15' 00" | 4' 00" |
| **F-5** | **FITZ SUSTAINABLE FORESTRY MANAGEMENT LTD., MANITOWANING, ON** | | | | | | | |
| | Wyn Cooper | TB | 1973 | D | 25* | 48' 00" | 13' 00" | 4' 00" |
| **F-6** | **FRASER SHIPYARDS, INC., SUPERIOR, WI** | | | | | | | |
| | Brenda L. | TB | 1941 | D | 11* | 36' 00" | 10' 00" | 3' 08" |
| | *(Harbour I '41 - '58, Su-Joy III '58 -'78)* | | | | | | | |
| | Maxine Thompson | TB | 1959 | D | 30* | 47' 04" | 13' 00" | 6' 06" |
| | *(Susan A. Fraser '59 - '78)* | | | | | | | |
| | Murray R. | TB | 1946 | D | 17* | 42' 10" | 12' 00" | 4' 07" |
| | Phil Milroy | TB | 1957 | D | 41* | 47' 11" | 16' 08" | 8' 04" |
| | *(Merchant of St. Marys '57-'60, Barney B. Barstow '57 - '78)* | | | | | | | |
| | Reuben Johnson | TB | 1912 | D | 71* | 78' 00" | 17' 00" | 11' 00" |
| | *(Buffalo {1} '12 - '28, USCOE Churchill '28 - '48, Buffalo {1} '48 - '74, Todd Fraser '74 - '78)* | | | | | | | |
| | Todd L. | TB | 1965 | D | 22* | 42' 10" | 12' 00" | 5' 06" |
| | *(Robert W. Fraser '65 - '78)* | | | | | | | |
| | Troy L. Johnson | TB | 1959 | D | 24* | 42' 08" | 12' 00" | 5' 05" |
| | Wally Kendzora | TB | 1956 | D | 24* | 43' 00" | 12' 00" | 5' 06" |
| | Wells Larson | TB | 1953 | D | 22* | 42' 10" | 12' 00" | 5' 06" |
| | *(E. C. Knudsen '53 - '74)* | | | | | | | |
| **F-7** | **FROST ENGINEERING CO., FRANKFORT, MI** | | | | | | | |
| | Captain George | TB | 1929 | D | 61* | 63' 00" | 17' 00" | 7' 08" |
| | *(USCOE Captain George '29 - '68, Captain George '68 - '73, Kurt R. Luetdke '73 - '91)* | | | | | | | |
| **G-1** | **GABRIEL MARINE, DETROIT, MI** | | | | | | | |
| | Elmer Dean | TB | 1998 | D | 45* | 68' 00" | 16' 08" | 6' 00" |
| **G-2** | **GAELIC TUG BOAT CO., GROSSE ILE, MI** | | | | | | | |
| | Carolyn Hoey | TB | 1951 | D | 146* | 90' 00" | 25' 00" | 11' 00" |
| | *(Atlas '51 - '84 Susan Hoey {1} '84 - '85, Atlas '85 - '87)* | | | | | | | |

| Fleet #. | Fleet Name / Vessel Name | Type of Vessel | Year Built | Type of Engine | Cargo Cap. or Gross* | Overall Length | Breadth | Depth or Draft* |
|---|---|---|---|---|---|---|---|---|
| | G.T.B. No. 2 | DH | 1968 | B | 1,600 | 195' 00" | 35' 00" | 12' 00" |
| | L.S.C. 236 | TK | 1946 | B | 10,000 | 195' 00" | 35' 00" | 10' 06" |
| | Marysville | TK | 1973 | B | 16,000 | 200' 00" | 50' 00" | 12' 06" |
| | *(N.M.S. No. 102 '73 - '81)* | | | | | | | |
| | Patricia Hoey {2} | TB | 1949 | D | 146* | 88' 06" | 25' 00" | 11' 00" |
| | *(Propeller '49 - '82, Bantry Bay '82 - '91)* | | | | | | | |
| | Roger Stahl | TB | 1944 | D | 148* | 110' 00" | 26' 05" | 15' 05" |
| | *(USCGC Kennebec [WYT-61] '44 - '44, USCGC Kaw [WYT-61] '44 - '80, Kaw '80 - '97)* | | | | | | | |
| | Shannon | TB | 1944 | D | 145* | 101' 00" | 28' 00" | 13' 00" |
| | *(USS Connewango [YT / YTB / YTM-388] '44 - '77)* | | | | | | | |
| | Susan Hoey {3} | TB | 1950 | D | 146* | 82' 00" | 25' 00" | 10' 07" |
| | *(Navajo {1} '50 - '53, Seaval '53 - '64, Mary T. Tracy '64 - '69, Yankee '69 - '70, Minn '70 - '74, William S. Bell '74 - '83, Newcastle '83 - '93, Laura Lynn '93 - '99)* | | | | | | | |
| | William Hoey {2} | TB | 1924 | D | 99* | 85' 00" | 21' 06" | 10' 09" |
| | *(Martha C. '24 - '52, Langdon C. Hardwicke '52 - '82, Wabash {2} '82 - '93, Katie Ann {1} '93 - '99)* | | | | | | | |
| **G-3** | **GALACTICA 001 ENTERPRISE LTD., TORONTO, ON** | | | | | | | |
| | Galactica 001 | ES | 1957 | D | 67* | 50' 00" | 16' 00" | 6' 03" |
| **G-4** | **GALCON MARINE LTD., TORONTO, ON** | | | | | | | |
| | Kenteau | TB | 1937 | D | 15* | 54' 07" | 16' 04" | 4' 02" |
| **G-5** | **GALLAGHER MARINE CONSTRUCTION CO., INC., ESCANABA, MI** | | | | | | | |
| | Bee Jay | TB | 1939 | D | 19* | 45' 00" | 13' 00" | 7' 00" |
| **G-6** | **GANANOQUE BOAT LINE LTD., GANANOQUE, ON** | | | | | | | |
| | Thousand Islander | ES | 1972 | D | 200* | 96' 11" | 22' 01" | 5' 05" |
| | Thousand Islander II | ES | 1973 | D | 200* | 99' 00" | 22' 01" | 5' 00" |
| | Thousand Islander III | ES | 1975 | D | 376* | 118' 00" | 28' 00" | 6' 00" |
| | Thousand Islander IV | ES | 1976 | D | 347* | 110' 09" | 28' 04" | 10' 08" |
| | Thousand Islander V | ES | 1979 | D | 246* | 88' 00" | 24' 00" | 5' 00" |
| **G-7** | **GANNON UNIVERSITY, ERIE, PA** | | | | | | | |
| | Environaut | RV | 1950 | D | 17* | 55' 00" | 13' 06" | 3' 10"* |
| **G-8** | **GEO. GRADEL CO., SANDUSKY, OH** | | | | | | | |
| | Amber Jean | TB | 1942 | D | 59* | 61' 00" | 18' 02" | 8' 02" |
| | Mighty Jake | TB | 1969 | D | 15* | 36' 00" | 12' 03" | 7' 03" |
| | Mighty Jessie | TB | 1954 | D | 57* | 61' 02" | 18' 00" | 7' 03" |
| | Mighty Jimmy | TB | 1945 | D | 27* | 56' 00" | 15' 10" | 7' 00" |
| | Mighty John III | TB | 1962 | D | 24* | 45' 00" | 15' 00" | 5' 10" |
| | Pioneerland | TB | 1943 | D | 45* | 59' 06" | 17' 00" | 7' 06"* |
| | Prairieland | TB | 1955 | D | 29* | 50' 00" | 15' 07" | 6' 05"* |
| | The Clyde | | 1922 | B | 704* | 150' 00" | 40' 00" | 12' 00" |
| | Timberland | TB | 1946 | D | 19* | 44' 00" | 13' 05" | 6' 11"* |
| **G-9** | **GEORGIAN BAY CRUISE CO. INC., PARRY SOUND, ON** | | | | | | | |
| | Chippewa {5} | PA | 1954 | D | 47* | 65' 00" | 16' 00" | 6' 06" |
| **G-10** | **GILLESPIE OIL & TRANSIT, INC., ST. JAMES, MI** | | | | | | | |
| | American Girl | PK | 1922 | D | 40 | 64' 00" | 14' 00" | 8' 03" |
| | Oil Queen | TK | 1949 | B | 620 | 65' 00" | 16' 00" | 6' 00" |
| **G-11** | **GODERICH ELEVATORS LTD., GODERICH, ON** | | | | | | | |
| | Willowglen | BC | 1943 | R | 16,300 | 620' 06" | 60' 00" | 35' 00" |
| | *(Launched as Mesabi. Lehigh {3} '43 - '81, Joseph X. Robert '81 - '82)* | | | | | | | |
| | *(Last operated Dec. 21, 1992; In use as a grain storage vessel at Goderich, ON.)* | | | | | | | |
| **G-12** | **GOODTIME ISLAND CRUISES, INC., SANDUSKY, OH** | | | | | | | |
| | Goodtime I | ES | 1960 | D | 81* | 111' 00" | 29' 08" | 9' 05" |
| **G-13** | **GOODTIME TRANSIT BOATS, INC., CLEVELAND, OH** | | | | | | | |
| | Goodtime III | ES | 1990 | D | 95* | 161' 00" | 40' 00" | 11' 00" |

**Algonorth loads at Sarnia (top).**
*(Marc Dease)*

**Walter J. McCarthy Jr. at full speed on Lake Superior (right).**
*(Mike Sipper)*

**Freshly-painted Frontenac loads at Duluth (bottom).**
*(Glenn Blaszkiewicz)*

| Fleet #. | Fleet Name<br>Vessel Name | Type of<br>Vessel | Year<br>Built | Type of<br>Engine | Cargo Cap.<br>or Gross* | Overall<br>Length | Breadth | Depth or<br>Draft* |
|---|---|---|---|---|---|---|---|---|
| **G-14** | **GOWESH CANADA INC., TORONTO, ON** | | | | | | | |
| | Katran-2 | HY | 1995 | D | 135* | 113' 02" | 33' 10" | 5' 11" |
| | *(Seawing I '95 - '95)* | | | | | | | |
| | Katran-3 | HY | 1996 | D | 135* | 113' 02" | 33' 10" | 5' 11" |
| | Seaflight I | HY | 1994 | D | 135* | 113' 02" | 33' 10" | 5' 11" |
| | *(Katran-1 '94 - '98)* | | | | | | | |
| | Seaflight II | HY | 1996 | D | 135* | 113' 02" | 33' 10" | 5' 11" |
| | *(Katran-4 '96 - '98)* | | | | | | | |
| **G-15** | **GRAMPA WOO EXCURSIONS, BEAVER BAY, MN** | | | | | | | |
| | Grampa Woo III | ES | 1978 | D | 99* | 115' 00" | 22' 00" | 5' 00"* |
| **G-16** | **GRAND VALLEY STATE UNIVERSITY, ALLENDALE, MI**<br>**ROBERT B. ANNIS WATER RESOURCES INSTITUTE** | | | | | | | |
| | D. J. Angus | RV | 1986 | D | 14* | 45' 00" | 14' 00" | 4' 00"* |
| | W. G. Jackson | RV | 1996 | D | 80* | 64' 10" | 20' 00" | 5' 00"* |
| **G-17** | **GRAVEL & LAKE SERVICES LTD., THUNDER BAY, ON** | | | | | | | |
| | Donald Mac | TB | 1914 | D | 69* | 71' 00" | 17' 00" | 10' 00" |
| | F. A. Johnson | TB | 1953 | B | 439* | 150' 00" | 32' 00" | 10' 00" |
| | *(Capt. Charles T. Parker '52 - '54, Rapid Cities '54 - '69, S. P. Renolds '69 - '70)* | | | | | | | |
| | George N. Carleton | TB | 1943 | D | 97* | 82' 00" | 21' 00" | 11' 00" |
| | *(HMCS Glenlea [W-25] '43 - '45, Bansaga '45 - '64)* | | | | | | | |
| | Peninsula | TB | 1944 | D | 261* | 111' 00" | 27' 00" | 13' 00" |
| | *(HMCS Norton [W-31] '44 - '45, W.A.C. 1 '45 - '46)* | | | | | | | |
| | Robert John | TB | 1945 | D | 98* | 82' 00" | 20' 01" | 11' 00" |
| | *(HMCS Gleneagle [W-40] '45 - '46, Bansturdy '46 - '65)* | | | | | | | |
| | Wolf River | BC | 1956 | D | 5,880 | 349' 02" | 43' 07" | 25' 04" |
| | *(Tecumseh {2} '56 - '67, New York News {3} '67 - '86, Stella Desgagnes '86 - '93, Beam Beginner '94 - '95)* | | | | | | | |
| **G-18** | **GREAT LAKES ASSOCIATES, INC., ROCKY RIVER, OH** | | | | | | | |
| | Kinsman Independent {3} | BC | 1952 | T | 18,800 | 642' 03" | 67' 00" | 35' 00" |
| | *(Charles L. Hutchinson {3} '52 - '62, Ernest R. Breech '62 - '88)* | | | | | | | |
| **G-19** | **GREAT LAKES DOCK & MATERIALS, MUSKEGON, MI** | | | | | | | |
| | Fischer Hayden | TB | 1967 | D | 64* | 54' 00" | 22' 1" | 7' 1" |
| | *(Gloria G. Cheramie, Joyce P. Crosby)* | | | | | | | |
| | Duluth | TB | 1954 | D | 82* | 70' 00" | 20' 00" | 9' 08" |
| | *(U. S. Army ST-2015 '54 - '62)* | | | | | | | |
| **G-20** | **GREAT LAKES FLEET, INC., DULUTH, MN - A DIV. OF GREAT LAKES TRANSPORTATION LLC** | | | | | | | |
| | Arthur M. Anderson | SU | 1952 | T | 25,300 | 767' 00" | 70' 00" | 36' 00" |
| | *(Lengthened 120' - '75) (Converted to a self-unloader, '82)* | | | | | | | |
| | Cason J. Callaway | SU | 1952 | T | 25,300 | 767' 00" | 70' 00" | 36' 00" |
| | *(Lengthened 120' - '74) (Converted to a self-unloader, '82)* | | | | | | | |
| | Edgar B. Speer | SU | 1980 | D | 73,700 | 1,004' 00" | 105' 00" | 56' 00" |
| | Edwin H. Gott | SU | 1979 | D | 74,100 | 1,004' 00" | 105' 00" | 56' 00" |
| | *(Converted from shuttle self-unloader to deck-mounted self-unloader '96)* | | | | | | | |
| | John G. Munson {2} | SU | 1952 | T | 25,550 | 768' 03" | 72' 00" | 36' 00" |
| | *(Lengthened 102' - '76)* | | | | | | | |
| | Philip R. Clarke | SU | 1952 | T | 25,300 | 767' 00" | 70' 00" | 36' 00" |
| | *(Lengthened 120' - '74) (Converted to a self-unloader, '82)* | | | | | | | |
| | Roger Blough | SU | 1972 | D | 43,900 | 858' 00" | 105' 00" | 41' 06" |
| | *GLF GREAT LAKES CORP., DULUTH, MN - A DIVISION OF GREAT LAKES FLEET, INC.* | | | | | | | |
| | Presque Isle {2} | IT | 1973 | D | 1,578* | 153' 03" | 54' 00" | 31' 03" |
| | Presque Isle {2} | SU | 1973 | B | 57,500 | 974' 06" | 104' 07" | 46' 06" |
| | **[ITB Presque Isle OA dimensions together]** | | | | | 1,000' 00" | 104' 07" | 46' 06" |
| **G-21** | **THE GREAT LAKES GROUP, CLEVELAND, OH**<br>*THE GREAT LAKES TOWING CO., CLEVELAND, OH - DIVISION OF THE GREAT LAKES GROUP* | | | | | | | |
| | Alabama {2} | TB | 1916 | D | 98* | 81' 00" | 21' 03" | 12' 05" |

| Fleet #. | Fleet Name / Vessel Name | Type of Vessel | Year Built | Type of Engine | Cargo Cap. or Gross* | Overall Length | Breadth | Depth or Draft* |
|---|---|---|---|---|---|---|---|---|
| | Arizona | TB | 1931 | D | 98* | 84' 04" | 20' 00" | 12' 06" |
| | Arkansas {2} | TB | 1909 | D | 98* | 81' 00" | 21' 03" | 12' 05" |
| | *(Yale '09 - '48)* | | | | | | | |
| | California | TB | 1926 | D | 98* | 81' 00" | 20' 00" | 12' 06" |
| | Colorado | TB | 1928 | D | 98* | 84' 04" | 20' 00" | 12' 06" |
| | Delaware {4} | TB | 1924 | D | 98* | 81' 00" | 20' 00" | 12' 06" |
| | Florida | TB | 1926 | D | 99* | 81' 00" | 20' 00" | 12' 06" |
| | *(Florida '26 - '83, Pinellas '83 - '84)* | | | | | | | |
| | Idaho | TB | 1931 | D | 98* | 84' 00" | 20' 00" | 12' 06" |
| | Illinois {2} | TB | 1914 | D | 99* | 81' 00" | 20' 00" | 12' 06" |
| | Indiana | TB | 1911 | D | 97* | 81' 00" | 20' 00" | 12' 06" |
| | Iowa | TB | 1915 | D | 98* | 81' 00" | 20' 00" | 12' 06" |
| | Kansas | TB | 1927 | D | 98* | 81' 00" | 20' 00" | 12' 06" |
| | Kentucky {2} | TB | 1929 | D | 98* | 84' 04" | 20' 00" | 12' 06" |
| | Louisiana | TB | 1917 | D | 98* | 81' 00" | 20' 00" | 12' 06" |
| | Maine {1} | TB | 1921 | D | 96* | 81' 00" | 20' 00" | 12' 06" |
| | *(Maine {1} '21 - '82, Saipan '82 - '83, Hillsboro '83 - '84)* | | | | | | | |
| | Massachusetts | TB | 1928 | D | 98* | 84' 04" | 20' 00" | 12' 06" |
| | Milwaukee | DB | 1924 | B | 1,095 | 172' 00" | 40' 00" | 11' 06" |
| | Minnesota {1} | TB | 1911 | D | 98* | 81' 00" | 20' 00" | 12' 06" |
| | Mississippi | TB | 1916 | D | 98* | 81' 00" | 20' 00" | 12' 06" |
| | Missouri {2} | TB | 1927 | D | 149* | 88' 04" | 24' 06" | 12' 03" |
| | *(Rogers City {1} '27 - '56, Dolomite {1} '56 - '81, Chippewa {7} '81 - '90)* | | | | | | | |
| | Montana | TB | 1929 | D | 98* | 84' 04" | 20' 00" | 12' 06" |
| | Nebraska | TB | 1929 | D | 98* | 84' 04" | 20' 00" | 12' 06" |
| | New Jersey | TB | 1924 | D | 98* | 81' 00" | 20' 00" | 12' 06" |
| | *(New Jersey '24 - '52, Petco-21 '52 - '53)* | | | | | | | |
| | New York | TB | 1913 | D | 98* | 81' 00" | 20' 00" | 12' 06" |
| | North Carolina {2} | TB | 1952 | D | 145* | 87' 09" | 24' 01" | 10' 07" |
| | *(Limestone '52 - '83, Wicklow '83 - '90)* | | | | | | | |
| | North Dakota | TB | 1910 | D | 97* | 81' 00" | 20' 00" | 12' 06" |
| | *(John M. Truby '10 - '38)* | | | | | | | |
| | Ohio {3} | TB | 1903 | D | 194* | 118' 00" | 24' 00" | 13' 06" |
| | *(M.F.D. No. 15 '03 - '52, Laurence C. Turner '52 - '73)* | | | | | | | |
| | Oklahoma | TB | 1913 | D | 97* | 81' 00" | 20' 00" | 12' 06" |
| | *(T. C. Lutz {2} '13 - '34)* | | | | | | | |
| | Pennsylvania {3} | TB | 1911 | D | 98* | 81' 00" | 20' 00" | 12' 06" |
| | Rhode Island | TB | 1930 | D | 98* | 84' 04" | 20' 00" | 12' 06" |
| | South Carolina | TB | 1925 | D | 102* | 86' 00" | 21' 00" | 11' 00" |
| | *(Welcome {2} '25 - '53, Joseph H. Callan '53 - '72, South Carolina '72 - '82, Tulagi '82 - '83)* | | | | | | | |
| | Superior {3} | TB | 1912 | D | 147* | 97' 00" | 22' 00" | 12' 00" |
| | *(Richard Fitzgerald '12 - '46)* | | | | | | | |
| | Tennessee | TB | 1917 | D | 98* | 81' 00" | 20' 00" | 12' 06" |
| | Texas | TB | 1916 | D | 97* | 81' 00" | 20' 00" | 12' 06" |
| | Vermont | TB | 1914 | D | 98* | 81' 00" | 20' 00" | 12' 06" |
| | Virginia {2} | TB | 1914 | D | 97* | 81' 00" | 20' 00" | 12' 06" |
| | Washington {1} | TB | 1925 | D | 97* | 81' 00" | 20' 00" | 12' 06" |
| | Wisconsin {4} | TB | 1897 | D | 105* | 90' 03" | 21' 00" | 12' 03" |
| | *(America {3} 1897 - '82, Midway '82 - '83)* | | | | | | | |
| | Wyoming | TB | 1929 | D | 104 | 84' 04" | 20' 00" | 12' 06" |

**G-22 GREAT LAKES MARINE ENGINEERING & SALVAGE, INC., ALPENA, MI**

| | Atlas | RV | 1941 | D | 157* | 90' 07" | 21' 04" | 11' 00" |
|---|---|---|---|---|---|---|---|---|

**G-23 GREAT LAKES MARITIME ACADEMY - NORTHWESTERN MICHIGAN COLLEGE, TRAVERSE CITY, MI**

| | Anchor Bay | TV | 1953 | D | 23* | 45' 00" | 13' 00" | 7' 00"* |
|---|---|---|---|---|---|---|---|---|
| | *(USCOE Anchor Bay '53 - ?)* | | | | | | | |
| | Northwestern {2} | TV | 1969 | D | 12* | 55' 00" | 15' 00" | 6' 06" |
| | *(USCOE North Central '69 - '98)* | | | | | | | |

| Fleet #. | Fleet Name<br>Vessel Name | Type of<br>Vessel | Year<br>Built | Type of<br>Engine | Cargo Cap.<br>or Gross* | Overall<br>Length | Breadth | Depth or<br>Draft* |
|---|---|---|---|---|---|---|---|---|
| | State of Michigan | TV | 1986 | D | 1,914* | 224' 00" | 43' 00" | 20' 00" |
| | (USCG Persistence '86-'02) | | | | | | | |
| **G-24** | **GREAT LAKES RESPONSE CORP. LTD., OTTAWA, ON** | | | | | | | |
| | Dover Light | EV | 1968 | B | 7,870 | 146' 05" | 50' 00" | 13' 07" |
| | (Jackson Purchase '68 - '83, Eliza S-1877 '83 - '86) | | | | | | | |
| | S.M.T.B. No. 7 | EV | 1969 | B | 7,502 | 150' 00" | 33' 00" | 14' 00" |
| **G-25** | **GREAT LAKES SCHOONER CO., TORONTO, ON** | | | | | | | |
| | Challenge | ES | 1980 | W | 76* | 96' 00" | 16' 06" | 8' 00" |
| | Kajama | ES | 1930 | W | 263* | 128' 09" | 22' 09" | 11' 08" |
| **G-26** | **GREAT LAKES SHIPWRECK HISTORICAL SOCIETY, SAULT STE. MARIE, MI** | | | | | | | |
| | David Boyd | RV | 1982 | D | 26* | 47' 00" | 17' 00" | 3' 00"* |
| **G-27** | **GREAT LAKES TRANSPORT LTD., HALIFAX, NS** | | | | | | | |
| | Jane Ann IV | TBA | 1978 | D | 954* | 137' 06" | 42' 08" | 21' 04" |
| | (Ouro Fino '78 - '81, Bomare '81 - '93, Tignish Sea '93 - '98) | | | | | | | |
| | Sarah Spencer | SU | 1959 | B | 23,200 | 611" 03" | 72' 00" | 40' 00" |
| | (Adam E. Cornelius {3} '59 - '89, Capt. Edward V. Smith '89 - '91, Sea Barge One '91 - '96;<br>(Engine removed, converted to a self-unloading barge, '89) | | | | | | | |
| **G-28** | **GREG RUDNICK, CLEVELAND, OH** | | | | | | | |
| | Forest City | BB | 1934 | D | 22* | 44' 04" | 11' 11" | 4' 09" |
| **H-1** | **HALRON OIL CO., INC., GREEN BAY, WI** | | | | | | | |
| | Mr. Micky | TK | 1940 | B | 10,500 | 195' 00" | 35' 00" | 10' 00" |
| **H-2** | **HAMILTON HARBOUR COMMISSIONERS, HAMILTON, ON** | | | | | | | |
| | Judge McCombs | TB | 1948 | D | 10* | 36' 00" | 10' 03" | 4' 00" |
| **H-3** | **HANNAH MARINE CORP., LEMONT, IL** | | | | | | | |
| | David E. | TB | 1945 | D | 602* | 149' 00" | 33' 00" | 16' 00" |
| | (U. S. Army LT-815 '45 - '64, Henry Foss '64 - '84, Kristin Lee '84 - '93, Kristin Lee Hannah '93 - 2001) | | | | | | | |
| | Daryl C. Hannah {2} | TB | 1956 | D | 268* | 102' 00" | 28' 00" | 8' 00" |
| | (Cindy Jo '56 - '66, Katherine L. '66 - '93) | | | | | | | |
| | Donald C. Hannah | TB | 1962 | D | 191* | 91' 00" | 29' 00" | 11' 06" |
| | E-63 | TK | 1980 | B | 60,000 | 407' 00" | 60' 00" | 20' 00" |
| | Hannah 1801 | TK | 1967 | B | 18,550 | 240' 00" | 50' 00" | 12' 00" |
| | (BRI 5 '67 - '88, CT-75 '88 - '92) | | | | | | | |
| | Hannah 1802 | TK | 1967 | B | 18,550 | 240' 00" | 50' 00" | 12' 00" |
| | (BRI 6 '67 - '87, CT-76 '87 - '92) | | | | | | | |
| | Hannah 2801 | TK | 1980 | B | 28,665 | 275' 00" | 54' 00" | 17' 06" |
| | (O.L.S.-30 '80 - '90) | | | | | | | |
| | Hannah 2901 | TK | 1962 | B | 17,400 | 264' 00" | 52' 06" | 12' 06" |
| | Hannah 2902 | TK | 1962 | B | 17,360 | 264' 00" | 52' 06" | 12' 06" |
| | Hannah 2903 | TK | 1962 | B | 17,350 | 264' 00" | 52' 06" | 12' 06" |
| | (2903 '62 - '90) | | | | | | | |
| | Hannah 3601 | TK | 1972 | B | 35,360 | 290' 00" | 60' 00" | 18' 03" |
| | Hannah 5101 | TK | 1978 | B | 49,660 | 360' 00" | 60' 00" | 22' 06" |
| | James A. Hannah | TB | 1945 | D | 593* | 149' 00" | 33' 00" | 16' 00" |
| | (U. S. Army LT-820 '45 - '65, Muskegon {1} '65 - '71) | | | | | | | |
| | Kristin Lee Hannah | TB | 1953 | D | 397* | 111' 10" | 35' 00" | 8' 04" |
| | Mark Hannah | TRA | 1969 | D | 191* | 127' 05" | 32' 01" | 14' 03" |
| | (Lead Horse '69 - '73, Gulf Challenger '73 - '80, Challenger {2} '80 - '93) | | | | | | | |
| | Mary E. Hannah | TB | 1945 | D | 612* | 149' 00" | 33' 00" | 16' 00" |
| | (U. S. Army LT-821 '45 - '47, Brooklyn '47 - '66, Lee Reuben '66 - '75) | | | | | | | |
| | No. 25 | TK | 1949 | B | 19,500 | 254' 00" | 54' 00" | 11' 00" |
| | No. 26 | TK | 1949 | B | 19,500 | 254' 00" | 54' 00" | 11' 00" |
| | No. 28 | TK | 1957 | B | 20,725 | 240' 00" | 50' 00" | 12' 06" |
| | (Bay 220 '57 - '62, Tenneco 220 '62 - '70) | | | | | | | |
| | No. 29 {2} | TK | 1952 | B | 22,000 | 254' 00" | 54' 00" | 11' 06" |

*Mesabi Miner fights Detroit River ice on Dec. 28, 2000.* *(Paul Beesley)*

| Fleet #. | Fleet Name / Vessel Name | Type of Vessel | Year Built | Type of Engine | Cargo Cap. or Gross* | Overall Length | Breadth | Depth or Draft* |
|---|---|---|---|---|---|---|---|---|
| | Susan W. Hannah | TBA | 1977 | D | 174* | 121' 06" | 34' 06" | 18' 02" |
| | *(Lady Elda '77 - '78, Kings Challenger '78 - '78, ITM No. 1 '78 - '81, Kings Challenger '81 - '86)* | | | | | | | |
| | **GENERAL MARINE TOWING, SOUTH CHICAGO, IL - DIVISION OF HANNAH MARINE CORP.** | | | | | | | |
| | Mary Page Hannah {2} | TB | 1972 | D | 99* | 59' 08" | 24' 01" | 10' 03" |
| | *(Kings Squire '72 - '78, Juanita D. '78 - '79 Katherine L. '79 - '93)* | | | | | | | |
| | Hannah D. Hannah | TB | 1955 | D | 134* | 86' 00" | 24' 00" | 10' 00" |
| | *(Harbor Ace '55 - '61, Gopher State '61 - '71, Betty Gale '71 - '93)* | | | | | | | |
| | Peggy D. Hannah | TB | 1920 | D | 145* | 108' 00" | 25' 00" | 14' 00" |
| | *(William A. Whitney '20 - '92)* | | | | | | | |
| | Susan E. | TB | 1921 | D | 96* | 81' 00" | 20' 00" | 12' 06" |
| | *(Oregon {1} '21 - '78, Ste. Marie I '78 - '81, Sioux {2} '81 - '91)* | | | | | | | |
| | **HMC SHIP MANAGEMENT LTD., LEMONT, IL - AN AFFILIATE OF HANNAH MARINE CORP.** | | | | | | | |
| | C.T.C. No. 1 | CC | 1943 | R | 16,300 | 620' 06" | 60' 00" | 35' 00" |
| | *(Launched as McIntyre. Frank Purnell {1} '43 - '64, Steelton {3} '64 - '78, Hull No. 3 '78 - '79,* | | | | | | | |
| | *Pioneer {4} '79 - '82)* | | | | | | | |
| | *(Last operated Nov. 12, 1981; In use as a cement storage / transfer vessel in S. Chicago, IL.)* | | | | | | | |
| | Southdown Challenger | CC | 1906 | S | 10,250 | 552' 01" | 56' 00" | 31' 00" |
| | *(William P. Snyder '06 - '26, Elton Hoyt II {1} '26 - '52, Alex D. Chisholm '52 - '66, Medusa Challenger '66 - '99)* | | | | | | | |
| | *(Repowered, '50; Converted to a self-unloading cement carrier, '67)* | | | | | | | |
| | Southdown Conquest | CC | 1937 | B | 8,500 | 437' 06" | 55' 00" | 28' 00" |
| | *(Red Crown '37 - '62, Amoco Indiana '62 - '87, Medusa Conquest '87 - '99)* | | | | | | | |
| | *(Converted from a powered tanker to a self-unloading cement barge, '87)* | | | | | | | |
| **H-4** | **HARBOR LIGHT CRUISE LINES, INC., TOLEDO, OH** | | | | | | | |
| | Sandpiper | ES | 1984 | D | 19* | 65' 00" | 16' 00" | 4' 00" |
| **H-5** | **HARBOR TOWN RIVERBOAT CO., INC., ROCHESTER, NY** | | | | | | | |
| | Harbor Town | ES | 1997 | D | `71* | 64' 05" | 24' 00" | 5' 05" |
| **H-6** | **HARBOUR PRINCESS TOURS, PORT DOVER, ON** | | | | | | | |
| | Harbour Princess 1 | ES | | D | | 100' 00" | 22' 00" | 4' 05" |
| | *(Johnny B. ?-?, Garden City '89 - '00)* | | | | | | | |
| **H-7** | **HARLEQUIN CRUISE LINES, TORONTO, ON** | | | | | | | |
| | River Gambler | ES | 1992 | D | 332* | 100' 07" | 40' 00" | 4' 06" |
| **H-8** | **HARRAH'S CASINO, EAST CHICAGO, IN** | | | | | | | |
| | Showboat Mardi Gras | GA | 1996 | D | 12,182* | 340' 00" | 74' 00" | 17' 06" |
| **H-9** | **HARRY GAMBLE SHIPYARDS, PORT DOVER, ON** | | | | | | | |
| | H. A. Smith | TB | 1944 | D | 24* | 55' 00" | 16' 00" | 5' 06" |
| | J. A. Cornett | TB | 1937 | D | 60* | 65' 00" | 17' 00" | 9' 00" |
| **H-10** | **HERITAGE CRUISE LINES, PARRY SOUND, ON** | | | | | | | |
| | Georgian Clipper | PA | 1967 | D | 170* | 78' 08" | 12' 06" | 6' 00" |
| **H-11** | **HERITAGE HARBOR MARINE, GODERICH, ON** | | | | | | | |
| | Salvage Monarch | TB | 1959 | D | 219* | 97' 09" | 28' 00" | 14' 06" |
| | Seven Sisters | TB | 1954 | D | 225* | 101' 10" | 26' 00" | 13' 08" |
| | *(Charlie S. '54 - '75, Cathy McAllister '75-'02)* | | | | | | | |
| **H-12** | **HOLLY MARINE TOWING, CHICAGO, IL** | | | | | | | |
| | Chris Ann | TB | 1981 | D | 45* | 51' 09" | 17' 00" | 6' 01" |
| | *(Captain Robbie '81 - '90, Philip M. Pearse '90 - '97)* | | | | | | | |
| | Debra Ann | TB | 1960 | D | 36* | 46' 02" | 15' 02" | 6' 03" |
| | Holly Ann | TB | 1926 | D | 220* | 108' 00" | 26' 06" | 15' 00" |
| | *(Wm. A. Lydon '26 - '92)* | | | | | | | |
| | Katie Ann {3} | TB | 1962 | D | 84* | 60' 04" | 24' 00" | 8' 06" |
| | Margaret Ann | TB | 1954 | D | 131* | 82' 00" | 24' 06" | 11' 06" |
| | *(John A. McGuire '54 - '87, William Hoey {1} '87 - '94)* | | | | | | | |
| **H-13** | **HORNE TRANSPORTATION, WOLFE ISLAND, ON** | | | | | | | |
| | William Darrell | CF | 1952 | D | 66* | 66' 00" | 28' 00" | 6' 00" |

| Fleet #. | Fleet Name / Vessel Name | Type of Vessel | Year Built | Type of Engine | Cargo Cap. or Gross* | Overall Length | Breadth | Depth or Draft* |
|---|---|---|---|---|---|---|---|---|
| H- 14 | **HOTLINE INDUSTRIES, SUPERIOR, WI** | | | | | | | |
| | Marine Supplier | GR | 1950 | D | 51* | 58' 00" | 15' 00" | 7' 00" |
| | *(Ted '50 - '50, Kaner I '50 - '98)* | | | | | | | |
| H-15 | **HOWE ISLAND TOWNSHIP, KINGSTON, ON** | | | | | | | |
| | The Howe Islander | CF | 1946 | D | 13* | 53' 00" | 12' 00" | 3' 00" |
| H-16 | **HUFFMAN EQUIPMENT RENTAL AND CONTRACTING, EASTLAKE, OH** | | | | | | | |
| | Hamp Thomas | TB | 1968 | D | 22* | 43' 00" | 13' 00" | 4' 00" |
| | Paddy Miles | TB | 1934 | D | 16* | 45' 04" | 12' 04" | 4' 07" |
| H-17 | **HULLFORMS (CANADA), INC., WIARTON, ON** | | | | | | | |
| | Cloud Chaser | ES | 1979 | D | 62* | 67' 00" | 17' 00" | 11' 00" |
| I-1 | **ILLINOIS MARINE TOWING, INC., LEMONT, IL** | | | | | | | |
| | Aggie C | TB | 1977 | D | 89* | 81' 00" | 26' 00" | 6' 10"* |
| | Albert C | TB | 1971 | D | 47* | 61' 02" | 18' 00" | 5' 08"* |
| | Eileen C | TB | 1982 | D | 122* | 75' 00" | 26' 00" | 8' 00"* |
| | Mary C | TB | 1946 | D | 34* | 56' 02" | 18' 00" | 5' 00"* |
| | William C | TB | 1968 | D | 105* | 76' 06" | 24' 00" | 6' 06"* |
| I-2 | **IMPERIAL OIL LTD. - ESSO PETROLEUM CANADA DIVISION, DARTMOUTH, NS** | | | | | | | |
| | Imperial Dartmouth | RT | 1970 | D | 15,265 | 205' 06" | 40' 00" | 16' 00" |
| I-3 | **INLAND BULK TRANSFER, CLEVELAND, OH** | | | | | | | |
| | Benjamin Ridgeway | TB | 1969 | D | 51* | 53' 00" | 18' 05" | 7' 05" |
| | Frank Palladino Jr. | TB | 1980 | D | 89* | 100' 00" | 32' 00" | 13' 00" |
| | *(Lady Ida '80 - '92)* | | | | | | | |
| | Inland 2401 | DB | 1968 | B | 2,589 | 240' 00" | 72' 00" | 14' 00" |
| | *(OC 240 '68 - '77, Martech Enterprise '77 - '84, Enterprise '84 - '88, Stevens 2401 '88 - ?)* | | | | | | | |
| | James Palladino | TB | 1999 | D | 392* | 109' 11" | 34' 01" | 16' 01" |
| | Kellstone 1 | SU | 1957 | B | 9,000 | 396' 00" | 71' 00" | 22' 06" |
| | *(M-211 '57 - '81, Virginia '81 - '88, C-11 '88 - '93)* | | | | | | | |
| I-4 | **INLAND LAKES MANAGEMENT, INC., ALPENA, MI** | | | | | | | |
| | Alpena {2} | CC | 1942 | T | 15,550 | 519' 06" | 67' 00" | 35' 00" |
| | *(Leon Fraser '42 - '91 (Shortened 120' and converted to a self-unloading cement carrier, '91)* | | | | | | | |
| | E. M. Ford | CC | 1898 | Q | 7,100 | 428' 00" | 50' 00" | 28' 00" |
| | *(Presque Isle {1} 1898 - '56)* | | | | | | | |
| | *(Converted to a self-unloading cement carrier, '56; Last operated Sept. 16, 1996; In use as a cement storage and transfer vessel at Saginaw, MI.)* | | | | | | | |
| | J. A. W. Iglehart | CC | 1936 | T | 12,500 | 501' 06" | 68' 03" | 37' 00" |
| | *(Pan Amoco '36 - '55, Amoco '55 - '60, H. R. Schemn '60 - '65)* | | | | | | | |
| | *(Converted from a saltwater tanker to a self-unloading cement carrier, '56)* | | | | | | | |
| | Paul H. Townsend | CC | 1945 | D | 8,400 | 447' 00" | 50' 00" | 29' 00" |
| | *(USNS Hickory Coll '45 - '46, USNS Coastal Delegate '46 - '52)* | | | | | | | |
| | *(Converted from a saltwater cargo vessel to a self-unloading cement carrier, '52; Lengthened '58)* | | | | | | | |
| | S. T. Crapo | CC | 1927 | R | 8,900 | 402' 06" | 60' 03" | 29' 00" |
| | *(Last operated Sept. 4, 1996; In use as a cement storage / transfer vessel in Green Bay, WI.)* | | | | | | | |
| I-5 | **INLAND SEAS EDUCATION ASSOCIATION, SUTTONS BAY, MI** | | | | | | | |
| | Inland Seas | RV | 1994 | W | 41* | 61' 06" | 17' 00" | 7' 00" |
| I-6 | **THE INTERLAKE STEAMSHIP CO., RICHFIELD, OH** | | | | | | | |
| | Charles M. Beeghly | SU | 1959 | T | 31,000 | 806' 00" | 75' 00" | 37' 06" |
| | *(Shenango II '59 - '67) (Lengthened 96' -, '72; Converted to a self-unloader, '81)* | | | | | | | |
| | Elton Hoyt 2nd {2} | SU | 1952 | T | 22,300 | 698' 00" | 70' 00" | 37' 00" |
| | *(Lengthened 72'- '57; Converted to a self-unloader, '80; Last operated Jan. 11, 2001 – 5 year survey expires March, 2005; Laid up in Superior, WI.)* | | | | | | | |
| | Herbert C. Jackson | SU | 1959 | T | 24,800 | 690' 00" | 75' 00" | 37' 06" |
| | *(Converted to a self-unloader, '75)* | | | | | | | |
| | James R. Barker | SU | 1976 | D | 63,300 | 1,004' 00" | 105' 00" | 50' 00" |

| Fleet #. | Fleet Name / Vessel Name | Type of Vessel | Year Built | Type of Engine | Cargo Cap. or Gross* | Overall Length | Breadth | Depth or Draft* |
|---|---|---|---|---|---|---|---|---|
| | Mesabi Miner | SU | 1977 | D | 63,300 | 1,004' 00" | 105' 00" | 50' 00" |
| | Paul R. Tregurtha | SU | 1981 | D | 68,000 | 1,013' 06" | 105' 00" | 56' 00" |
| | *(William J. DeLancey '81 - '90)* | | | | | | | |

### INTERLAKE TRANSPORTATION, INC., RICHFIELD, OH - A DIV. OF THE INTERLAKE STEAMSHIP CO.

| | | | | | | | | |
|---|---|---|---|---|---|---|---|---|
| | Dorothy Ann | AT/TT | 1999 | D | 1,600* | 124' 03" | 44' 00" | 24' 00" |
| | Pathfinder {3} | SU | 1953 | B | 21,260 | 606' 02" | 70' 00" | 36' 00" |
| | *(J. L. Mauthe '53 - '98)* | | | | | | | |
| | *(Engine removed, converted from a powered bulk carrier to a self-unloading barge, '98)* | | | | | | | |
| | **[ATB Dorothy Ann / Pathfinder {3} OA dimensions together]** | | | | | 700' 00" | 70' 00" | 36' 00" |

### LAKES SHIPPING CO., INC., RICHFIELD, OH - A DIVISION OF THE INTERLAKE STEAMSHIP CO.

| | | | | | | | | |
|---|---|---|---|---|---|---|---|---|
| | John Sherwin {2} | BC | 1958 | T | 31,500 | 806' 00" | 75' 00" | 37' 06" |
| | *(Lengthened 96'- '73;  Last operated Nov. 16, 1981. In long-term layup at Superior, WI.)* | | | | | | | |
| | Kaye E. Barker | SU | 1952 | T | 25,900 | 767' 00" | 70' 00" | 36' 00" |
| | *(Edward B. Greene '52 - '85, Benson Ford {3} '85 - '89;)* | | | | | | | |
| | *(Lengthened 120'- '76; Converted to a self-unloader, '81)* | | | | | | | |
| | Lee A. Tregurtha | SU | 1942 | T | 29,300 | 826' 00" | 75' 00" | 39' 00" |
| | *(Laid down as Mobiloil, Launched as Samoset, USS Chiwawa [AO-68] '42 - '46, Chiwawa '46 - '61,* | | | | | | | |
| | *Walter A. Sterling '61 - '85, William Clay Ford {2} '85 - '89)* | | | | | | | |
| | *(Converted from a saltwater tanker to a Great Lakes bulk carrier, '61; Lengthend '96, '76; Converted* | | | | | | | |
| | *to a self-unloader, '78)* | | | | | | | |

### I-7    INTERNATIONAL MARINE SALVAGE CO. LTD., PORT COLBORNE, ON

| | | | | | | | | |
|---|---|---|---|---|---|---|---|---|
| | Canadian Venture | BC | 1965 | D | 28,050 | 730' 03" | 75' 00" | 39' 02" |
| | *(Lawrencecliffe Hall {2} '65 - '88, David K. Gardiner '88 - '94)* | | | | | | | |
| | *(Last operated Dec. 12, 2001. Scheduled for scrapping at Port Colborne, ON, in 2003.)* | | | | | | | |
| | Charlie E. | TB | 1943 | D | 32* | 63' 00" | 16' 06" | 7' 06" |
| | *(Kolbe '43 - '86,  Lois T. '86-'02)* | | | | | | | |
| | Comeaudoc | BC | 1960 | D | 26,750 | 730' 00" | 75' 06" | 37' 09" |
| | *(Murray Bay {2} '60 - '63) (Last operated Dec. 4, 1996. Scrapping underway at Port Colborne, ON)* | | | | | | | |
| | Kinsman Enterprise {2} | BC | 1927 | T | 16,100 | 631' 00" | 65' 00" | 33' 00" |
| | *(Harry Coulby {2} '27 - '89)* | | | | | | | |
| | *(Last operated Dec. 13, 1995. Scheduled for scrapping at Port Colborne, ON, in 2003.)* | | | | | | | |
| | Sea Castle | CC | 1909 | B | 2,600 | 260' 00" | 43' 00" | 25' 03" |
| | *(Kaministiquia {2} '09 - '16, Westoil '16 - '23, J. B. John {1} '23 - '51, John L. A. Galster '51 - '69)* | | | | | | | |
| | *(5 year survey expired November, 1983. Laid up in Muskegon, MI.)* | | | | | | | |

### I-8    INTERNATIONAL MARINE SYSTEMS LTD., MILWAUKEE, WI

| | | | | | | | | |
|---|---|---|---|---|---|---|---|---|
| | Iroquois {1} | ES | 1946 | D | 57* | 61' 09" | 21' 00" | 6' 04" |

### I-9    ISLAND EXPRESS BOAT LINES LTD., SANDUSKY, OH

| | | | | | | | | |
|---|---|---|---|---|---|---|---|---|
| | Island Rocket | PF | 1997 | D | 47* | 65' 00" | 18' 02" | 6' 00" |
| | Island Rocket II | PC | 1997 | D | 32* | 64' 07" | 19' 02" | 6' 05" |
| | Island Rocket III | PC | 1988 | D | 80* | 108' 00" | 29' 00" | 10' 02" |
| | *(Auk Nu - '02)* | | | | | | | |

### I-10    ISLAND FERRY SERVICES CORP., CHEBOYGAN, MI

| | | | | | | | | |
|---|---|---|---|---|---|---|---|---|
| | Polaris | PF | 1952 | D | 99* | 65' 00" | 36' 00" | 8' 00"* |

### I-11    (THE) ISLE ROYALE LINE, COPPER HARBOR, MI

| | | | | | | | | |
|---|---|---|---|---|---|---|---|---|
| | Isle Royale Queen III | PK | 1959 | D | 88* | 85' 00" | 18' 04" | 9' 05" |

### J-1    J. M. MARINE TOWING CORP., SYRACUSE, NY

| | | | | | | | | |
|---|---|---|---|---|---|---|---|---|
| | Dynamic | TB | 1958 | D | 19* | 34' 11" | 12' 00" | 4' 08"* |

### J-2    J. W. WESTCOTT CO., DETROIT, MI

| | | | | | | | | |
|---|---|---|---|---|---|---|---|---|
| | J. W. Westcott II | MB | 1949 | D | 11* | 46' 01" | 13' 04" | 4' 06" |
| | Joseph J. Hogan | MB | 1957 | D | 16* | 40' 00" | 12' 06" | 5' 00" |
| | *(USCOE Ottawa '57 - '95)* | | | | | | | |

### J-3    JACOBS INVESTMENTS - JRM, INC., CLEVELAND, OH

| | | | | | | | | |
|---|---|---|---|---|---|---|---|---|
| | Nautica Queen | ES | 1981 | D | 95* | 124' 00" | 31' 02" | 8' 10" |
| | *(Bay Queen '81 - '85, Arawanna Queen '85 - '88, Star of Nautica '88 - '92)* | | | | | | | |

**Lake Superior in the Welland Canal.** *(Alain Gindroz)*

| Fleet #. | Fleet Name<br>Vessel Name | Type of<br>Vessel | Year<br>Built | Type of<br>Engine | Cargo Cap.<br>or Gross* | Overall<br>Length | Breadth | Depth or<br>Draft* |
|---|---|---|---|---|---|---|---|---|
| **J-4** | **JOSEPH G. GAYTON, HARROW, ON** | | | | | | | |
| | Princess | TB | 1903 | D | 87* | 77' 00" | 20' 04" | 7' 11" |
| | *(Radiant '03 - '33, Anna Sheridan '33 - '62)* | | | | | | | |
| **J-5** | **JOSEPH MARTIN, BEAVER ISLAND, MI** | | | | | | | |
| | Shamrock {1} | TB | 1933 | D | 60* | 64' 00" | 18' 00" | 7' 04" |
| **J-6** | **JUBILEE QUEEN CRUISES, TORONTO, ON** | | | | | | | |
| | Jubilee Queen | ES | 1986 | D | 269* | 122' 00" | 23' 09" | 5' 05" |
| | *(Pioneer Princess III '86 - '89)* | | | | | | | |
| | Pioneer Princess | ES | 1984 | D | 74* | 56' 00" | 17' 01" | 3' 09" |
| | Pioneer Queen | ES | 1968 | D | 110* | 85' 00" | 30' 06" | 7' 03" |
| | *(Peche Island III '68 - '71, Papoose IV '71 - '96)* | | | | | | | |
| **J-7** | **JULIO CONTRACTING CO., HANCOCK, MI** | | | | | | | |
| | Winnebago | TB | 1945 | D | 14* | 40' 00" | 10' 02" | 4' 06" |
| **K-1** | **K & K WAREHOUSING, MENOMINEE, MI** | | | | | | | |
| | Manitowoc | DB | 1926 | B | | 371' 03" | 67' 03" | 22' 06" |
| | Viking I | DB | 1925 | B | | 360' 00" | 56' 03" | 21' 06" |
| | *(Ann Arbor No. 7 '25 - '64, Viking {2} '64 - '96)* | | | | | | | |
| | *(Under conversion from a powered carferry to a pulpwood barge at Marinette, WI, 2003 )* | | | | | | | |
| | William H. Donner | CS | 1914 | B | 9,400 | 524' 00" | 54' 00" | 30' 00" |
| | *(Last operated in 1969; In use as a cargo transfer vessel at Marinette, WI.)* | | | | | | | |
| **K-2** | **KADINGER MARINE SERVICE, INC., MILWAUKEE, WI** | | | | | | | |
| | David J. Kadinger | TB | 1969 | D | 98* | 65' 06" | 22' 00" | 8' 06" |
| | *(N. F. Candies ? - ?, Connie Guidry ? - '89)* | | | | | | | |
| | Jake M. Kadinger | TB | 1984 | D | 131* | 77' 09" | 24' oo" | 12'00" |
| | Jason A. Kadinger | TB | 1963 | D | 60* | 52' 06" | 19' 01" | 7' 04" |
| | Kayla D. Kadinger | PA | 1958 | D | 24* | 39' 00" | 11' 00" | 6' 05" |
| | Kyle D. Kadinger | TB | 1962 | D | 35* | 47' 00" | 16' 00" | 6' 03" |
| | Ruffy J. Kadinger | TB | 1981 | D | 74* | 55' 00" | 23' 00" | 7' 02" |
| **K-3** | **KCBX TERMINALS CO., CHICAGO, IL** | | | | | | | |
| | Matador VI | TB | 1971 | D | 31* | 42' 00" | 18' 00" | 6' 00"* |
| **K-4** | **KELLEYS ISLAND BOAT LINES, MARBLEHEAD, OH** | | | | | | | |
| | Carlee Emily | PA/CF | 1987 | D | 98* | 101' 00" | 34' 06" | 10' 00" |
| | *(Endeavor '87 - '02)* | | | | | | | |
| | Joelle Ann Marie | PA/CF | 1960 | D | 81* | 64' 06" | 33' 00" | 9' 00" |
| | *(Commuter '60 - '02)* | | | | | | | |
| | Juliet Alicia | PA/CF | 1969 | D | 95* | 100' 00" | 34' 03" | 8' 00" |
| | *(Kelley Islander '69 - '02)* | | | | | | | |
| | Kayla Marie | PA/CF | 1975 | D | 93* | 122' 00" | 40' 00" | 8' 00" |
| | *(R. Bruce Etherige '75 - '97)* | | | | | | | |
| | Shirley Irene | PA/CF | 1991 | D | 68* | 160' 00" | 46' 00" | 9' 00" |
| **K-5** | **KENT LINE LTD., SAINT JOHN, NB** | | | | | | | |
| | Irving Canada | TK | 1981 | D | 297,407 | 628' 06" | 90' 02" | 48' 03" |
| | Irving Eskimo | TK | 1980 | D | 292,960 | 629' 00" | 90' 03" | 48' 03" |
| | Kent Carrier | GC | 1971 | B | 8,128 | 363' 00" | 82' 02" | 22' 03" |
| | *(Saint John Carrier '71 - '79, Nitinat Carrier '79 - '84, Irving Carrier '84 - '92)* | | | | | | | |
| | Kent Express | GC | 1999 | D | 17,500 | 503' 11" | 83' 00" | 44' 04" |
| | Kent Sprint | GC | 2000 | D | 17,500 | 503' 11" | 83' 00" | 44' 04" |
| | Kent Transport | GC | 1971 | B | 7,366 | 362' 10" | 82' 02" | 22' 03" |
| | *(Rothesay Carrier '71 - '97)* | | | | | | | |
| | Kent Voyageur | GC | 1982 | D | 15,912 | 488' 10" | 78' 01" | 42' 00" |
| | *(Reed Voyageur '82 - '88, Daishowa Voyageur '88 - '96)* | | | | | | | |
| | Wellington Kent {2} | TK | 1980 | D | 120,790 | 433' 11" | 67' 04" | 30' 04" |
| | *(Irving Nordic '80 - '93)* | | | | | | | |

| Fleet #. | Fleet Name<br>Vessel Name | Type of<br>Vessel | Year<br>Built | Type of<br>Engine | Cargo Cap.<br>or Gross* | Overall<br>Length | Breadth | Depth or<br>Draft* |
|---|---|---|---|---|---|---|---|---|
| **K-6** | **KEWEENAW EXCURSIONS, INC., HOUGHTON, MI** | | | | | | | |
| | Keweenaw Star | ES | 1981 | D | 97* | 110' 00" | 23' 04" | 6' 03" |
| | *(Atlantic Star ? - ?)* | | | | | | | |
| **K-7** | **KEYSTONE GREAT LAKES, INC., BALA CYNWYD, PA** | | | | | | | |
| | Great Lakes {2} | TK | 1982 | B | 75,000 | 414' 00" | 60' 00" | 30' 00" |
| | *(Amoco Great Lakes '82 - '85)* | | | | | | | |
| | Michigan {10} | AT | 1982 | D | 293* | 107' 08" | 34' 00" | 16' 00" |
| | *(Amoco Michigan '82 - '85)* | | | | | | | |
| | **[ATB Michigan / Great Lakes {2} OA dimensions together]** | | | | | 454' 00" | 60' 00" | 30' 00" |
| **K-8** | **KINDRA LAKE TOWING LP., DOWNERS GROVE, IL** | | | | | | | |
| | Buckley | TB | 1958 | D | 94* | 95' 00" | 26' 00" | 11' 00" |
| | *(Linda Brooks '58 - '67, Eddie B. {2} '67 - '95)* | | | | | | | |
| | Morgan | TB | 1974 | D | 134* | 90' 00" | 30' 00" | 10' 06" |
| | *(Donald O' Toole '74 - '86, Bonesey B. '86 - '95)* | | | | | | | |
| | Old Mission | TB | 1945 | D | 94* | 85' 00" | 23' 00" | 10' 04" |
| | *(U. S. Army ST-880 '45 - '47, USCOE Avondale '47 - '64, Adrienne B. '64 - '95)* | | | | | | | |
| **K-9** | **KING COMPANY, INC., HOLLAND, MI** | | | | | | | |
| | Barry J | TB | 1943 | D | 42* | 46' 00" | 13' 00" | 7' 00" |
| | Carol Ann | TB | 1981 | D | 115* | 68' 00" | 24' 00" | 8' 08" |
| | Julie Dee | TB | 1903 | D | 59* | 63' 03" | 17' 05" | 9' 00" |
| | *(Bonita {1} '03 - '16, Chicago Harbor No. 4 '16 - '60, Eddie B. {1} '60 - '69, Seneca Queen '69 - '70,* | | | | | | | |
| | *Ludington '70 -?)* | | | | | | | |
| | Miss Edna | TB | 1935 | D | 29* | 36' 08" | 11' 02" | 4' 08" |
| | Muskegon {2} | TB | 1973 | D | 138* | 75' 00" | 24' 00" | 11' 06" |
| **K-10** | **KINGSTON 1,000 ISLANDS CRUISES, KINGSTON, ON** | | | | | | | |
| | Island Belle I | ES | 1988 | D | 150* | 65' 00" | 22' 00" | 8' 00" |
| | *(Spirit of Brockville '88 - '91)* | | | | | | | |
| | Island Queen | ES | 1975 | D | 300* | 96' 00" | 26' 00" | 11' 00" |
| | Island Star | ES | 1994 | D | 220* | 97' 00" | 30' 00" | 10' 00" |
| | *(Le Bateau-Mouche II '94 - '98)* | | | | | | | |
| **L-1** | **L. R. JACKSON FISHIERS LTD., PORT STANLEY, ON** | | | | | | | |
| | G. W. Jackson | FT | 1964 | D | 109* | 70' 02" | 23' 08" | 4' 00" |
| | L. R. Jackson | FT | 1982 | D | 146* | 63' 00" | 21' 00" | 6' 00 |
| **L-2** | **LAFARGE CORP., SOUTHFIELD, M** | | | | | | | |
| | J. B. Ford | CC | 1904 | R | 8,000 | 440' 00" | 50' 00" | 28' 00" |
| | *(Edwin F. Holmes '04 - '16, E. C. Collins '16 - '59)* | | | | | | | |
| | *(Converted to a self-unloading cement carrier, '59; Last operated Nov. 15, 1985. In use as a* | | | | | | | |
| | *cement storage and transfer vessel at Superior WI.)* | | | | | | | |
| **L-3** | **LAKE MICHIGAN CARFERRY SERVICE, INC., LUDINGTON, MI** | | | | | | | |
| | Badger [43] {2} | CF | 1953 | S | 4,244* | 410' 06" | 59' 06" | 24' 00" |
| | Spartan [42] {2} | CF | 1952 | S | 4,244* | 410' 06" | 59' 06" | 24' 00" |
| | *(Last operated Jan. 20, 1979. In long-term layup at Ludington, MI.)* | | | | | | | |
| **L-4** | **LAKE MICHIGAN CONTRACTORS, INC., HOLLAND, MI** | | | | | | | |
| | Art Lapish | TB | 1954 | D | 15* | 44' 03" | 12' 08" | 5' 04" |
| | Beaver State | TB | 1935 | D | 18* | 43' 07" | 12' 00" | 5' 02" |
| | Cherokee {3} | DB | 1943 | R | 1,500 | 155' 00" | 50' 00" | 13' 00" |
| | Curly B. | TB | 1956 | D | 131* | 84' 00" | 26' 00" | 9' 02" |
| | *(Waverly '56 - '74, Bother Collins '74 - '80)* | | | | | | | |
| | G. W. Falcon | TB | 1936 | D | 22* | 49' 07" | 13' 08" | 6' 02" |
| | Iroquois {2} | DS | 1950 | B | 495* | 120' 00" | 30' 00" | 7' 00" |
| | James Harris | TB | 1943 | D | 18* | 41' 09" | 12' 05" | 5' 07" |
| | John Henry | TB | 1954 | D | 66* | 70' 00" | 20' 06" | 9' 07" |
| | *(U. S. Army ST-2013 '54 - '80)* | | | | | | | |
| | Ojibway {2} | DS | 1954 | B | 517* | 120' 00" | 50' 00" | 10' 00" |

| Fleet #. | Fleet Name<br>Vessel Name | Type of<br>Vessel | Year<br>Built | Type of<br>Engine | Cargo Cap.<br>or Gross* | Overall<br>Length | Breadth | Depth or<br>Draft* |
|---|---|---|---|---|---|---|---|---|
| | Shirley Joy | TB | 1978 | D | 98* | 72' 00" | 26' 00" | 7' 06" |
| | *(Douglas B. Mackie '78 - '97)* | | | | | | | |
| | Sioux {1} | DS | 1954 | B | 518* | 120' 00" | 50' 00" | 10' 00" |
| **L-5** | **LAKE TOWING, INC., AVON, OH** | | | | | | | |
| | Jiggs | TB | 1911 | D | 45* | 61' 00" | 16' 00" | 8' 00" |
| | Johnson | TB | 1976 | D | 287* | 140' 06" | 40' 00" | 15' 06" |
| | Johnson II | TB | 1975 | D | 311* | 194' 00" | 40' 00" | 17' 00" |
| | Menominee | TB | 1967 | D | 344* | 108' 00" | 29' 00" | 14' 00" |
| | Wolverine | TB | 1952 | D | 13* | 40' 00" | 11' 00" | 4' 05" |
| | 2361 | BC | 1967 | B | 3,600 | 236' 00" | 50' 00" | 15' 10" |
| | 3403 | SU | 1963 | B | 9,500 | 340' 00" | 62' 06" | 25' 04" |
| **L-6** | **LAKES PILOTS ASSOCIATION, PORT HURON, MI** | | | | | | | |
| | Huron Belle | PB | 1979 | D | 21* | 50' 00" | 16' 00" | 7' 09" |
| | Huron Maid | PB | 1976 | D | 26* | 46' 00" | 16' 00" | 3' 05" |
| **L-7** | **LE BATEAU-MOUCHE AU VIEUX, MONTREAL, QC** | | | | | | | |
| | Le Bateau-Mouche | ES | 1992 | D | 190* | 108' 00" | 22' 00" | 3' 00" |
| **L-8** | **LE BRUN NORTHERN CONTRACTING, THUNDER BAY, ON** | | | | | | | |
| | Henry T. | DB | 1932 | B | 1,000 | 120' 00" | 44' 00" | 11' 00" |
| **L-9** | **LE GROUPE C.T.M.A. (NAVIGATION MADELEINE INC.), CAP-AUX-MEULES, QC** | | | | | | | |
| | C.T.M.A. Vacancier | PA/RR | 1973 | D | 11,481* | 388' 04" | 70' 02" | 43' 06" |
| | *(Aurella '80 - '82, Saint Patrick II '82 - '98, Egnatia II '98 - '00, Ville de Sete '00 - '01, City of Cork '01 - '02)* | | | | | | | |
| **L-10** | **LE GROUPE OCEAN, INC., QUEBEC, QC** | | | | | | | |
| | Basse-Cote | DB | 1932 | B | 400 | 201' 00" | 40' 00" | 12' 00" |
| | Betsiamites | SU | 1969 | B | 11,600 | 402' 00" | 75' 00" | 24' 00" |
| | Coucoucache | TB | 1934 | D | 95* | 34' 01" | 9' 05" | 4' 02" |
| | Jerry G. | TB | 1960 | D | 202* | 91' 06" | 27' 03" | 12' 06" |
| | Lac St-Francois | BC | 1979 | B | 1,200 | 195' 00" | 35' 00" | 12' 00" |
| | La Prairie | TB | 1975 | D | 110* | 73' 09" | 25' 09" | 11' 08" |
| | Navcomar #1 | DB | 1955 | B | 500 | 135' 00" | 35' 00" | 9' 00" |
| | Ocean Abys | DB | 1948 | B | 1,000 | 140' 00" | 40' 00" | 9' 00" |
| | Ocean Bravo | TB | 1970 | D | 320* | 110' 00" | 28' 06" | 17' 00" |
| | *(Takis V. '70 - '80, Donald P '80 - '80, Nimue '80 - '83, Donald P. '83 - '98)* | | | | | | | |
| | Ocean Charlie | TB | 1973 | D | 448* | 123' 02" | 31' 06" | 18' 09" |
| | *(Leonard W. '73 - '98)* | | | | | | | |
| | Ocean Delta | TB | 1973 | D | 722* | 136' 08" | 35' 08" | 22' 00" |
| | *(Sistella '73 - '78, Sandy Cape '78 - '80, Captain Ioannis S. '80 - '99)* | | | | | | | |
| | Ocean Echo II | AT | 1969 | D | 438* | 104' 08" | 35' 05" | 18' 00" |
| | *(Atlantic '69 - '75, Laval '75 - '96)* | | | | | | | |
| | Ocean Foxtrot | TB | 1971 | D | 700* | 184' 05" | 38' 05" | 16' 07" |
| | *(Polor Shore '71 - '77, Canmar Supplier VII '77 - '95)* | | | | | | | |
| | Ocean Golf | TB | 1959 | D | 159* | 103' 09" | 25' 10" | 11' 09" |
| | *(Launched as Stranton. Helen M. McAllister '59 - '97)* | | | | | | | |
| | Ocean Hercule | TB | 1976 | D | 448* | 120' 00" | 32' 00" | 19' 00" |
| | *(Stril Pilot '76 - '81, Spirit Sky '81 - '86, Ierland '86 - '89, Ierlandia '89 - '95, Charles Antoine '95 - '97)* | | | | | | | |
| | Ocean Intrepide | TT | 1998 | D | 302* | 80' 00" | 30' 01" | 14' 09" |
| | Ocean Jupiter {2} | TT | 1999 | D | 302* | 80' 00" | 30' 00" | 13' 04" |
| | Omni-Atlas | CS | 1913 | B | 479* | 133' 00" | 42' 00" | 10' 00" |
| | Omni-Richelieu | TB | 1969 | D | 144* | 83' 00" | 24' 06" | 13' 06" |
| | *(Port Alfred II '69 - '82)* | | | | | | | |
| | Omni St-Laurent | TB | 1957 | D | 161* | 99' 02" | 24' 09" | 12' 06" |
| | *(Diligent '57 - '89)* | | | | | | | |
| | Vezina No. 1 | TB | 1967 | D | 8.00* | 31' 01" | 11' 01" | 5' 02" |
| | Windoc {2} | BC | 1959 | D | 29,100 | 730' 00" | 75' 09" | 40' 02" |
| | *(Rhine Ore '59 - '76, Steelcliffe Hall '76 - '88) (Damaged by fire Aug. 11, 2001 after a bridge was<br>lowered on its superstructure. Laid up awaiting possible conversion to a barge at Montreal, 2002. )* | | | | | | | |

# ATLANTIC ERIE

**W**hen the Great Lakes, St. Lawrence and ocean-class self-unloader **Hon. Paul Martin** was launched Nov. 1, 1984, she was the largest vessel ever built at Collingwood Shipyards, Collingwood, Ont.

The new self-unloader, operated by Canada Steamship Lines, sailed April 6, 1985, on

### Vessel Spotlight

her maiden voyage to Thunder Bay to load grain for Quebec City, but it was not long before the vessel moved almost exclusively into saltwater trades. The vessel loaded gypsum at Halifax, Sept. 15, 1985, bound for Tampa and New Orleans, and returned to the Canadian East Coast with a load of salt from the Bahamas.

Reflecting the vessel's dual ocean and Great Lakes trade patterns, she was renamed **Atlantic Erie** in a ceremony held Dec. 6, 1988 at Savannah, Ga. Later that year her unloading boom broke while at Vancouver, B.C. The following spring, **Atlantic Erie** was reflagged at Nassau, the Bahamas, after which she resumed trading along the East Coast and Caribbean. She also began moving cargoes of gypsum from Mexico, bound for U.S. and Canadian West Coast ports.

After returning to Atlantic trade routes, **Atlantic Erie** handled cargoes to and from various ports in Europe. The vessel was reregistered in Canada in 1994, returning to the East Coast gypsum trade. She resumed some Great Lakes trading in mid-1996.

In 1997, **Atlantic Erie** and her fleet mates **Atlantic Huron** and **Nanticoke**, were rigged with special unloading gear required to carry and unload magnetite ore to ballast the Hibernia Oil Platform, located off the Grand Banks.

After drydocking at Les Mechins, Que., in 1998, **Atlantic Erie** emerged with a newly-painted red hull and a large website address, www.csl.ca, splashed on the side of her hull. – *George Wharton*

**Atlantic Erie in the St. Marys River, 2002.** *(Roger LeLievre; Inset: Jim Hoffman)*

| Fleet #. | Fleet Name / Vessel Name | Type of Vessel | Year Built | Type of Engine | Cargo Cap. or Gross* | Overall Length | Breadth | Depth or Draft* |
|---|---|---|---|---|---|---|---|---|
| | **THREE RIVERS BOATMEN LTD., A SUBSIDIARY OF LE GROUPE OCEAN, TROIS-RIVIERES, QC** | | | | | | | |
| | Andre H. | TB | 1963 | D | 317* | 126' 00" | 28' 06" | 15' 06" |
| | (Foundation Valiant '63 - '73, Point Valiant {1} '73 - '95) | | | | | | | |
| | Avantage | TB | 1969 | D | 367* | 116' 10" | 32' 09" | 16' 03" |
| | (Sea Lion '69 - '97) | | | | | | | |
| | Duga | TB | 1977 | D | 403* | 111' 00" | 33' 00" | 16' 01" |
| | Escorte | TT | 1964 | D | 120* | 85' 00" | 23' 08" | 11' 00"* |
| | (USS Menasha [YTB / YTM-773, YTM-761] '64 - '92, Menasha {1} '92 - '95) | | | | | | | |
| | R. F. Grant | TB | 1969 | D | 78* | 71' 00" | 17' 00" | 8' 00" |
| L-11 | **LEE MARINE LTD., SOMBRA, ON** | | | | | | | |
| | Hammond Bay | ES | 1992 | D | 43* | 54' 00" | 16' 00" | 3' 00" |
| | (Scrimp & Scrounge '92 - '95) | | | | | | | |
| | Nancy A. Lee | TB | 1939 | D | 9* | 40' 00" | 12' 00" | 3' 00" |
| L-12 | **LES BATEAUX BLANCS DU ST. LAURENT** | | | | | | | |
| | Richelieu | CF | 1961 | D | 882* | 200' 00" | 70' 06" | 10' 00" |
| | (Trois Rivieres '61 - '00) | | | | | | | |
| L-13 | **LES EQUIPMENTS VERREAULT INC., LES MECHINS, QC** | | | | | | | |
| | Epinette II | TB | 1965 | D | 75* | 61' 03" | 20' 01" | 8' 05" |
| L-14 | **LOCK TOURS CANADA BOAT CRUISES, SAULT STE. MARIE, ON** | | | | | | | |
| | Chief Shingwauk | ES | 1965 | D | 109* | 70' 00" | 24' 00" | 4' 06" |
| L-15 | **LOWER LAKES TOWING LTD., PORT DOVER, ON** | | | | | | | |
| | Cuyahoga | SU | 1943 | D | 15,675 | 620' 00" | 60' 00" | 35' 00" |
| | (J. Burton Ayers '43 - '95) Converted to a self-unloader, '74; Repowered; '01) | | | | | | | |
| | Mississagi | SU | 1943 | D | 15,800 | 620' 06" | 60' 00" | 35' 00" |
| | (Hill Annex '43 - '43, George A. Sloan '43 - '01) Converted to a self-unloader, '67; Repowered, '85) | | | | | | | |
| | Saginaw {3} | SU | 1953 | T | 20,200 | 639' 03" | 72' 00" | 36' 00" |
| | (John J. Boland {3} '53 - '99) | | | | | | | |
| | **LOWER LAKES TRANS. CO., WILLIAMSVILLE, NY - SUBSIDIARY OF LOWER LAKES TOWING LTD.** | | | | | | | |
| | Calumet | SU | 1929 | D | 12,450 | 603' 09" | 60' 00" | 32' 00" |
| | (Myron C. Taylor '29 - '01) Converted to a self-unloader, 56; Repowered, '68) | | | | | | | |
| | Invincible | TBA | 1979 | D | 180* | 100' 00" | 35' 00" | 22' 06" |
| | (R. W. Sesler '79 - '91) | | | | | | | |
| | Maumee | SU | 1929 | D | 12,650 | 604' 09" | 60' 00" | 32' 00" |
| | (William G. Clyde '29 - '61, Calcite II '61 - '01) Converted to a self-unloader, '61; Repowered, "64) | | | | | | | |
| | **LAKE SERVICE SHIPPING CO. - OWNER** | | | | | | | |
| | McKee Sons | SU | 1945 | B | 19,900 | 579' 02" | 71' 06" | 38' 06" |
| | (USNS Marine Angel '45 - '52) | | | | | | | |
| | (Converted from saltwater vessel to a self-unloading Great Lakes bulk carrier, '53; Engine removed and converted to a self-unloading barge, '91) | | | | | | | |
| L-16 | **LUEDTKE ENGINEERING CO., FRANKFORT, MI** | | | | | | | |
| | Alan K. Luedtke | TB | 1944 | D | 149* | 86' 04" | 23' 00" | 10' 03" |
| | (U. S. Army ST-527 '44 - '55, USCOE Two Rivers '55 - '90) | | | | | | | |
| | Ann Marie | TB | 1954 | D | 119* | 71' 00" | 19' 06" | 9' 06" |
| | (Lewis Castle '54 - '97, Apache '97 - 2001) | | | | | | | |
| | Chris E. Luedtke | TB | 1936 | D | 18* | 45' 00" | 12' 03" | 6' 00" |
| | Erich R. Luedtke | TB | 1939 | D | 18* | 45' 00" | 12' 03" | 6' 00" |
| | Gretchen B. | TR | 1943 | D | 18* | 45' 00" | 12' 03" | 6' 00" |
| | Karl E. Luedtke | TB | 1928 | D | 32* | 59' 03" | 14' 09" | 8' 00" |
| | Kurt Luedtke | TB | 1956 | D | 96* | 72' 00" | 22' 06" | 7' 06" |
| | (Jere C. '56 - '90) | | | | | | | |
| M-1 | **M. C. M. MARINE, INC., SAULT STE. MARIE, MI** | | | | | | | |
| | Drummond Islander II | CF | 1961 | D | 97* | 65' 00" | 36' 00" | 9' 00" |
| | Mackinaw City | TB | 1943 | D | 23* | 38' 00" | 11' 05" | 4' 07" |
| | Mohawk | TB | 1945 | D | | 65' 00" | 19' 00" | 10' 06" |

| Fleet #. | Fleet Name<br>Vessel Name | Type of<br>Vessel | Year<br>Built | Type of<br>Engine | Cargo Cap.<br>or Gross* | Overall<br>Length | Breadth | Depth or<br>Draft* |
|---|---|---|---|---|---|---|---|---|
| | Ojibway | SB | 1945 | D | 65* | 53' 00" | 28' 00" | 7' 00" |
| | William C. Gaynor | TB | 1956 | D | 146* | 94' 00" | 27' 00" | 11' 09" |
| | *(William C. Gaynor '56 - '88, Captain Barnaby '88 - '02)* | | | | | | | |
| M-2 | **MacDONALD MARINE LTD., GODERICH, ON** | | | | | | | |
| | Debbie Lyn | TB | 1950 | D | 10* | 45' 00" | 14' 00" | 10' 00" |
| | *(Skipper '50 - '60)* | | | | | | | |
| | Donald Bert | TB | 1953 | D | 11* | 45' 00" | 14' 00" | 10' 00" |
| | Dover | TB | 1931 | D | 70* | 84' 00" | 17' 00" | 6' 00" |
| | *(Earleejune '31 - ?, Iveyrose ? -?)* | | | | | | | |
| | Ian Mac | TB | 1955 | D | 12* | 45' 00" | 14' 00" | 10' 00" |
| M-3 | **MADELINE ISLAND FERRY LINE, INC., LaPOINTE, WI** | | | | | | | |
| | Bayfield {2} | PA/CF | 1952 | D | 83* | 120' 00" | 43' 00" | 10' 00" |
| | *(Charlotte '52 - '99)* | | | | | | | |
| | Island Queen {2} | PA/CF | 1966 | D | 90* | 75' 00" | 34' 09" | 10' 00" |
| | Madeline | PA/CF | 1984 | D | 97* | 90' 00" | 35' 00" | 8' 00" |
| | Nichevo II | PA/CF | 1962 | D | 89* | 65' 00" | 32' 00" | 8' 09" |
| M-4 | **MAID OF THE MIST STEAMBOAT CO. LTD., NIAGARA FALLS, ON** | | | | | | | |
| | Maid of the Mist {2} | ES | 1987 | D | 54* | 65' 00" | 16' 00" | 7' 00" |
| | Maid of the Mist IV | ES | 1976 | D | 74* | 72' 00" | 16' 00" | 7' 00" |
| | Maid of the Mist V | ES | 1983 | D | 74* | 72' 00" | 16' 00" | 7' 00" |
| | Maid of the Mist VI | ES | 1990 | D | 155* | 78' 09" | 29' 06" | 7' 00" |
| | Maid of the Mist VII | ES | 1997 | D | 160* | 80' 00" | 30' 00" | 7' 00" |
| M-5 | **MALCOLM MARINE, ST. CLAIR, MI** | | | | | | | |
| | Manitou {2} | TB | 1943 | D | 491* | 110' 00" | 26' 05" | 11' 06" |
| | *(USCGC Manitou [WYT-60] '43 - '84)* | | | | | | | |
| M-6 | **MANITOU ISLAND TRANSIT, LELAND, MI** | | | | | | | |
| | Manitou Isle | PA/PK | 1946 | D | 10 | 52' 00" | 14' 00" | 8' 00" |
| | *(Namaycush '46 - '59)* | | | | | | | |
| | Mishe-Mokwa | PA/CF | 1966 | D | 49* | 65' 00" | 17' 06" | 8' 00" |
| | *(LaSalle '66 - '80)* | | | | | | | |
| M-7 | **MANSON CONSTRUCTION CO., INC., BUFFALO, NY** | | | | | | | |
| | Burro | TB | 1965 | D | 19* | 36' 00" | 13' 03" | 5' 01" |
| | J. G. II | TB | 1944 | D | 16* | 42' 03" | 13' 00" | 5' 06" |
| | Marcey | TB | 1966 | D | 22* | 42' 00" | 12' 06" | 6' 10" |
| M-8 | **MARINE ATLANTIC, INC., MONCTON, NB** | | | | | | | |
| | Atlantic Freighter | RR | 1978 | D | 8,661 | 495' 05" | 71' 01" | 48' 01" |
| | *(Tor Felicia '78 - '78, Merzario Grecia '78 - '83, Stena Grecia '83 - '86)* | | | | | | | |
| | Caribou | CF | 1986 | D | 27,213* | 587' 04" | 84' 01" | 27' 06" |
| | Joseph & Clara Smallwood | CF | 1989 | D | 27,614* | 587' 03" | 84' 01" | 22' 02" |
| M-9 | **MARINE MANAGEMENT, INC., CHICAGO, IL** | | | | | | | |
| | Baldy B. | TB | 1932 | D | 36* | 62' 00" | 16' 01" | 7' 00" |
| | Nicole S. | TB | 1949 | D | 146* | 88' 07" | 24' 10" | 10' 09" |
| | *(Evening Star '49 - '86, Protector '86 - '94)* | | | | | | | |
| M-10 | **MARINE TECH LLC., DULUTH, MN** | | | | | | | |
| | Alton Andrew | CS | 1958 | B | | 70' 00" | 50' 00 | 6' 00" |
| | Callie M. | TB | 1910 | D | 51* | 64' 03" | 16' 09" | 8' 06" |
| | *(Chattanooga '10 - '79, Howard T. Hagen '79 - '94, Nancy Ann '94 - 2001)* | | | | | | | |
| | Dean R. Smith | DR | 1985 | B | 338* | 120' 00" | 48' 00" | 7' 00" |
| | *(No. 2 '85 - '94, B. Yetter '94 - '01)* | | | | | | | |
| | Tilly | TB | 1943 | T | 82* | 81' 09" | 24' 00" | 9' 09" |
| | *(DPC-86 '43 - '46, Lewis No. 8 '46 - '81, Tipperary '81 - '90)* | | | | | | | |
| M-11 | **MARIPOSA CRUISE LINE, TORONTO, ON** | | | | | | | |
| | Captain Matthew Flinders | ES | 1982 | D | 696* | 144' 00" | 40' 00" | 8' 06" |

| Fleet #. | Fleet Name<br>Vessel Name | Type of Vessel | Year Built | Type of Engine | Cargo Cap. or Gross* | Overall Length | Breadth | Depth or Draft* |
|---|---|---|---|---|---|---|---|---|
| | Mariposa Belle | ES | 1970 | D | 195* | 93' 00" | 23' 00" | 8' 00" |
| | *(Niagara Belle '70 - '73)* | | | | | | | |
| | Rosemary | ES | 1960 | D | 52* | 68' 00" | 15' 06" | 6' 08" |
| | Showboat Royal Grace | ES | 1988 | D | 135* | 58' 00" | 18' 00" | 4' 00" |
| | Torontonian | ES | 1962 | D | 68* | 68' 00" | 18' 06" | 6' 08" |
| | *(Shiawassie '62 - '82)* | | | | | | | |
| **M-12** | **McASPHALT MARINE TRANSPORTATION LTD., SCARBOROUGH, ON** | | | | | | | |
| | Everlast | AB | 1977 | D | 1,361* | 143' 04" | 44' 04" | 21' 04" |
| | *(Bilibino '77 - '96)* | | | | | | | |
| | McAsphalt 401 | TK | 1966 | B | 48,000 | 300' 00" | 60' 00" | 23' 00" |
| | *(Pittson 200 '66 - '73, Pointe Levy '73 - '87)* | | | | | | | |
| | Norman McLeod | TK | 2001 | B | 70,000 | 379' 02" | 71' 06" | 30' 02" |
| | **[ATB Everlast / Norman McLeod OA dimensions together]** | | | | | 500' 00" | 71' 06" | 30' 02" |
| | ***McKEIL MARINE LTD., HAMILTON, ON - VESSEL CHARTERED BY McASPHALT MARINE*** | | | | | | | |
| | John Spence | TB | 1972 | D | 719* | 171' 00" | 38' 00" | 15' 01" |
| | *(Mary B. VI '72 - '81, Mary B. '81 - '82, Mary B. VI '82 - '83, Artic Tuktu '83 - '94)* | | | | | | | |
| **M-13** | **McCUE & OTHERS, CEDAR POINT, ON** | | | | | | | |
| | Indian Maiden | PF | 1987 | D | 128* | 74' 00" | 23' 00" | 8' 00" |
| **M-14** | **McKEIL MARINE LTD. (McKEIL WORK BOATS LTD.) , HAMILTON, ON** | | | | | | | |
| | Argue Martin | TB | 1895 | D | 71* | 69' 00" | 19' 06" | 9' 00" |
| | *(Ethel 1895 - '38, R. C. Co. Tug No.1 '38 - '58, R. C. L. Tug No. 1 '58 - '62)* | | | | | | | |
| | Atomic | TB | 1945 | D | 96* | 82' 00" | 20' 00" | 10' 00" |
| | Beaver D. | TB | 1955 | D | 15* | 36' 02" | 14' 09" | 4' 04" |
| | Bonnie B. III | TB | 1969 | D | 308* | 100' 03" | 32' 00" | 17' 00" |
| | *(Esso Oranjestad '69 - '85, Oranjestad '85 - '86, San Nicolas '86 - '87, San Nicolas I '87 - '88)* | | | | | | | |
| | Capt. Ralph Tucker | TK | 1966 | D | 81,764 | 440' 00" | 60' 00" | 31' 00" |
| | *(Imperial Acadia '66 - '97, Algoscotia '97 - '01, Ralph Tucker '01 - '01)* | | | | | | | |
| | Carrol C I | TB | 1969 | D | 291* | 100' 03" | 32' 00" | 17' 00" |
| | *(Launched as Esso Oranjestad II, Esso San Nicolas '69 - '86, San Nicolas '86 - '87, Carrol C '87 - '88)* | | | | | | | |
| | Colinette | TB | 1943 | D | 64* | 65' 00" | 16' 00" | 7' 00" |
| | *(Ottawa {1} '43 - '57, Lac Ottawa '57 - '66)* | | | | | | | |

**Tug Seneca at Duluth.** *(Franz VonRiedel)*

| Fleet #. | Fleet Name / Vessel Name | Type of Vessel | Year Built | Type of Engine | Cargo Cap. or Gross* | Overall Length | Breadth | Depth or Draft* |
|---|---|---|---|---|---|---|---|---|
| | Congar | TK | 1948 | B | | 324' 01" | 42' 09" | 17' 03" |
| | (Imperial London '48-'77, Tegucigalpa '77-'80) | | | | | | | |
| | CSL Trillium | BC | 1966 | B | 18,064 | 489' 10" | 75' 00" | 37' 05" |
| | (Caribbean '66 - '92, Pacnav Princess '92 - '94, CSL Trillium I '94 - '95)  (Laid up at Hamilton, ON.) | | | | | | | |
| | Dalmig | CF | 1957 | D | 538* | 175' 10" | 40' 01" | 11' 10" |
| | (Pierre de Saurel '57 - '87) | | | | | | | |
| | Doug McKeil {2} | TB | 1943 | D | 196* | 130' 00" | 30' 00" | 15' 01" |
| | (U. S. Army LT-643 '44 - '77, Taurus '77 - '90, Gaelic Challenge '90 - '95, Frankie D. '95 - '97, Dawson B. '97 - '98) | | | | | | | |
| | Erie West | DB | 1951 | B | 1,800 | 290' 00" | 50' 00" | 12' 00" |
| | (Dover Light) | | | | | | | |
| | Escuminac | TB | 1948 | D | 8.7* | 33' 04" | 9' 08" | 4' 05" |
| | Evans McKeil | TB | 1936 | D | 284* | 110' 07" | 25' 06" | 11' 06" |
| | (Alhajuela '36 - '70, Barbara Ann {2} '70 - '89) | | | | | | | |
| | Flo-Mac | TB | 1960 | D | 15* | 40' 00" | 13' 00" | 6' 00" |
| | Florence McKeil | TB | 1962 | D | 207* | 98' 05" | 26' 00" | 9' 07" |
| | (T. 4 '62 - ?, Foundation Viceroy ? - '72, Feuille D' Erable '72 - '97) | | | | | | | |
| | Glenevis | TB | 1944 | D | 91* | 80' 06" | 20' 00" | 9' 07" |
| | (HMCS Glenevis [W-65 / YTM-502] '44 - '77) | | | | | | | |
| | Greta V | TB | 1951 | D | 14* | 44' 00" | 12' 00" | 5' 00" |
| | Jarrett McKeil | TB | 1956 | D | 197* | 91' 08" | 27' 04" | 13' 06" |
| | (Robert B. No. 1 '56 - '97) | | | | | | | |
| | Jean Raymond | DB | 1941 | B | 6,800 | 409' 00" | 57' 00" | 18' 00" |
| | Jerry Newberry | TB | 1956 | D | 244* | 98' 00" | 28' 02" | 14' 04" |
| | (Foundation Victor '56 - '73, Point Victor '73 - '77, Kay Cole '77 - '95) | | | | | | | |
| | Josee M. | RT | 1963 | D | 9,415 | 175' 00" | 36' 00" | 14' 00" |
| | (Imperial Lachine '63 - '03) | | | | | | | |
| | King Fish | TB | 1955 | D | 18* | 55' 00" | 16' 00" | 6' 08" |
| | (Duchess V '55 - '00) | | | | | | | |
| | Kristin | TB | 1944 | D | 261* | 111' 00" | 27' 00" | 13' 00" |
| | (HMCS Riverton [W-47 / ATA-528] '44 - '79, Techno St-Laurent '79 - '02) | | | | | | | |
| | Lac Como | TB | 1944 | D | 63* | 65' 00" | 16' 10" | 7' 10" |
| | (Tanac 74 '44 - '64) | | | | | | | |
| | Lac Erie | TB | 1944 | D | 65* | 65' 00" | 16' 10" | 7' 07" |
| | (Tanmac '44 - '74) | | | | | | | |
| | Lac Manitoba | TB | 1944 | D | 65* | 65' 00" | 16' 10" | 7' 07" |
| | (Tanac 75 '44 - '52, Manitoba '52 - '57) | | | | | | | |
| | Lac Vancouver | TB | 1943 | D | 65* | 65' 00" | 16' 10" | 7' 07" |
| | (Vancouver '43 - '74) | | | | | | | |
| | Lorena 1 | GC | 1961 | D | 5,039 | 404' 01" | 60' 05" | 36' 06" |
| | (French River '61 - '81, Jensen Star '81 - '86, Woodland '86 - '91, Woodlands '91 - '98)  (Laid up at Hamilton, ON.) | | | | | | | |
| | Manco | TB | 1951 | D | 263* | 100' 00" | 28' 00" | 10' 00" |
| | Maritime Trader | DB | 1969 | B | 2,636* | 250' 00" | 76' 01" | 16' 01" |
| | (Barge 252 '69 - '82, Genmar 252 '82 - '87, McAllister 252 '87 - '99) | | | | | | | |
| | McLeary's Spirit | TK | 1969 | B | 13,920 | 379' 09" | 63' 03" | 33' 08" |
| | (LeVent '69-'02) | | | | | | | |
| | Miss Shawn Simpson | ES | 1956 | D | 23* | 55' 02" | 13' 02" | 5' 00" |
| | Ocean Hauler | TB | 1943 | B | 3,781* | 344' 00" | 69' 00" | 96' 00" |
| | Paul E. No. 1 | TB | 1945 | D | 97* | 80' 00" | 20' 00" | 9' 0/" |
| | (W.A.C. 4 '45 - '46, E. A. Rockett '46 - '76) | | | | | | | |
| | Progress | TB | 1948 | D | 123* | 86' 00" | 21' 00" | 10' 00" |
| | (P. J. Murer '48 - '81, Michael D. Misner '81 - '93, Thomas A. Payette '93 - '96) | | | | | | | |
| | Salvager | TB | 1961 | D | 429* | 120' 00" | 32' 09" | 18' 09" |
| | (M. Moran '61 - '70, Port Arthur '70 - '72, M. Moran '72 - '00) | | | | | | | |
| | Salty Dog No. 1 | TK | 1945 | B | 88,735 | 313' 00" | 68' 03" | 26' 07" |
| | (Fort Hoskins '45 - '66, Ocean Hauler 10 '66 - '79, ATC 610 '79 - '91) | | | | | | | |
| | Salvor | TB | 1963 | D | 426* | 120' 00" | 32' 09" | 18' 09" |
| | (Esther Moran '63 - '00) | | | | | | | |

| Fleet #. | Fleet Name<br>Vessel Name | Type of<br>Vessel | Year<br>Built | Type of<br>Engine | Cargo Cap.<br>or Gross* | Overall<br>Length | Breadth | Depth or<br>Draft* |
|---|---|---|---|---|---|---|---|---|
| | Sault au Couchon | DH | 1969 | B | 10,000 | 422' 11" | 74' 10" | 25' 07" |
| | St. Clair {2} | TF | 1927 | B | 27 rail cars | 400' 00" | 54' 00" | 22' 00" |
| | *(Pere Marquette 12 '27 - '70)* | | | | | | | |
| | Stormont | TB | 1953 | D | 108* | 80' 00" | 20' 00" | 9' 07" |
| | Tony Mackay | TB | 1973 | D | 366* | 127' 00" | 30' 05" | 14' 05" |
| | *(Point Carroll '73 - 2001)* | | | | | | | |
| | William J. Moore | TB | 1970 | D | 564* | 135' 00" | 34' 09" | 19' 04" |
| | *(Warrawee '70 - '76, Seaspan Raider '76 - '87, Raider '87 - '87, Raider IV '87 - '88, Alice A. '88 -'02)* | | | | | | | |
| | Wyatt McKeil | TB | 1950 | D | 237* | 102' 06" | 26' 00" | 13' 06" |
| | *(Otis Wack '50 - '97)* | | | | | | | |

*MONTREAL BOATMAN, POINTE AUX TREMBLE, QC - A SUBSIDIARY OF McKEIL MARINE LTD.*

| | | | | | | | | |
|---|---|---|---|---|---|---|---|---|
| | Aldo H. | TB | 1979 | D | 37* | 56' 04" | 15' 04" | 6' 02" |
| | Boatman No. 3 | TB | 1965 | D | 13* | 33' 08" | 11' 00" | 6' 00" |
| | Boatman No. 4 | TB | 1967 | D | 15* | 43' 03" | 14' 01" | 5' 09" |
| | Boatman No. 6 | TB | 1979 | D | 39* | 56' 07" | 18' 07" | 6' 03" |
| | Pilot 1 | TB | 1994 | D | 14* | 32' 01" | 5' 08" | 2' 06" |

*REMORQUEURS & BARGES MONTREAL LTEE, SALABERRY-DE-VALLEYFIELD, QC*
*A SUBSIDIARY OF McKEIL MARINE LTD.*

| | | | | | | | | |
|---|---|---|---|---|---|---|---|---|
| | Condarrell | CS | 1953 | D | 3,017 | 259' 00" | 43' 06" | 21' 00" |
| | *(D. C. Everest '53 - '81)* | | | | | | | |
| | Connie E. | TB | 1974 | D | 9* | 30' 00" | 11' 00" | 6' 00" |
| | Dufresne M-58 | TB | 1944 | D | 40* | 58' 08" | 14' 08" | 6' 02" |
| | Pacific Standard | TB | 1967 | D | 451* | 127' 08" | 31' 00" | 15' 06" |
| | *(Irishman '67 - '76, Kwakwani '76 - '78, Lorna B. '78 - '81)* | | | | | | | |
| | Techno Venture | TB | 1939 | D | 470* | 138' 03" | 30' 07" | 15' 01" |
| | *(HMS Dragonet [Z-82] '39 - '61, Foundation Venture '61 - '73, M.I.L. Venture '73 - '79)* | | | | | | | |
| | Willmac | TB | 1959 | D | 16* | 40' 00" | 13' 00" | 3' 07" |

**M-15**   **McLEOD BROTHERS MECHANICAL, SAULT STE. MARIE, ON**

| | | | | | | | | |
|---|---|---|---|---|---|---|---|---|
| | Kam | TB | 1927 | D | 33* | 52' 00" | 13' 00" | 5' 06"* |
| | *(North Shore Supply '27 - '74)* | | | | | | | |

**M-16**   **McMULLEN & PITZ CONSTRUCTION CO., MANITOWOC, WI**

| | | | | | | | | |
|---|---|---|---|---|---|---|---|---|
| | Dauntless | TB | 1937 | D | 25* | 52' 06" | 15' 06" | 5' 03" |
| | Erich | TB | 1943 | D | 19* | 45' 00" | 12' 07" | 5' 09" |

**M-17**   **McNALLY MARINE, INC., TORONTO, ON**

| | | | | | | | | |
|---|---|---|---|---|---|---|---|---|
| | Bagotville | TB | 1964 | D | 65* | 65' 00" | 18' 06" | 10' 00" |
| | Canadian | DR | 1954 | B | 1,087* | 173' 08" | 49' 08" | 13' 04" |
| | Canadian Argosy | DR | 1978 | B | 951* | 149' 09" | 54' 01" | 10' 08" |
| | Carl M. | TB | 1957 | D | 21* | 47' 00" | 14' 06" | 6' 00" |
| | Idus Atwell | DR | 1962 | B | 366* | 100' 00" | 40' 00" | 8' 05" |
| | John Holden | DR | 1954 | B | 148* | 89' 08" | 30' 01" | 6' 02" |
| | Le Tareau | TB | 1985 | D | 25* | 36' 04" | 14' 07" | 5' 09" |
| | Manistique | TB | 1954 | D | 16* | 38' 00" | 12' 01" | 3' 02" |
| | Mister Joe | TB | 1964 | D | 70* | 61' 00" | 19' 00" | 7' 02" |
| | Paula M. | TB | 1959 | D | 12* | 46' 06" | 16' 01" | 4' 10" |
| | R. C. L. No. II | TB | 1958 | D | 20* | 42' 09" | 14' 03" | 5' 09" |
| | Sandra Mary | TB | 1962 | D | 97* | 80' 00" | 21' 00" | 10' 09" |
| | *(Flo Cooper '62 - '00)* | | | | | | | |
| | Whithy | TB | 1978 | D | 24* | 45' 00" | 14' 00" | 5' 00" |

**M-18**   **MENASHA TUGBOAT CO., SARNIA, ON**

| | | | | | | | | |
|---|---|---|---|---|---|---|---|---|
| | Menasha {2} | TB | 1949 | D | 147* | 78' 00" | 24' 00" | 9' 08" |
| | *(W. C. Harms '49 - '54, Hamilton '54 - '86, Ruby Casho '86 - '88, W. C. Harms '88 - '97)* | | | | | | | |

**M-19**   **MERCURY CRUISE LINES, PALATINE, IL**

| | | | | | | | | |
|---|---|---|---|---|---|---|---|---|
| | Chicago's First Lady | ES | 1991 | D | 62* | 96' 00" | 22' 00" | 9' 00" |
| | Chicago's Little Lady | ES | 1999 | D | | 68' 00" | 23' 00" | 8' 06"* |
| | Skyline Princess | ES | 1956 | D | 56* | 59' 04" | 16' 00" | 4' 08" |

Spruceglen, formerly the Fraser, makes her first trip under her new name on Dec. 17, 2002. *(Rene Beauchamp)*

| Fleet #. | Fleet Name<br>Vessel Name | Type of<br>Vessel | Year<br>Built | Type of<br>Engine | Cargo Cap.<br>or Gross* | Overall<br>Length | Breadth | Depth or<br>Draft* |
|---|---|---|---|---|---|---|---|---|
| | Skyline Queen | ES | 1959 | D | 45* | 61' 05" | 16' 10" | 6' 00" |
| **M-20** | **MICHIGAN DEPARTMENT OF NATURAL RESOURCES, LANSING, MI** | | | | | | | |
| | Channel Cat | RV | 1968 | D | 24* | 46' 00" | 13' 06" | 4' 00" |
| | Chinook | RV | 1947 | D | 26* | 50' 00" | 12' 00" | 5' 00" |
| | Judy | RV | 1950 | D | | 40' 00" | 12' 00" | 3' 06" |
| | Steelhead | RV | 1967 | D | 70* | 63' 00" | 16' 04" | 6' 06" |
| **M-21** | **MIDDLE BASS BOAT LINE, MIDDLE BASS, OH** | | | | | | | |
| | Victory | PA/CF | 1960 | D | 14* | 63' 07" | 15' 03" | 4' 08" |
| **M-22** | **MILLER BOAT LINE, INC., PUT-IN-BAY, OH** | | | | | | | |
| | Islander {3} | PA/CF | 1983 | D | 92* | 90' 03" | 38' 00" | 8' 03" |
| | Put-In-Bay {3} | PA/CF | 1997 | D | 95* | 96' 00" | 38' 06" | 9' 06" |
| | South Bass | PA/CF | 1989 | D | 95* | 96' 00" | 38' 06" | 9' 06" |
| | Wm. Market | PA/CF | 1993 | D | 95* | 96' 00" | 38' 06" | 8' 09" |
| **M-23** | **MILWAUKEE BULK TERMINALS, INC., MILWAUKEE, WI** | | | | | | | |
| | MBT 10 | DH | 1994 | B | 1,960 | 200' 00" | 35' 00" | 13' 00" |
| | MBT 20 | DH | 1994 | B | 1,960 | 200' 00" | 35' 00" | 13' 00" |
| | MBT 33 | DH | 1976 | B | 3,793 | 240' 00" | 52' 06" | 14' 06"* |
| **M-24** | **MONTREAL SHIPPING, INC., STEPHENVILLE, NF** | | | | | | | |
| | Point Viking | TB | 1962 | D | 207* | 98' 05" | 27' 10" | 13' 05" |
| | (Foundation Viking '62 - '75) | | | | | | | |
| **M-25** | **MORTON SALT CO., CHICAGO, IL** | | | | | | | |
| | Morton Salt 74 | DB | 1974 | B | 2,101 | 195' 00" | 35' 00" | 12' 00" |
| **M-26** | **MUSIQUE AQUATIQUE CRUISE LINES, INC., TORONTO, ON** | | | | | | | |
| | Harbour Star | ES | 1978 | D | 45* | 63' 06" | 15' 09" | 3' 09" |
| **M-27** | **MUSKOKA LAKES NAVIGATION & HOTEL CO. LTD., GRAVENHURST, ON** | | | | | | | |
| | Segwun | PA | 1887 | R | 168* | 128' 00" | 24' 00" | 7' 06" |
| | (Nipissing {2} 1887 - '25) | | | | | | | |
| | Wanda III | PA | 1915 | R | 60* | 94' 00" | 12' 00" | 5' 00" |
| | Wenonah II | PA | 2001 | D | 470* | 127' 00" | 28' 00" | 6' 00"* |
| **N-1** | **NADRO MARINE SERVICES LTD., PORT DOVER, ON** | | | | | | | |
| | Ecosse | TB | 1979 | D | 146* | 91' 00" | 26' 01" | 8' 06" |
| | (R & L No. 1 '79 - '96) | | | | | | | |
| | Intrepid III | TB | 1976 | D | 39* | 66' 00" | 17' 00" | 7' 06" |
| | Miseford | TB | 1915 | D | 116* | 85' 00" | 20' 00" | 10' 06" |
| | Nadro Clipper | TB | 1939 | D | 64* | 70' 00" | 23' 00" | 6' 06" |
| | (Stanley Clipper '39 - '94) | | | | | | | |
| | Seahound | TB | 1941 | D | 60* | 65' 06" | 17' 00" | 7' 00" |
| | ([Unnamed] '41 - '56, Sea Hound '56 - '80, Carolyn Jo '80 - '00) | | | | | | | |
| | Terry S. | TB | 1958 | D | 16* | 52' 00" | 17' 00" | 6' 00" |
| | Vac | TB | 1942 | D | 37* | 65' 00" | 21' 00" | 6' 06" |
| | Vigilant 1 | TB | 1944 | D | 111* | 76' 08" | 20' 09" | 10' 02" |
| | (HMCS Glenlivet [W-43] '44 - '75, Glenlivet II '75 - '77, Canadian Franko '77 - '82, Glenlivet II '82 - '00) | | | | | | | |
| **N-2** | **NAUTICAL ADVENTURES, TORONTO, ON** | | | | | | | |
| | Empire Sandy | ES/3S | 1943 | D/W | 434* | 140' 00" | 32' 08" | 14' 00" |
| | (Empire Sandy '43 - '40, Ashford '48 - '52, Chris M '52 - '79) | | | | | | | |
| | Wayward Princess | ES | 1976 | D | 325* | 92' 00" | 26' 00" | 10' 00" |
| | (Cayuga II '76 - '82) | | | | | | | |
| **N-3** | **NELSON CONSTRUCTION CO., LaPOINTE, WI** | | | | | | | |
| | Eclipse | TB | 1937 | D | 23* | 47' 00" | 13' 00" | 6' 00" |
| **N-4** | **NELVANA YACHT CHARTERS, TORONTO, ON** | | | | | | | |
| | Nelvana {1} | ES | 1963 | D | 61* | 55' 10" | 16' 00" | 5' 00" |

| Fleet #. | Fleet Name / Vessel Name | Type of Vessel | Year Built | Type of Engine | Cargo Cap. or Gross* | Overall Length | Breadth | Depth or Draft* |
|---|---|---|---|---|---|---|---|---|
| **N-5** | **NEWFOUNDLAND TRANSSHIPMENT LTD., ST. JOHN, NF** | | | | | | | |
| | Placentia Hope | TT | 1998 | D | 925* | 125' 00" | 42' 08" | 17' 05" |
| | Placentia Pride | TT | 1998 | D | 925* | 125' 00" | 42' 08" | 17' 05" |
| **N-6** | **NIAGARA STEAMSHIP CO., NIAGARA ON THE LAKE, ON** | | | | | | | |
| | Pumper | ES | 1903 | R | 25* | 60' 00" | 14' 06" | 7' 06" |
| | *(Planet '03 - '29, Racey '29 - '57, Paul Evans '57 - '80, Racey '80 - '?)* | | | | | | | |
| **N-7** | **NICHOLSON TERMINAL & DOCK CO., RIVER ROUGE, MI** | | | | | | | |
| | Charles E. Jackson | TB | 1956 | D | 12* | 35' 00" | 10' 06" | 5' 01" |
| | Detroit {1} | TF | 1904 | B | 22 cars | 308' 00" | 76' 09" | 19' 06" |
| **N-8** | **NORTH CHANNEL DIVING & MARINE (GARDINER MARINE), RICHARD'S LANDING, ON** | | | | | | | |
| | Joyce K. Gardiner | | 1962 | D | 71* | 72' 00" | 19' 00" | 12' 00" |
| | *(Angus M. '62 - '92, Omni Sorel '92-'02)* | | | | | | | |
| | Opeongo | TB | 1947 | D | 21* | 50' 00" | 13' 00" | 6' 00"* |
| | Tolsma Bay | TB | 1910 | D | 49* | 65' 00" | 16' 06" | 8' 00"* |
| | *(Willard L '10 - '89)* | | | | | | | |
| **N-9** | **NORTHERN MARINE TRANSPORTATION, SAULT STE. MARIE, MI** | | | | | | | |
| | Linda Jean | PB | 1950 | D | 17* | 38' 00" | 10' 00" | 5' 00" |
| | Soo River Belle | PB | 1961 | D | 25* | 40' 00" | 14' 00" | 6' 00" |
| **N-10** | **NORTHUMBERLAND FERRIES LTD. / BAY FERRIES LTD., CHARLOTTETOWN, PEI** | | | | | | | |
| | Confederation {2} | CF | 1993 | D | 8,060* | 374' 08" | 61' 07" | 17' 09" |
| | Holiday Island | CF | 1971 | D | 3,037* | 325' 00" | 67' 06" | 16' 06" |
| | *(Launched as William Pope)* | | | | | | | |
| | Incat 046 | CF | 1997 | D | 5,060* | 300' 00" | 85' 03" | 12' 01" |
| | *(Devil Cat '97 - '98)* | | | | | | | |
| | Princess of Acadia | CF | 1971 | D | 10,051* | 480' 01" | 66' 00" | 12' 06" |
| | *(Launched as Princess of Nova)* | | | | | | | |
| **N-12** | **NORTHWEST MARINE, INC., WAUWATOSA, WI** | | | | | | | |
| | Islay | TB | 1892 | D | 19* | 60' 00" | 13' 00" | 5' 00"* |
| | *(Islay 1892 - '47, Bayfield {1} '47 - '83)* | | | | | | | |
| **O-1** | **OAK GROVE MARINE AND TRANSPORTATION, INC., CLAYTON, NY** | | | | | | | |
| | Maple Grove | PK | 1954 | D | 55 | 75' 00" | 21' 00" | 5' 06"* |
| | Oak Grove | PK | 1953 | D | 18 | 53' 02" | 14' 00" | 4' 00"* |
| **O-2** | **ODYSSEY CRUISES, CHICAGO, IL** | | | | | | | |
| | Odyssey II | ES | 1993 | D | 101* | 200' 00" | 41' 00" | 9' 00"* |
| **O-3** | **OGLEBAY NORTON MARINE SERVICES CO., CLEVELAND, OH** | | | | | | | |
| | Armco | SU | 1953 | T | 25,500 | 767' 00" | 70' 00" | 36' 00" |
| | *(Lengthened by 120' - '74; Converted to a self-unloader, '82)* | | | | | | | |
| | Buckeye {3} | SU | 1952 | T | 22,300 | 698' 00" | 70' 00" | 37' 00" |
| | *(Sparrows Point '52 - '90) (Lengthened by 72' - '58; Converted to a self-unloader, '80)* | | | | | | | |
| | Columbia Star | SU | 1981 | D | 78,850 | 1,000' 00" | 105' 00" | 56' 00" |
| | Courtney Burton | SU | 1953 | T | 22,300 | 690' 00" | 70' 00" | 37' 00" |
| | *(Ernest T. Weir {2} '53 - '78; Converted to a self-unloader, '81)* | | | | | | | |
| | David Z. Norton {3} | SU | 1973 | D | 19,650 | 630' 00" | 68' 00" | 36' 11" |
| | *(William R. Roesch '73 - '95)* | | | | | | | |
| | Earl W. Oglebay | SU | 1973 | D | 19,650 | 630' 00" | 68' 00" | 36' 11" |
| | *(Paul Thayer '73 - '95)* | | | | | | | |
| | Fred R. White Jr. | SU | 1979 | D | 23,800 | 636' 00" | 68' 00" | 40' 00" |
| | Joseph H. Frantz | SU | 1925 | D | 13,600 | 618' 00" | 62' 00" | 32' 00" |
| | *(Repowered, converted to a self-unloader, '65; Last operated Dec. 10, 2001. Laid up at Toledo.)* | | | | | | | |
| | Middletown | SU | 1942 | T | 26,300 | 730' 00" | 75' 00" | 39' 03" |
| | *(Laid down as Marquette. USS Neshanic [AO-71] '42 - '47, Gulfoil '47 - '61, Pioneer Challenger '61 - '62)* | | | | | | | |
| | *(Converted from saltwater tanker to Great Lakes bulk carrier, '61; Converted to a self-unloader, '82)* | | | | | | | |
| | Oglebay Norton | SU | 1978 | D | 78,850 | 1,000' 00" | 105' 00" | 56' 00" |

| Fleet #. | Fleet Name<br>Vessel Name | Type of<br>Vessel | Year<br>Built | Type of<br>Engine | Cargo Cap.<br>or Gross* | Overall<br>Length | Breadth | Depth or<br>Draft* |
|---|---|---|---|---|---|---|---|---|
| | Reserve | SU | 1953 | T | 25,500 | 767' 00" | 70' 00" | 36' 00" |
| | *(Lengthened 120'-'75; Converted to a self-unloader, '83)* | | | | | | | |
| | Wolverine {4} | SU | 1974 | D | 19,650 | 630' 00" | 68' 00" | 36' 11" |
| | ***ERIE SAND STEAMSHIP CO., ERIE, PA – A SUBSIDIARY OF OGLEBAY NORTON MARINE*** | | | | | | | |
| | J. S. St. John | SC | 1945 | D | 680 | 174' 00" | 32' 02" | 15' 00" |
| | *(USS YO-178 '45 - '51, Lake Edward '51 - '67)* | | | | | | | |
| | Richard Reiss | SU | 1943 | D | 14,900 | 620' 06" | 60' 03" | 35' 00" |
| | *(Launched as Adirondack, Richard J. Reiss {2} '43 - '86)* | | | | | | | |
| | *(Converted to a self-unloader, '64; Repowered, '76; Last operated Dec. 18, '01; Laid up at Erie, PA.)* | | | | | | | |
| | Day Peckinpaugh | PA | 1921 | D | 1,490 | 254' 00" | 36' 00" | 14' 00" |
| | *(Interwaterways Line Incorporated 101 '21 - '32, I.L.I. 101 '32 - '36, Richard J. Barnes '36 - '58)* | | | | | | | |
| | *(Last operated Sept. 9, 1994; Laid up at Erie, PA.)* | | | | | | | |
| O-4 | **ONTARIO MINISTRY OF TRANSPORTATION & COMMUNICATION, KINGSTON, ON** | | | | | | | |
| | Amherst Islander {2} | PA/CF | 1955 | D | 184* | 106' 00" | 38' 00" | 10' 00" |
| | Frontenac II | PA/CF | 1962 | D | 666* | 181' 00" | 45' 00" | 10' 00" |
| | *(Charlevoix {2} '62 - '92)* | | | | | | | |
| | Glenora | PA/CF | 1952 | D | 209* | 127' 00" | 33' 00" | 9' 00" |
| | *(The St. Joseph Islander '52 - '74)* | | | | | | | |
| | The Quinte Loyalist | PA/CF | 1954 | D | 209* | 127' 00" | 32' 00" | 8' 00" |
| | Wolfe Islander III | PA/CF | 1975 | D | 985* | 205' 00" | 68' 00" | 6' 00" |
| O-5 | **ONTARIO WATERWAY CRUISES, INC., ORILLIA, ON** | | | | | | | |
| | Kawartha Voyager | PA | 1983 | D | 264* | 108' 00" | 22' 00" | 5' 00" |
| O-6 | **ORILLIA BOAT CRUISES LTD., ORILLIA, ON** | | | | | | | |
| | Island Princess {1} | ES | 1989 | D | 194* | 65' 00" | 27' 00" | 5' 00" |
| O-7 | **OSBORNE MATERIALS CO., MENTOR, OH** | | | | | | | |
| | John R. Emery | SC | 1905 | D | 490 | 140' 00" | 33' 00" | 14' 00" |
| | *(Trenton {1} '05 - '25)* | | | | | | | |
| | Emmet J. Carey | SC | 1948 | D | 900 | 114' 00" | 23' 00" | 11' 00" |
| | *(Beatrice Ottinger '48 - '63, James B. Lyons '63 - '88)* | | | | | | | |
| | F. M. Osborne {2} | SC | 1910 | D | 500 | 150' 00" | 29' 00" | 11' 03" |
| | *(Grand Island {1} '10 - '58, Lesco '58 - '75)* | | | | | | | |
| O-8 | **OWEN SOUND TRANSPORTATION CO. LTD., OWEN SOUND, ON** | | | | | | | |
| | Chi-Cheemaun | PA/CF | 1974 | D | 6,991* | 365' 05" | 61' 00" | 21' 00" |
| | ***PELEE ISLAND TRANSPORTATION SERVICES, PELEE ISLAND, ON*** | | | | | | | |
| | ***A DIVISION OF OWEN SOUND TRANSPORTATION CO. LTD.*** | | | | | | | |
| | Jiimaan | CF | 1992 | D | 2,830* | 176' 09" | 42' 03" | 13' 06" |
| | Pelee Islander | CF | 1960 | D | 334* | 145' 00" | 32' 00" | 10' 00" |
| P-1 | **PARKWAY BOAT LINES, IVY LEA, ON** | | | | | | | |
| | Miss Ivy Lea II | ES | | D | | 66' 00" | 15' 00" | 5' 00" |
| | Miss Ivy Lea III | ES | | D | | 48' 00" | 12' 00" | 5' 00" |
| P-2 | **PENETANGUISHENE 30,000 ISLAND CRUISES, PENETANGUISHENE, ON** | | | | | | | |
| | Georgian Queen | ES | 1918 | D | 249* | 119' 00" | 36' 00" | 16' 06" |
| | *(Victoria '18 - '18, Murray Stewart '18 - '48, David Richard '48 - '79)* | | | | | | | |
| P-3 | **PENETANGUISHENE MIDLAND COACH LINE 30,000 ISLAND BOAT CRUISES, MIDLAND, ON** | | | | | | | |
| | Miss Midland | ES | 1974 | D | 119* | 68' 07" | 19' 04" | 6' 04" |
| | Serendipity Princess | ES | 1982 | D | 93* | 69' 00" | 23' 00" | 4' 03"* |
| | *(Trent Voyageur '82 - '87, Serendipity Lady '87 - '95)* | | | | | | | |
| P-4 | **PERE MARQUETTE SHIPPING CO., LUDINGTON, MI** | | | | | | | |
| | Pere Marquette 41 | SU | 1941 | B | 4,545 | 403' 00" | 58' 00" | 23' 06" |
| | *(City of Midland 41 '41 - '97; Converted from powered train / carferry to self-unloading barge, '97)* | | | | | | | |
| | Undaunted | AT | 1944 | D | 860* | 143' 00" | 33' 01" | 18' 00" |
| | *(USS Undaunted [ATR-126, ATA-199] '44 - '63, USMA Kings Pointer '63 - '93, Krystal K. '93 - '97)* | | | | | | | |
| | **[ATB Undaunted / Pere Marquette 41 OA dimensions together]** | | | | | 493' 06" | 58' 00" | 23' 06" |

# OLD TIMERS

**Hullett unloaders at work on Cleveland-Cliffs' H. L. Gobeille at Huron, Ohio, in the 1950s.**
*(Dave Glick photo, Richard I. Weiss Collection)*

**Passenger liner Juniata in the Soo Locks. We know her (or at least her hull) today as Milwaukee Clipper.**
*(Thomas Manse Collection)*

**Otto M. Reiss upbound in 1966. She was scrapped in 1973.** *(Ken Niemi Collection)*

| Fleet #. | Fleet Name<br>Vessel Name | Type of<br>Vessel | Year<br>Built | Type of<br>Engine | Cargo Cap.<br>or Gross* | Overall<br>Length | Breadth | Depth or<br>Draft* |
|---|---|---|---|---|---|---|---|---|
| **P-5** | **PICTURED ROCKS CRUISES, INC., MUNISING, MI** | | | | | | | |
| | Grand Island {2} | ES | 1989 | D | 51* | 68' 00" | 16' 01" | 5' 01" |
| | Miners Castle | ES | 1974 | D | 72* | 68' 00" | 17' 00" | 5' 00" |
| | Miss Superior | ES | 1984 | D | 76* | 68' 00" | 17' 00" | 5' 00" |
| | Pictured Rocks | ES | 1972 | D | 47* | 60' 00" | 14' 00" | 4' 04" |
| **P-6** | **PIER WISCONSIN, MILWAUKEE, WI** | | | | | | | |
| | Denis Sullivan | TV/ES | 1994 | W | 99* | 138' 00" | 24' 00" | 8' 09" |
| **P-7** | **PIERRE GAGNE CONTRACTING LTD., THUNDER BAY, ON** | | | | | | | |
| | M A C Gagne | BC | 1964 | B | 30,500 | 730' 00" | 75' 02" | 44' 08" |
| | *(Saguenay {2} '64 - '98) (Last operated Nov. 30, 1992. Hull laid up at Thunder Bay, ON.)* | | | | | | | |
| **P-8** | **PLAUNT TRANSPORTATION CO., INC., CHEBOYGAN, MI** | | | | | | | |
| | Kristen D. | CF | 1988 | D | 83* | 64' 11" | 36' 00" | 6' 05" |
| **P-9** | **PORT CITY PRINCESS CRUISES, INC., MUSKEGON, MI** | | | | | | | |
| | Port City Princess | ES | 1966 | D | 79* | 64' 09" | 30' 00" | 5' 06" |
| | *(Island Queen {1} '66 - '87)* | | | | | | | |
| **P-10** | **PORT MANSION ENTERTAINMENT GROUP, ST. CATHARINES, ON** | | | | | | | |
| | Dalhousie Princess | ES | 1975 | D | 281* | 106' 00" | 24' 00" | 8' 02" |
| | *(Island Queen {3} '75 - '79, Miss Kingston II '79 - '84, M/V Montreal '84 - '01)* | | | | | | | |
| **P-11** | **PORTOFINO ON THE RIVER, WYANDOTTE, MI** | | | | | | | |
| | Friendship | ES | 1968 | D | 110* | 85' 00" | 30' 06" | 7' 03" |
| | *(Peche Island V '68 - '71, Papoose V '71 - '82)* | | | | | | | |
| **P-12** | **PRESIDENT RIVERBOAT CASINO, INC., ST. LOUIS, MO** | | | | | | | |
| | Majestic Star {2} | GA | 1997 | D | 12,805* | 330' 00" | 76' 00" | 20' 00" |
| **P-13** | **PROTEUS CO., CHICAGO, IL.** | | | | | | | |
| | Atchafalaya | DR | 1980 | D | 760* | 196' 08" | 40' 06" | 16' 04" |
| **P-14** | **PROTHERO, TORONTO, ON** | | | | | | | |
| | Kajama | ES | 1930 | D/W | 263* | 128' 09" | 23' 01" | 12' 00" |
| | *(Wilfried '30 - '64)* | | | | | | | |
| **P-15** | **PURVIS MARINE LTD., SAULT STE. MARIE, ON** | | | | | | | |
| | Adanac | TB | 1913 | D | 108* | 80' 03" | 19' 02" | 10' 06" |
| | *(Edward C. Whalen '13 - '66, John McLean '66 - '95)* | | | | | | | |
| | Anglian Lady | TB | 1953 | D | 398* | 136' 06" | 30' 00" | 14' 01" |
| | *(Hamtun '53 - '72, Nathalie Letzer '72 - '88)* | | | | | | | |
| | Avenger IV | TB | 1962 | D | 293* | 120' 00" | 30' 05" | 17' 05" |
| | *(Avenger '62 - '85)* | | | | | | | |
| | Charles W. Johnson | DB | 1915 | B | 1,685 | 245' 00" | 43' 00" | 14' 00" |
| | *(Iocolite '15 - '47, Imperial Kingston '47 - '61)* | | | | | | | |
| | Chief Wawatam | DB | 1911 | B | 4,500 | 347' 00" | 62' 03" | 15' 00" |
| | *(Converted from a powered trainferry to a self-unloading barge, '88)* | | | | | | | |
| | G.L.B. No. 1 | DB | 1953 | B | 3,215 | 305' 00" | 50' 00" | 12' 00" |
| | *(Joe Baugh Jr. '53 - '66, ORG 5503 '66 - '75)* | | | | | | | |
| | G.L.B. No. 2 | DB | 1953 | B | 3,215 | 305' 02" | 50' 00" | 12' 00" |
| | *(Jane Newfield '53 - '66, ORG 6502 '66 - '75)* | | | | | | | |
| | Goki | TB | 1940 | D | 24* | 57' 00" | 12' 08" | 7' 00" |
| | Malden | DB | 1946 | B | 1,075 | 150' 00" | 41' 09" | 10' 03" |
| | Martin E. Johnson | TB | 1959 | D | 26* | 46' 00" | 16' 00" | 5' 09" |
| | Osprey | TB | 1944 | D | 36* | 45' 00" | 13' 06" | 7' 00" |
| | P.M.L. Alton | DB | 1951 | B | 150 | 93' 00" | 30' 00" | 8' 00" |
| | P.M.L. Salvager | DB | 1945 | B | 5,200 | 341' 00" | 54' 00" | 27' 00" |
| | *([Unnamed] '45 - '55, Balsambranch '55 - '73, M.I.L. Balsam '73 - '77, Techno Balsam '77 - '77, DDS Salvager '77 - '88)* | | | | | | | |
| | P.M.L. 357 | DB | 1944 | B | 600 | 138' 00" | 38' 00" | 11' 00" |

| Fleet #. | Fleet Name / Vessel Name | Type of Vessel | Year Built | Type of Engine | Cargo Cap. or Gross* | Overall Length | Breadth | Depth or Draft* |
|---|---|---|---|---|---|---|---|---|
| | P.M.L. 2501 | TK | 1980 | B | 25,000 | 302' 00" | 52' 00" | 17' 00" |
| | *(CTCO 2505 '80 - '96)* | | | | | | | |
| | P.M.L. 9000 | DB | 1968 | B | 5,051* | 400' 00" | 76' 00" | 20' 00" |
| | *(Palmer '68 - '00)* | | | | | | | |
| | Quedoc {3} | BC | 1965 | D | 28,050 | 730' 00" | 75' 00" | 39' 02" |
| | *(Beavercliffe Hall '65 - '88)* | | | | | | | |
| | *(Last operated Dec. 20, 1991; Scheduled for scrapping at Sault Ste. Marie, ON, in 2003.)* | | | | | | | |
| | Reliance | TB | 1974 | D | 708* | 148' 04" | 35' 07" | 21' 06" |
| | *(Sinni '74 - '81, Irving Cedar '81 - '96, Atlantic Cedar '96-'02)* | | | | | | | |
| | Rocket | TB | 1901 | D | 39* | 70' 00" | 15' 00" | 8' 00" |
| | Sheila P. | TB | 1940 | D | 15* | 40' 00" | 14' 00" | |
| | Tecumseh II | DB | 1976 | B | 2,500 | 180' 00" | 54' 00" | 12' 00" |
| | *(U-727 '76 - '94)* | | | | | | | |
| | Wilfred M. Cohen | TB | 1948 | D | 284* | 104' 00" | 28' 00" | 14' 06" |
| | *(A. T. Lowmaster '48 - '75)* | | | | | | | |
| | W. I. Scott Purvis | TB | 1938 | D | 206* | 96' 06" | 26' 04" | 10' 04" |
| | *(Orient Bay '38 - '75, Guy M. No. 1 '75 - '90)* | | | | | | | |
| | W. J. Ivan Purvis | TB | 1938 | D | 191* | 100' 00" | 25' 06" | 9' 00" |
| | *(Magpie '38 - '66, Dana T. Bowen '66 - '75)* | | | | | | | |
| | Yankcanuck {2} | CS | 1963 | D | 4,760 | 324' 03" | 49' 00" | 26' 00" |
| **P-16** | **PUT-IN-BAY BOAT LINE CO., PORT CLINTON, OH** | | | | | | | |
| | Jet Express | PC | 1989 | D | 93* | 92' 08" | 28' 06" | 8' 04" |
| | Jet Express II | PC | 1992 | D | 85* | 92' 06" | 28' 06" | 8' 04" |
| | Jet Express III | PC | 2001 | D | 70* | 78' 02" | 27' 06" | 8' 02" |
| **R-1** | **RAYMOND BURTON BERKSHIRE, PLACENTIA, NF** | | | | | | | |
| | Paradise Sound | GC | 1969 | D | 430 | 137' 04" | 25' 00" | 11' 01" |
| | *(Tower Duchess '69 - '84)* | | | | | | | |
| | Placentia Sound | GC | 1969 | D | 713 | 173' 11" | 29' 00" | 12' 01" |
| | *(Apollo 1 '69 - '80, Arklow River '80 - '82, Cynthia June '82 - '86, Tora '86 - '88, Greeba River '88 - '97)* | | | | | | | |
| **R-2** | **RAYMOND MICHAEL DAVIS, TOBERMORY, ON** | | | | | | | |
| | Dawn Light | TB | 1891 | D | 64* | 75' 00" | 24' 00" | 12' 00" |
| | *(Le Roy Brooks 1891 - '25, Henry Stokes '25 - '54, Aburg '54 - '81)* | | | | | | | |
| **R-3** | **RIGEL SHIPPING CANADA, INC., SHEDIAC, NB** | | | | | | | |
| | Diamond Star | TK | 1992 | D | 68,019 | 405' 11" | 58' 01" | 34' 09" |
| | *(Elbestern '92 - '93)* | | | | | | | |
| | Emerald Star | TK | 1992 | D | 68,019 | 405' 11" | 58' 01" | 34' 09" |
| | *(Emsstern '92 - '92)* | | | | | | | |
| | Jade Star | TK | 1993 | D | 68,019 | 405' 11" | 58' 01" | 34' 09" |
| | *(Jadestern '93 - '94)* | | | | | | | |
| **R-4** | **ROCKPORT BOAT LINE (1994) LTD., ROCKPORT, ON** | | | | | | | |
| | Ida M. | ES | 1970 | D | 29* | 55' 00" | 14' 00" | 3' 00" |
| | Ida M. II | ES | 1973 | D | 116* | 63' 02" | 22' 02" | 5' 00" |
| **R-5** | **ROEN SALVAGE CO., STURGEON BAY, WI** | | | | | | | |
| | Chas Asher | TB | 1967 | D | 10* | 50' 00" | 18' 00" | 8' 00" |
| | John R. Asher | TB | 1943 | D | 93* | 70' 00" | 20' 00" | 8' 06" |
| | *(U. S. Army ST-71 '43 - '46, Russell 8 '46 - '64, Reid McAllister '64 - '67, Donegal '67 - '85)* | | | | | | | |
| | Louie S. | TB | 1956 | D | 43* | 37' 00" | 12' 00" | 5' 00" |
| | Spuds | TB | 1944 | D | 19* | 42' 00" | 12' 06" | 6' 00" |
| | Stephen M. Asher | TB | 1954 | D | 60* | 65' 00" | 19' 01" | 5' 04" |
| | *(Captain Bennie '54 - '82, Dumar Scout '82 - '87)* | | | | | | | |
| | Timmy A. | TB | 1953 | D | 12* | 33' 06" | 10' 08" | 5' 02" |
| **R-6** | **ROYAL CANADIAN YACHT CLUB, TORONTO, ON** | | | | | | | |
| | Elsie D. | PA | 1958 | D | 9* | 34' 07" | 10' 08" | 3' 06" |
| | Esperanza | PA | 1953 | D | 14* | 38' 06" | 11' 02" | 4' 06" |

**Wilfred Sykes enroute from Marquette to Detroit with taconite, Sept. 2, 2002.** *(Jim Hoffman)*

| Fleet #. | Fleet Name<br>Vessel Name | Type of<br>Vessel | Year<br>Built | Type of<br>Engine | Cargo Cap.<br>or Gross* | Overall<br>Length | Breadth | Depth or<br>Draft* |
|---|---|---|---|---|---|---|---|---|
| | Hiawatha | PA | 1895 | D | 46* | 56' 01" | 14' 04" | 6' 02" |
| | Kwasind | PA | 1912 | D | 47* | 70' 08" | 15' 09" | 5' -5" |
| **R-7** | **RUSSELL ISLAND TRANSIT CO., ALGONAC, MI** | | | | | | | |
| | Islander {2} | CF | 1982 | D | | 41' 00" | 15' 00" | 3' 06" |
| **R-8** | **RYBA MARINE CONSTRUCTION CO., CHEBOYGAN, MI** | | | | | | | |
| | Alcona | TB | 1957 | D | 18* | 40' 00" | 12' 06" | 5' 06" |
| | Amber Mae | TB | 1922 | D | 67* | 65' 00" | 14' 01" | 10' 00" |
| | *(E. W. Sutton '22 - '52, Venture '52 - '00)* | | | | | | | |
| | Harbor Master | CS | 1979 | B | 100* | 70' 00" | 27' 00" | 4' 00" |
| | Jarco 1402 | CS | 1981 | B | 473* | 140' 00" | 39' 00" | 9' 00" |
| | Kathy Lynn | D | 1944 | D | 140* | 85' 00" | 24' 00" | 9' 06" |
| | *(U. S. Army ST-693 '44 - '79, Sea Islander '79 - '91)* | | | | | | | |
| | Relief | CS | 1924 | B | 1,000 | 160' 00" | 40' 00" | 9' 00" |
| | Rochelle Kaye | TB | 1963 | D | 52* | 51' 06" | 19' 04" | 7' 00" |
| | *(Jaye Anne '63 - ?, Katanni ? - '97)* | | | | | | | |
| | Tonawanda | CS | 1935 | B | 600 | 120' 00" | 45' 00" | 8' 00" |
| **S-1** | **SANKORE MARINE IMMERSION HIGH SCHOOL, DETROIT, MI** | | | | | | | |
| | Sea-Born | ES | 1961 | D | 55* | 65' 00" | 17' 00" | 5' 00" |
| | *(Falcon '61 - '65, Bucky '65 - '68, Holiday '68 - '72, Speedy IV '72 - '74, Capt. Bill Van '74 - '76,<br>Pilot II '76 - '77, Capt. Eddie B. '77 - '94, Huron Lady '94 - '01)* | | | | | | | |
| **S-2** | **SAWMILL CREEK RESORT, HURON, OH** | | | | | | | |
| | Sawmill Explorer | ES | 1953 | D | 12* | 65' 00" | 17' 00" | 4' 00" |
| | *(Cedar Point II '53 - '89, Dispatch '89'-??)* | | | | | | | |
| **S-3** | **SCOTLUND STIVERS, MARINETTE, WI** | | | | | | | |
| | Arthur K. Atkinson | PA | 1917 | D | 3,241* | 384' 00" | 56' 00" | 20' 06" |
| | *(Ann Arbor No. 6 '17 - '59) Last operated in April, 1982. Laid up in Ludington, MI.)* | | | | | | | |
| **S-4** | **SEA FOX THOUSAND ISLANDS BOAT TOURS, KINGSTON, ON** | | | | | | | |
| | General Brock III | ES | 1977 | D | 56* | 50' 05" | 15' 04" | |
| | *(Miss Peterborough)* | | | | | | | |
| | Island Heritage | ES | 1929 | D | 21* | 63' 09" | 9' 08" | 4' 09" |
| | *(Miss Ivy Lea No. 1)* | | | | | | | |
| | Sea Fox II | ES | 1988 | D | 55* | 39' 08" | 20' 00" | 2' 00"* |
| **S-5** | **SEA SERVICE L. L. C., SUPERIOR, WI** | | | | | | | |
| | Sea Colt | TB | 1984 | D | 23* | 38' 00" | 11' 06" | 8' 00" |
| | *(Clara '84 - '95)* | | | | | | | |
| | Sea Bear | PB | 1959 | D | | 45' 00" | | |
| | *(Narrows ?? - '02)* | | | | | | | |
| | Sea Eagle | PB | | D | | | | |
| **S-6** | **SEAWAY MARINE TRANSPORT, ST. CATHARINES, ON**<br>*PARTNERSHIP BETWEEN ALGOMA CENTRAL CORP. AND UPPER LAKES GROUP, INC.*<br>*SEE RESPECTIVE FLEETS FOR VESSELS INVOLVED* | | | | | | | |
| **S-7** | **SELVICK MARINE TOWING CORP., STURGEON BAY, WI** | | | | | | | |
| | Carla Anne Selvick | TB | 1908 | D | 191* | 96' 00" | 23' 00" | 11' 02" |
| | *(S.O. Co. No. 19 '08 - '16, S.T. Co. No. 19 '16 - '18, Socony 19 '18 - '47, Esso Tug No. 4 '47 - '53,<br>McAllister 44 '53 - '55, Roderick McAllister '55 - '84)* | | | | | | | |
| | Escort II | TB | 1955 | D | 26* | 50' 00" | 15' 00" | 7' 03" |
| | Jacquelyn Nicole | TB | 1913 | D | 96* | 81' 00" | 20' 00" | 12' 06" |
| | *(Michigan {4} '13 - '78, Ste. Marie II '78 - '81, Dakota '81 - '92. Ethel E. '92-'02)* | | | | | | | |
| | Jimmy L. | TB | 1939 | D | 148* | 110' 00" | 25' 00" | 13' 00" |
| | *(USCGC Naugatuck [WYT / WYTM-92] '39 - '80, Timmy B. '80 - '84)* | | | | | | | |
| | Mary Page Hannah {1} | TB | 1950 | D | 461* | 143' 00" | 33' 01" | 14' 06" |
| | *(U. S. Army ATA-230 '49 - '72, G. W. Codrington '72 - '73, William P. Feeley {2} '73 - '73,<br>William W. Stender '73 - '78)* | | | | | | | |

| Fleet #. | Fleet Name<br>Vessel Name | Type of<br>Vessel | Year<br>Built | Type of<br>Engine | Cargo Cap.<br>or Gross* | Overall<br>Length | Breadth | Depth or<br>Draft* |
|---|---|---|---|---|---|---|---|---|
| | Moby Dick | DB | 1952 | B | 835 | 121' 00" | 33' 02" | 10' 06" |
| | Sharon M. Selvick | TB | 1945 | D | 28* | 45' 06" | 13' 00" | 7' 01" |
| | Susan L. | TB | 1944 | D | 163* | 86' 00" | 23' 00" | 10' 04" |
| | *(U. S. Army ST-709 '44 - '47, USCOE Stanley '47 - '99)* | | | | | | | |
| | William C. Selvick | TB | 1944 | D | 142* | 85' 00" | 22' 11" | 10' 04" |
| | *(U. S. Army ST-500 '44 - '49, Sherman H. Serre '49 - '77)* | | | | | | | |
| **S-8** | **SERVICES MARITIMES LAVIOLETTE INC., TROIS RIVIERES, QC** | | | | | | | |
| | Barge Laviolette | BC | 1965 | B | 7,573 | 498' 00" | 75' 00" | 39' 03" |
| | *(Grain storage barge constucted from bow and cargo section of powered vessel Canadian Explorer, '01.)* | | | | | | | |
| **S-9** | **SHAMROCK CHARTERING CO., GROSSE POINT, MI** | | | | | | | |
| | Helene | ES | 1927 | D | 109* | 106' 00" | 17' 00" | 6' 06"* |
| **S-10** | **SHELL CANADIAN TANKERS LTD., MONTREAL, QC** | | | | | | | |
| | Horizon Montreal | RT | 1958 | D | 32,900 | 315' 00" | 45' 07" | 24' 07" |
| | *(Tyee Shell '58 - '69, Arctic Trader '69 - '83, Rivershell {4} '83 - '95)* | | | | | | | |
| **S-11** | **SHEPARD MARINE CONSTRUCTION, ST. CLAIR SHORES, MI** | | | | | | | |
| | Robin Lynn | TB | 1952 | D | 146* | 85' 00" | 25' 00" | 11' 00" |
| | *(Bonita '52-'85, Susan Hoey {2} '85'-'95, Blackie B '95-'97, Susan Hoey {3 }'97-'98)* | | | | | | | |
| **S-12** | **SHEPLER'S MACKINAC ISLAND FERRY SERVICE, MACKINAW CITY, MI** | | | | | | | |
| | Capt. Shepler | PF | 1986 | D | 71* | 78' 00" | 21' 00" | 7' 10" |
| | Felicity | PF | 1972 | D | 84* | 65' 00" | 18' 01" | 8' 03" |
| | Sacre Bleu | PK | 1959 | D | 92* | 94' 10" | 31' 00" | 9' 09" |
| | *(Put-In-Bay {2} '59 - '94)* | | | | | | | |
| | The Hope | PF | 1975 | D | 87* | 77' 00" | 20' 00" | 8' 03" |
| | The Welcome | PF | 1969 | D | 66* | 60' 06" | 16' 08" | 8' 02" |
| | Wyandot | PF | 1979 | D | 99* | 77' 00" | 20' 00" | 8' 00" |
| **S-13** | **SHIPWRECK TOURS, INC., MUNISING, MI** | | | | | | | |
| | Miss Munising | ES | 1967 | D | 50* | 60' 00" | 14' 00" | 4' 04" |
| **S-14** | **SHORELINE CONTRACTORS INC., CLEVELAND, OH** | | | | | | | |
| | Eagle | TB | 1943 | D | 31* | 57' 09" | 14' 05" | 6' 10" |
| **S-15** | **SHORELINE SIGHTSEEING CO., CHICAGO, IL** | | | | | | | |
| | Allons-Y | PF | 1978 | D | 25" | 40' 00" | 12' 00" | 8' 00" |
| | Andiamo | PF | 1980 | D | 25* | 40' 00" | 12' 00" | 8' 00" |
| | Blue Dog | PF | 1981 | D | 31* | 47' 07" | 18' 00" | 5' 05" |
| | *(Miss Ocean World)* | | | | | | | |
| | Cap Streeter | ES | 1987 | D | 28* | 63' 06" | 24' 04" | 7' 07" |
| | Evening Star | ES | 2001 | D | | 83' 00" | 23' 00" | |
| | Shoreline II | ES | 1987 | D | 89* | 75' 00" | 26' 00" | 7' 01" |
| | South Shore | CF | 1945 | D | 67* | 64' 10" | 24' 00" | 9' 06" |
| | Star of Chicago {2} | ES | 1999 | D | | 64' 10" | 22' 08" | 7' 05" |
| **S-16** | **SIVERTSON'S GRAND PORTAGE - ISLE ROYALE TRANSPORTATION LINES, SUPERIOR, WI** | | | | | | | |
| | A. E. Clifford | FT | 1946 | D | 33* | 45' 00" | 15' 00" | 7' 00" |
| | Provider | FT | 1959 | D | | 46' 00" | 13' 05" | 5' 05" |
| | Sharon Jon | FT | 1943 | D | 17* | 32' 04" | 11' 06" | 5' 00" |
| | Voyageur II | ES | 1970 | D | | 63' 00" | 18' 00" | 5' 00" |
| | Wenonah | FS | 1960 | D | 91* | 70' 07" | 19' 04" | 9' 07" |
| | *(Jamaica '60 - '64)* | | | | | | | |
| **S-17** | **SOCIETE DES TRAVERSIERS DU QUEBEC, QUEBEC, QC** | | | | | | | |
| | Alphonse desJardins | CF | 1971 | D | 1,741* | 214' 00" | 71' 06" | 20' 00" |
| | Armand Imbeau | CF | 1980 | D | 1,285* | 203' 07" | 72' 00" | 18' 04" |
| | Camille Marcoux | CF | 1974 | D | 6,122* | 310' 00" | 62' 09" | 39' 00" |
| | Catherine-Legardeur | CF | 1985 | D | 1,348* | 205' 09" | 71' 10" | 18' 10" |
| | Felix-Antoine Savard | CF | 1997 | D | 2,489* | 272' 00" | 70' 00" | |

| Fleet #. | Fleet Name / Vessel Name | Type of Vessel | Year Built | Type of Engine | Cargo Cap. or Gross* | Overall Length | Breadth | Depth or Draft* |
|---|---|---|---|---|---|---|---|---|
| | Grue des Iles | CF | 1981 | D | 447* | 155' 10" | 41' 01" | 12' 06" |
| | Jos Deschenes | CF | 1980 | D | 1,287* | 203' 07" | 72' 00" | 18' 04" |
| | Joseph Savard | CF | 1985 | D | 1,445* | 206' 00" | 71' 10" | 18' 10" |
| | Lomer Gouin | CF | 1971 | D | 1,741* | 214' 00" | 71' 06" | 20' 00" |
| | Lucien L. | CF | 1967 | D | 867* | 220' 10" | 61' 06" | 15' 05" |
| | Radisson {1} | CF | 1954 | D | 1,043* | 164' 03" | 72' 00" | 10' 06" |
| **S-18** | **SOCIETE DU PORT DE MONTREAL, MONTREAL, QC** | | | | | | | |
| | Maisonneuve | TB | 1972 | D | 103* | 63' 10" | 20' 07" | 9' 03" |
| **S-19** | **SOO LOCKS BOAT TOURS, SAULT STE. MARIE, MI** | | | | | | | |
| | Bide-A-Wee {3} | ES | 1955 | D | 99* | 64' 07" | 23' 00" | 7' 11" |
| | Hiawatha {2} | ES | 1959 | D | 99* | 64' 07" | 23' 00" | 7' 11" |
| | Holiday | ES | 1957 | D | 99* | 64' 07" | 23' 00" | 7' 11" |
| | LeVoyageur | ES | 1959 | D | 70* | 65' 00" | 25' 00" | 7' 00" |
| | Nokomis | ES | 1959 | D | 70* | 65' 00" | 25' 00" | 7' 00" |
| **S-20** | **SPECIALTY RESTAURANTS CORP., ANAHEIM, CA** | | | | | | | |
| | Lansdowne | TF | 1884 | B | 1,571* | 319' 00" | 41' 03" | 13' 00" |
| | *(Last operated in 1974. Superstructure of former Detroit River, sidewheel-driven train ferry gutted at Erie, PA, in 2002. Now undergoing conversion to a floating restaurant.)* | | | | | | | |
| **S- 21** | **SPIRIT CRUISE LINE LTD., TORONTO, ON** | | | | | | | |
| | Northern Spirit I | ES | 1983 | D | 489* | 136' 00" | 31' 00" | 9' 00" |
| | *(New Spirit '83 - '89, Pride of Toronto '89 - '92)* | | | | | | | |
| | Oriole | ES | 1987 | D | 200* | 75' 00" | 23' 00" | 9' 00" |
| **S-22** | **SPIRIT LAKE MARINA, DULUTH, MN** | | | | | | | |
| | John V. II | TB | 1942 | D | 12* | 40' 00" | 10' 00" | 3' 05" |
| **S-23** | **ST. LAWRENCE CRUISE LINES, INC., KINGSTON, ON** | | | | | | | |
| | Canadian Empress | PA | 1981 | D | 463* | 108' 00" | 30' 00" | 8' 00" |
| **S-24** | **ST. LAWRENCE SEAWAY DEVELOPMENT CORP., MASSENA, NY** | | | | | | | |
| | Robinson Bay | TB | 1958 | D | 213* | 103' 00" | 26' 10" | 14' 06" |
| | Performance | TB | 1997 | D | | 50' 00" | | |
| **S-25** | **ST. LAWRENCE SEAWAY MANAGEMENT CORP., CORNWALL, ON** | | | | | | | |
| | VM/S Hercules | GL | 1962 | D | 2,107 | 200' 00" | 75' 00" | 18' 08" |
| | VM/S Iroquois | TB | 1974 | D | 20* | 30' 08" | | |
| | VM/S Maisonneuve | TB | 1974 | D | 56* | 58' 03" | | |
| | VM/S St. Lambert | TB | 1974 | D | 20* | 30' 08" | | |
| | VM/S St. Louis III | TB | 1977 | D | 15* | 34' 04" | | |
| **S-26** | **STANTON CRUISE LINES, THUNDER BAY, ON** | | | | | | | |
| | Pioneer II | ES | 1959 | D | 28* | 52' 01" | 11' 08" | 3' 09" |
| | *(Witte-De-With '59-'72, Miss Algonquin Park '72-'74, David H. Simpson '74-'90, London Princess '90 - '02)* | | | | | | | |
| **S-27** | **STAR LINE MACKINAC ISLAND FERRY, ST. IGNACE, MI** | | | | | | | |
| | Cadillac {5} | PF | 1990 | D | 73* | 64' 07" | 20' 00" | 7' 07" |
| | Joliet {3} | PF | 1993 | D | 83* | 64' 08" | 22' 00" | 8' 03" |
| | La Salle {4} | PF | 1983 | D | 55* | 65' 00" | 20' 00" | 7' 05" |
| | Marquette {5} | PF | 1979 | D | 55* | 62' 03" | 22' 00" | 7' 01" |
| | Nicolet {2} | PF | 1985 | D | 51* | 65' 00" | 20' 00" | 7' 05" |
| | Radisson {2} | PF | 1988 | D | 97* | 80' 00" | 23' 06" | 7' 00" |
| **S-28** | **STAR OF SAUGATUCK BOAT CRUISES, SAUGATUCK, MI** | | | | | | | |
| | Star of Saugatuck | ES | 1978 | D | 12* | 57' 00" | 14' 00" | 2' 04" |
| **S-29** | **STEPHEN HUME, DETROIT, MI** | | | | | | | |
| | Queen City {2} | PA | 1911 | D | 248* | 116' 00" | 23' 00" | 12' 07" |
| | *(Polana '11 - '30, Jalobert '30 - '54, Macassa {2} '54 - '65; Last operated 1982. Laid up at Detroit, MI.)* | | | | | | | |

**H. Lee White northbound with a cargo of limestone.** *(Roger LeLievre)*

**American Girl is based on Beaver Island in Lake Michigan.**
*(John Vournakis)*

**Herbert C. Jackson leaves Grand Haven.** *(Don Geske)*

| Fleet #. | Fleet Name / Vessel Name | Type of Vessel | Year Built | Type of Engine | Cargo Cap. or Gross* | Overall Length | Breadth | Depth or Draft* |
|---|---|---|---|---|---|---|---|---|
| **S-30** | **STEVEN WALLACE, PENETANGUISHENE, ON** | | | | | | | |
| | Georgian Storm | TB | 1931 | D | 167* | 91' 00" | 24' 02" | 12' 00" |
| | *(Capitaine Simard '31 - '57, Renee Simard '57 - '86)* | | | | | | | |
| **T-1** | **T & T DREDGING, INC., GRAND RAPIDS, MI** | | | | | | | |
| | Bonnie G. Selvick | TB | 1928 | D | 95* | 86' 00" | 21' 00" | 12' 00" |
| | *(E. James Fucik '28 - '77)* | | | | | | | |
| | Louise | DR | | B | | | | |
| | Wolverine | TB | 1952 | D | 22* | 42' 05" | 14' 00" | 7' 00" |
| **T- 2** | **TALISMAN ENERGY INC., CALGARY, AL** | | | | | | | |
| | J.R. Rouble | TB | 1958 | D | 562* | 123' 06" | 49' 08" | 16' 00" |
| | *(Mr. Neil)* | | | | | | | |
| | Miss Libby | DV | 1972 | B | 924* | 160' 01" | 54' 01" | 11' 01" |
| | Mr. Chris | DV | 1973 | B | 1,022* | 160' 01" | 54' 01" | 11' 01" |
| | Sarah No. 1 | TB | 1969 | D | 43* | 72' 01" | 17' 03" | 6' 08" |
| | Timesaver II | PD | 1964 | B | 510* | 91' 08" | 70' 08" | 9' 01" |
| **T-3** | **TEE DEE ENTERPRISES, INC., CHICAGO, IL** | | | | | | | |
| | Anita Dee 1 | ES | 1972 | D | 97* | 90' 00" | 21' 00" | 8' 10" |
| | *(M/V Happy Dolphin '72 - '84, Spirit of Toledo '84 - ?)* | | | | | | | |
| | Anita Dee II | ES | 1990 | D | 81* | 140' 00" | 33' 00" | 8' 06" |
| **T-4** | **THOMAS W. MARSHALL, TORONTO, ON** | | | | | | | |
| | Still Watch | SV | 1960 | D | 390* | 134' 02" | 28' 00" | 13' 09" |
| | *(CCGS Ville Marie '60 - '85, Heavenbound '85 - '95)* | | | | | | | |
| **T-5** | **THORNTON CONSTRUCTION CO., INC., HANCOCK, MI** | | | | | | | |
| | Shannon 66-5 | TB | 1950 | D | 21* | 49' 00" | 16' 00" | 5' 00"* |
| **T-6** | **THUNDER BAY MARINE SERVICE LTD., THUNDER BAY, ON** | | | | | | | |
| | Agoming | CS | 1926 | B | 155* | 100' 00" | 34' 00" | 9' 00" |
| | Coastal Cruiser | TB | 1939 | D | 29* | 65' 00" | 18' 00" | 12' 00" |
| | Robert W. | TB | 1949 | D | 48* | 60' 00" | 16' 00" | 8' 06" |
| | Rosalee D. | TB | 1943 | D | 22* | 55' 00" | 16' 00" | 10' 00" |
| **T-7** | **THUNDER BAY TUG SERVICES LTD., THUNDER BAY, ON** | | | | | | | |
| | Glenada | TB | 1943 | D | 107* | 80' 06" | 25' 00" | 10' 01" |
| | *(HMCS Glenada [W-30] '43 - '45)* | | | | | | | |
| | Point Valour | TB | 1958 | D | 246* | 97' 08" | 28' 02" | 13' 10" |
| | *(Foundation Valour '58 - '83)* | | | | | | | |
| **T-8** | **TOM ERHART - TERRACE INN HOTEL, PETOSKEY, MI** | | | | | | | |
| | Bay Pride | ES | 1987 | D | 27* | 42' 00" | 14' 00" | 7' 00" |
| **T-9** | **TORONTO DRY-DOCK CORP., TORONTO, ON** | | | | | | | |
| | Menier Consol | FD | 1962 | B | 2,575* | 304' 07" | 49' 06" | 25' 06" |
| **T-10** | **TORONTO FIRE DEPARTMENT, TORONTO, ON** | | | | | | | |
| | Wm. Lyon Mackenzie | FB | 1964 | D | 102* | 81' 01" | 20' 00" | 10' 00" |
| **T-11** | **TORONTO PORT AUTHORITY, TORONTO, ON** | | | | | | | |
| | Fred Scandrett | TB | 1963 | D | 52* | 62' 00" | 17' 00" | 8' 00" |
| | *(C. E. "Ted" Smith '63 - '70)* | | | | | | | |
| | Maple City | CF | 1951 | D | 135* | 70' 06" | 36' 04" | 5' 11" |
| | Ned Hanlan II | TB | 1966 | D | 26* | 41' 06" | 14' 01" | 5' 05" |
| | Osprey | TB | 1991 | D | 5* | 25' 09" | 8' 08" | 3' 06" |
| | William Rest | TB | 1961 | D | 62* | 65' 00" | 18' 06" | 10' 06" |
| | Windmill Point | CF | 1954 | D | 118* | 65' 00" | 36' 00" | 10' 00" |
| **T-12** | **TORONTO TOURS LTD., TORONTO, ON** | | | | | | | |
| | Miss Kim Simpson | ES | 1960 | D | 33* | 90' 02" | 13' 04" | 3' 09" |
| | Shipsands | ES | 1972 | D | 23* | 58' 03" | 12' 01" | 4' 09" |

| Fleet #. | Fleet Name / Vessel Name | Type of Vessel | Year Built | Type of Engine | Cargo Cap. or Gross* | Overall Length | Breadth | Depth or Draft* |
|---|---|---|---|---|---|---|---|---|
| **T-13** | **TRANSPORT DESGAGNES, INC., QUEBEC, QC** | | | | | | | |
| | **CROISIERES NORDIK, INC., QUEBEC, QC - A DIVISION OF TRANSPORT DESGAGNES, INC.** | | | | | | | |
| | Nordik Passeur | RR | 1962 | D | 627 | 285' 04" | 62' 00" | 20' 01" |
| | *(Confederation {1} '62 - '93, Hull 28 '93 - '94) (5 year survey expired 1994 – Laid up in Quebec, QC.)* | | | | | | | |
| | **DESGAGNES SHIPPING INT., INC., QUEBEC, QC - A DIV. OF TRANSPORT DESGAGNES, INC.** | | | | | | | |
| | Anna Desgagnes | RR | 1986 | D | 17,850 | 565' 00" | 75' 00" | 45' 00" |
| | *(Truskavets '86 - '96, Anna Desgagnes '96 - '98, PCC Panama '98 - '99)* | | | | | | | |
| | **DESGAGNES TANKER, INC., QUEBEC, QC - A DIVISION OF TRANSPORT DESGAGNES, INC.** | | | | | | | |
| | Maria Desgagnes | TK | 1999 | D | 95,607 | 393' 08" | 68' 11" | 40' 04" |
| | *(Kilchem Asia '99 - '99)* | | | | | | | |
| | Petrolia Desgagnes | TK | 1975 | D | 97,725 | 441' 05" | 56' 06" | 32' 10" |
| | *(Jorvan '75 - '79, Lido '79 - '84, Ek-Sky '84 - '98)* | | | | | | | |
| | Thalassa Desgagnes | TK | 1976 | D | 104,667 | 441' 05" | 56' 06" | 32' 10" |
| | *(Joasla '76 - '79, Orinoco '79 - '82, Rio Orinoco '82 - '93)* | | | | | | | |
| | Vega Desgagnes | TK | 1982 | D | 82,417 | 461' 11" | 69' 08" | 35' 01" |
| | *(Shelltrans '82 - '94, Acila '94 - '99, Bacalan '99 - '01)* | | | | | | | |
| | **GROUP DESGAGNES, INC., QUEBEC, QC - A DIVISION OF TRANSPORT DESGAGNES, INC.** | | | | | | | |
| | Amelia Desgagnes | GC | 1976 | D | 7,126 | 355' 00" | 49' 00" | 30' 06" |
| | *(Soodoc {2} '76 - '90)* | | | | | | | |
| | Catherine Desgagnes | GC | 1962 | D | 8,350 | 410' 03" | 56' 04" | 31' 00" |
| | *(Gosforth '62 - '72, Thorold {4} '72 - '85)* | | | | | | | |
| | Cecelia Desgagnes | GC | 1971 | D | 7,875 | 374' 10" | 54' 10" | 34' 06" |
| | *(Carl Gorthon '71 - '81, Federal Pioneer '81 - '85)* | | | | | | | |
| | Jacques Desgagnes | GC | 1960 | D | 1,250 | 208' 10" | 36' 00" | 14' 00" |
| | *(Loutre Consol '60 - '77)* | | | | | | | |
| | Mathilda Desgagnes | GC | 1959 | D | 6,920 | 360' 00" | 51' 00" | 30' 02" |
| | *(Eskimo '59 - '80)* | | | | | | | |
| | Melissa Desgagnes | GC | 1975 | D | 7,000 | 355' 00" | 49' 00" | 30' 06" |
| | *(Ontadoc {2} '75 - '90)* | | | | | | | |
| | Nordik Express | CF | 1974 | D | 1,697 | 219' 11" | 44' 00" | 16' 01" |
| | *(Theriot Offshore IV '74 - '77, Scotoil 4 '77 - '79, Tartan Sea '79 - '87)* | | | | | | | |
| **T-14** | **TRANSPORT IGLOOLIK, INC., MONTREAL, QC** | | | | | | | |
| | Aivik | HL | 1980 | D | 4,860 | 359' 08" | 63' 08" | 38' 09" |
| | *(Mont Ventoux '80 - '90, Aivik '90 - '91, Unilifter '91 - '92)* | | | | | | | |
| **T-15** | **TRANSPORT NANUK, INC., MONTREAL, QC** | | | | | | | |
| | Umiavut | GC | 1988 | D | 9,682 | 371' 02" | 63' 01" | 37' 00" |
| | *(Completed as Newca, Kapitan Silin '88 - '92, Lindengracht '92 - '00)* | | | | | | | |
| **T-16** | **TRAVERSE TALL SHIP CO., TRAVERSE CITY, MI** | | | | | | | |
| | Manitou {1} | ES/2S | 1983 | W | 78* | 114' 00" | 21' 00" | 9' 00" |
| | Westwind | ES/2S | 1992 | W | 43* | 66' 00" | 14' 00" | 8' 06" |
| **T-17** | **30,000 ISLANDS CRUISE LINES, INC., PARRY SOUND, ON** | | | | | | | |
| | Island Queen V {3} | ES | 1990 | D | 526* | 130' 00" | 35' 00" | 6' 06" |
| **U-1** | **UNCLE SAM BOAT TOURS, ALEXANDRIA, NY** | | | | | | | |
| | Alexandria Belle | ES | 1988 | D | 72* | 104' 00" | 32' 00" | 7' 08"* |
| | Island Duchess | ES | 1988 | D | 60* | 110' 00" | 27' 08" | 8' 08"* |
| | Island Wanderer | ES | 1971 | D | 57* | 62' 05" | 22' 00" | 7' 02" |
| | Uncle Sam 7 | ES | 1976 | D | 55* | 60' 04" | 22' 00" | 7' 01" |
| **U-2** | **UNITED STATES ARMY CORPS OF ENGINEERS, CHICAGO, IL - GREAT LAKES / OHIO RIVER DIV.** | | | | | | | |
| | **UNITED STATES ARMY CORPS OF ENGINEERS, BUFFALO, NY - BUFFALO DISTRICT** | | | | | | | |
| | Cheraw | TB | 1970 | D | 356* | 109' 00" | 30' 06" | 16' 03" |
| | *(USS Cheraw [YTB-802] '70 - '96)* | | | | | | | |
| | Koziol | TB | 1973 | D | 356* | 109' 00" | 30' 06" | 16' 03" |
| | *(USS Chetek [YTB-827] '73 - '96, Chetek '96 - '00)* | | | | | | | |
| | McCauley | CS | 1948 | B | | 112' 00" | 52' 00" | 3' 00"* |
| | Simonsen | CS | 1954 | B | | 142' 00" | 58' 00" | 5' 00"* |

**George A. Stinson, upbound for another National Steel cargo.** *(Gene Onchulenko)*

# GEORGE A. STINSON

**G**eorge A. Stinson, the seventh of the 13 Great Lakes 1,000-footers built, is the only one dedicated to a particular run. If you see her heading downbound, it's a sure bet she's carrying taconite from Lake Superior ports to the National Steel Corp.'s mill on Zug Island, near Detroit. To signify her affiliation, the **Stinson** displays the National Steel red "N" logo next to her name, on either side of her bow.

## Vessel Spotlight

Built in 1978 for National Steel, the **Stinson** 's bow and stern sections were completed at American Ship Building Co., Lorain, Ohio, while its mid-body was built at Amship's Toledo yard. The new vessel was christened Aug. 21, 1978, in Detroit to honor National Steel's chairman of the board. Not only was the vessel the only 1,000-footer in National Steel's fleet, she was the fleet's first self-unloader. Managed by the Hanna Mining Co., the **Stinson** departed on its maiden voyage Oct. 14, 1978, in ballast for Superior, Wis., to load iron ore pellets for Zug Island.

Only three months into her career, the **Stinson** struck a wall at the Poe Lock at Sault Ste. Marie, causing an estimated $200,000 in damages. On April 17, 1983, the unloading boom collapsed due to a mechanical failure while at Detroit. She continued operating as a straight-decker until the boom was replaced later that year. On April 20, 1984, the Stinson ran aground in the St. Clair River near Marine City, Mich., due to an ice jam. Part of her cargo of ore pellets was lightered into fleetmate **Paul H. Carnahan** before she could be freed.

Skar-Ore Corp., Cleveland, assumed ownership of the vessel in 1986, followed by Stinson, Inc. in 1989 with M. A. Hanna Co. as agents for both owners. With Stinson, Inc. retaining ownership, the vessel was leased to Interlake Steamship Co. in 1992. In 1996, when the lease expired, American Steamship Co. leased the vessel, and continues to manage her. The recent pooling of American Steamship and Oglebay Norton fleets did not include the **Stinson** due to her dedicated National Steel operation. – *George Wharton*

| Fleet #. | Fleet Name / Vessel Name | Type of Vessel | Year Built | Type of Engine | Cargo Cap. or Gross* | Overall Length | Breadth | Depth or Draft* |
|---|---|---|---|---|---|---|---|---|
| | Wheeler | DR | 1982 | B | 10,353 | 384' 00" | 78' 00" | 39' 00" |

**UNITED STATES ARMY CORPS OF ENGINEERS, CHICAGO, IL - CHICAGO DISTRICT**

| Fleet #. | Fleet Name / Vessel Name | Type of Vessel | Year Built | Type of Engine | Cargo Cap. or Gross* | Overall Length | Breadth | Depth or Draft* |
|---|---|---|---|---|---|---|---|---|
| | Kenosha | TB | 1954 | D | 82* | 70' 00" | 20' 00" | 9' 08" |
| | *(U. S. Army ST-2011 '54 - '65)* | | | | | | | |
| | Manitowoc | CS | 1976 | B | | 132' 00" | 44' 00" | 8' 00"* |
| | Racine | TB | 1931 | D | 61* | 66' 03" | 18' 05" | 7' 08" |

**UNITED STATES ARMY CORPS OF ENGINEERS, DETROIT, MI - DETROIT DISTRICT**

| Fleet #. | Fleet Name / Vessel Name | Type of Vessel | Year Built | Type of Engine | Cargo Cap. or Gross* | Overall Length | Breadth | Depth or Draft* |
|---|---|---|---|---|---|---|---|---|
| | D. L. Billmaier | TB | 1968 | D | 356* | 109' 00" | 30' 06" | 16' 03" |
| | *(USS Natchitoches [YTB-799] '68 - '95)* | | | | | | | |
| | Demolen | TB | 1974 | D | 356* | 109' 00" | 30' 06" | 16' 03" |
| | *(USS Metacom [YTB-829] '74 - '01, Metacom '01 - '02)* | | | | | | | |
| | Fairchild | TB | 1953 | D | 23* | 45' 00" | 13' 00" | 7' 00"* |
| | Forney | TB | 1944 | D | 163* | 86' 00" | 23' 00" | 10' 04" |
| | *(U. S. Army ST-707 '44 - '60)* | | | | | | | |
| | Harvey | CS | 1961 | B | | 122' 00" | 40' 00" | 4' 10" |
| | H. J. Schwartz | CS | 1995 | B | | 150' 00" | 48' 00" | 11' 00" |
| | Huron | CS | 1954 | B | | 100' 00" | 34' 00" | 4' 06"* |
| | James M. Bray | SV | 1924 | D | 194* | 128' 00" | 31' 00" | 8' 00" |
| | *(Deck Cargo Barge 20 '24 - '85)* | | | | | | | |
| | Michigan | CS | 1971 | B | | 120' 00" | 33' 00" | 3' 06"* |
| | Nicolet | CS | 1971 | B | | 120' 00" | 42' 00" | 5' 00"* |
| | Owen M. Frederick | TB | 1942 | D | 56* | 65' 00" | 17' 00" | 7' 06" |
| | Paj | SV | 1955 | D | 151* | 120' 06" | 34' 02" | 6' 05" |
| | *(Deck Cargo Barge No. 30 '55 - '86)* | | | | | | | |
| | Paul Bunyan | GL | 1945 | B | | 150' 00" | 65' 00" | 12' 06" |
| | Tawas Bay | TB | 1953 | D | 23* | 45' 00" | 13' 00" | 7' 00"* |
| | Veler | CS | 1991 | B | 613* | 150' 00" | 46' 00" | 10' 06" |
| | Whitefish Bay | TB | 1953 | D | 23* | 45' 00" | 13' 00" | 7' 00"* |

**U-3   UNITED STATES COAST GUARD 9TH COAST GUARD DISTRICT, CLEVELAND, OH**

| Fleet #. | Fleet Name / Vessel Name | Type of Vessel | Year Built | Type of Engine | Cargo Cap. or Gross* | Overall Length | Breadth | Depth or Draft* |
|---|---|---|---|---|---|---|---|---|
| | Acacia   **[WLB-406]** | BT | 1944 | D | 1,025* | 180' 00" | 37' 00" | 17' 04" |
| | *(Launched as USCGC Thistle [WAGL-406]) (Scheduled to be decommissioned in 2005.)* | | | | | | | |
| | Adler   **[WLB-216]** | BT | 2004 | D | 2,000* | 225' 09" | 46' 00" | 19' 08" |
| | *(To be commissioned in January 2004 and stationed at Charlevoix, MI.)* | | | | | | | |
| | Biscayne Bay **[WTGB-104]** | IB | 1979 | D | 662* | 140' 00" | 37' 06" | 12' 00"* |
| | Bramble   **[WLB-392]** | BT | 1944 | D | 1,025* | 180' 00" | 37' 00" | 17' 04" |
| | *(Scheduled to be decommissioned in 2003.)* | | | | | | | |
| | Bristol Bay   **[WTGB-102]** | IB | 1979 | D | 662* | 140' 00" | 37' 06" | 12' 00"* |
| | Buckthorn   **[WLI-642]** | BT | 1963 | D | 200* | 100' 00" | 24' 00" | 4' 08"* |
| | CGB-12000 | BT | 1991 | B | 700* | 120' 00" | 50' 00" | 6' 00"* |
| | CGB-12001 | BT | 1991 | B | 700* | 120' 00" | 50' 00" | 6' 00"* |
| | Hollyhock   **[WLB-215]** | BT | 2003 | D | 2,000* | 225' 09" | 46' 00" | 19' 08" |
| | *(To be commissioned in September 2003 and stationed at Port Huron, MI.)* | | | | | | | |
| | Katmai Bay **[WTGB-101]** | IB | 1978 | D | 662* | 140' 00" | 37' 06" | 12' 00"* |
| | Mackinaw   **[WAGB-83]** | IB | 1944 | D | 5,252* | 290' 00" | 74' 00" | 29' 00" |
| | *(Launched as USCGC Manitowoc [WAG-83]) (Scheduled to be decommissioned in 2006.)* | | | | | | | |
| | Mackinaw   **[WLBB-30]** | IB | 2005 | D | 15'06"* | 240' 00" | 58' 00" | 15' 05"* |
| | *(To be commissioned in 2005 and stationed at Cheboygan, MI.)* | | | | | | | |
| | Mobile Bay **[WTGB-103]** | IB | 1979 | D | 662* | 140' 00" | 37' 06" | 12' 00"* |
| | Neah Bay   **[WTGB-105]** | IB | 1900 | D | 662* | 140' 00" | 37' 06" | 12' 00"* |
| | Sundew   **[WLB-404]** | BT | 1944 | D | 1,025" | 180' 00" | 37' 00" | 17' 04" |
| | *(Scheduled to be decommissioned in 2003.)* | | | | | | | |

**NEW BUILDINGS FOR USCG – "JUNIPER" CLASS / MARINETTE MARINE**

| Fleet #. | Fleet Name / Vessel Name | Type of Vessel | Year Built | Type of Engine | Cargo Cap. or Gross* | Overall Length | Breadth | Depth or Draft* |
|---|---|---|---|---|---|---|---|---|
| | Fir   **[WLB-213]** | BT | 2003 | D | 2,000* | 225' 09" | 46' 00" | 19' 08" |
| | *(To be commissioned in June 2003 and stationed at Astoria, OR in the 13th Coast Guard District.)* | | | | | | | |
| | Hickory   **[WLB-212]** | BT | 2003 | D | 2,000* | 225' 09" | 46' 00" | 19' 08" |
| | *(To be commissioned in Jan. 2003 and stationed at Homer, AK in the 17th Coast Guard District.)* | | | | | | | |

**Summer sunset on board Southdown Challenger.** *(Dustin Sadowski)*

| Fleet #. | Fleet Name<br>Vessel Name | Type of<br>Vessel | Year<br>Built | Type of<br>Engine | Cargo Cap.<br>or Gross* | Overall<br>Length | Breadth | Depth or<br>Draft* |
|---|---|---|---|---|---|---|---|---|
| **U-4** | **UNITED STATES DEPARTMENT OF THE INTERIOR, ANN ARBOR, MI** | | | | | | | |
| | **GREAT LAKES SCIENCE CENTER** | | | | | | | |
| | Grayling | RV | 1977 | D | 198* | 75' 00" | 22' 00" | 9' 10" |
| | Kaho | RV | 1961 | D | 83* | 64' 10" | 17' 10" | 9' 00" |
| | Kiyi | RV | 1999 | D | 290* | 107' 00" | 27' 00" | 12' 02" |
| | Musky II | RV | 1960 | D | 25* | 45' 00" | 14' 04" | 5' 00" |
| | Siscowet | RV | 1946 | D | 54* | 57' 00" | 14' 06" | 7' 00" |
| | Sturgeon | RV | 1977 | D | 325* | 100'00" | 25' 05" | 10' 00" |
| **U-5** | **UNITED STATES ENVIRONMENTAL PROTECTION AGENCY, DULUTH, MN. & CHICAGO, IL** | | | | | | | |
| | Bluewater | RV | 1970 | D | 22* | 50' 00" | 14' 00" | 3' 0" |
| | Lake Explorer | RV | 1962 | D | 69* | 82' 10" | 17' 07" | 5' 11"* |
| | *(USCGC Point Roberts [WPB-82332] '62 - '92)* | | | | | | | |
| | Lake Guardian | RV | 1981 | D | 282* | 180' 00" | 40' 00" | 11' 00" |
| | *(Marsea Fourteen '81 - '90)* | | | | | | | |
| | Mudpuppy | RV | 1988 | D | 6* | 32' 00" | 8' 00" | 2' 00" |
| **U-6** | **UNITED STATES NATIONAL PARK SERVICE - ISLE ROYALE NATIONAL PARK, HOUGHTON, MI** | | | | | | | |
| | Beaver | GC | 1952 | B | 550 | 110' 00" | 32' 00" | 6' 05" |
| | Charlie Mott | PF | 1953 | D | 28* | 56' 00" | 14' 00" | 4' 07" |
| | Greenstone | TK | 1977 | B | 30 | 81' 00" | 24' 00" | 6' 01" |
| | J. E. Colombe | TB | 1953 | D | 25* | 45' 00" | 12' 05" | 5' 03" |
| | Ranger III | PK | 1958 | D | 140 | 165' 00" | 34' 00" | 15' 03" |
| **U-7** | **UNITED STATES NAVAL SEA CADET CORPS - FC SHERMAN DIVISION, PORT HURON, MI** | | | | | | | |
| | Greyfox  **[TWR-825]** | TV | 1985 | D | 213* | 120' 00" | 25' 00" | 12' 00"* |
| | *(USS TWR-825 '85 - '97)* | | | | | | | |
| | Pride of Michigan  **[YP-673]** | TV | 1977 | D | 70* | 80' 06" | 17' 08" | 5' 03"* |
| | *(USS YP-673 '77 - '89)* | | | | | | | |
| **U-8** | **UNIVERSITE DU QUEBEC, RIMOUSKI, QC** | | | | | | | |
| | Alcide C. Horth | RV | 1965 | D | 135* | 89' 02" | 22' 09" | 11' 00" |
| | *(Villmont No. 2 '65 - '83, Raymond Moore '83 - '90)* | | | | | | | |
| **U-9** | **UNIVERSITY OF MICHIGAN - CENTER FOR GREAT LAKES & AQUATIC SCIENCES, ANN ARBOR, MI** | | | | | | | |
| | Laurentian | RV | 1977 | D | 129* | 80' 00" | 21' 06" | 11' 00" |

| Fleet #. | Fleet Name / Vessel Name | Type of Vessel | Year Built | Type of Engine | Cargo Cap. or Gross* | Overall Length | Breadth | Depth or Draft* |
|---|---|---|---|---|---|---|---|---|
| U-10 | **UNIVERSITY OF MINNESOTA - DULUTH, DULUTH, MN** | | | | | | | |
| | Blue Heron | RV | 1985 | D | 175* | 119' 06" | 28' 00" | 15' 06" |
| | *(Fairtry '85 - '97)* | | | | | | | |
| U-11 | **UNIVERSITY OF WISCONSIN - GREAT LAKES WATER INSTITUTE, MILWAUKEE, WI** | | | | | | | |
| | Neeskay | RV | 1952 | D | 75* | 71' 00" | 17' 06" | 7' 06"* |
| | *(? '52 - '66, Northstar '66 - '69)* | | | | | | | |
| U-12 | **UNIVERSITY OF WISCONSIN, SUPERIOR, WI** | | | | | | | |
| | L. L. Smith Jr. | RV | 1950 | D | 38* | 57' 06" | 16' 06" | 6' 06" |
| U-13 | **UPPER LAKES GROUP, INC., TORONTO, ON** | | | | | | | |

U-13 (continued):

*\* INDICATES VESSELS OPERATED BY SEAWAY MARINE TRANSPORT, ST. CATHARINES, ON*
*A PARTNERSHIP BETWEEN ALGOMA CENTRAL CORP. AND UPPER LAKES GROUP, INC.*
***HAMILTON MARINE & ENGINEERING LTD., - A DIVISION OF UPPER LAKES GROUP, INC.***

| Fleet #. | Fleet Name / Vessel Name | Type of Vessel | Year Built | Type of Engine | Cargo Cap. or Gross* | Overall Length | Breadth | Depth or Draft* |
|---|---|---|---|---|---|---|---|---|
| | James E. McGrath | TB | 1963 | D | 90* | 77' 00" | 20' 00" | 10' 09" |

***JACKES SHIPPING, INC., TORONTO, ON - A DIVISION OF UPPER LAKES GROUP, INC.***

| | Gordon C. Leitch* {2} | BC | 1968 | D | 29,700 | 730' 00" | 75' 00" | 42' 00" |
|---|---|---|---|---|---|---|---|---|
| | *(Ralph Misener '68 - '94) (Converted from a self-unloader to a bulk carrier, '77)* | | | | | | | |

***PROVMAR FUELS, INC., HAMILTON, ON - A DIVISION OF UPPER LAKES GROUP, INC.***

| | Hamilton Energy | TK | 1965 | D | 8,622 | 201' 05" | 34' 01" | 14' 09" |
|---|---|---|---|---|---|---|---|---|
| | *(Partington '65 - '79, Shell Scientist '79 - '81, Metro Sun '81 - '85)* | | | | | | | |
| | Provmar Terminal | TK | 1959 | B | 60,000 | 403' 05" | 55' 06" | 28' 05" |
| | *(Varangnes '59 - '70, Tommy Wiborg '70 - '74, Ungava Transport '74 - '85)* | | | | | | | |
| | *(Last operated in 1984; In use as a fuel storage barge at Hamilton, ON.)* | | | | | | | |
| | Provmar Terminal II | TK | 1948 | B | 73,740 | 408' 08" | 53' 00" | 26' 00" |
| | *(Imperial Sarnia {2} '48 - '89; Last operated 1986 - In use as a fuel storage barge at Hamilton, ON.)* | | | | | | | |

***ULS CORPORATION, TORONTO, ON - A DIVISION OF UPPER LAKES GROUP, INC.***

| | Canadian Enterprise* | SU | 1979 | D | 35,100 | 730' 00" | 75' 08" | 46' 06" |
|---|---|---|---|---|---|---|---|---|
| | Canadian Leader* | BC | 1967 | T | 28,300 | 730' 00" | 75' 00" | 39' 08" |
| | *(Feux - Follets '67 - '72)* | | | | | | | |
| | Canadian Mariner* | BC | 1963 | T | 27,700 | 730' 00" | 75' 00" | 39' 03" |
| | *(Newbrunswicker '63 - '68, Grande Hermine '68 - '72)* | | | | | | | |
| | Canadian Miner* | BC | 1966 | D | 28,050 | 730' 00" | 75' 00" | 39' 01" |
| | *(Maplecliffe Hall '66 - '88, Lemoyne {2} '88 - '94)* | | | | | | | |
| | Canadian Navigator* | SU | 1967 | D | 30,925 | 728' 11" | 75' 10" | 40' 06" |
| | *(Demeterton '67 - '75, St. Lawrence Navigator '75 - '80)* | | | | | | | |
| | *(Coverted from a saltwater bulk carrier '80; Converted to a self-unloader, '97)* | | | | | | | |
| | Canadian Olympic* | SU | 1976 | D | 35,100 | 730' 00" | 75' 00" | 46' 06" |
| | Canadian Progress* | SU | 1968 | D | 32,700 | 730' 00" | 75' 00" | 46' 06" |
| | Canadian Prospector* | BC | 1964 | D | 30,500 | 730' 00" | 75' 10" | 40' 06" |
| | *(Carlton '64 - '75, Federal Wear '75 - '75, St. Lawrence Prospector '75 - '79)* | | | | | | | |
| | *(Converted from a saltwater bulk carrier, '79)* | | | | | | | |
| | Canadian Provider* | BC | 1963 | T | 27,450 | 730' 00" | 75' 00" | 39' 02" |
| | *(Murray Bay {3} '63 - '94)* | | | | | | | |
| | Canadian Ranger* | GU | 1943/67 | D | 25,900 | 729' 10" | 75' 00" | 39' 03" |
| | *([**Fore Section**] Grande Ronde '43 - '48, Kate N. L. '48 - '61, Hilda Marjanne '61 - '84) (Coverted from a saltwater bulk carrier '61) ([**Stern Section**] Chimo '67 - '83)* | | | | | | | |
| | *Canadian Ranger was built by joining of the stern section (pilothouse, engine room, machinery) of the former coastal package freighter Chimo with the bow and mid-body of the laker Hilda Marjanne in 1984; Converted to a self- unloader, '88; Last operated Dec. 3, 2000; Laid up at Montreal, QC.)* | | | | | | | |
| | Canadian Transfer* | SU | 1943/65 | D | 22,204 | 650' 06" | 60' 00" | 35' 00" |
| | *([**Fore Section**] J. H. Hillman Jr. '43 - '74, Crispin Oglebay {2} '74 - '95, Hamilton Transfer '95 - '98)* | | | | | | | |
| | *(Converted to a self-unloader, '74) [**Stern Section**] Cabot {1} '65 - '83, Canadian Explorer '83 - '98)* | | | | | | | |
| | *Canadian Transfer was built by joining the stern section of Canadian Explorer (engine room, machinery) with the bow and mid-body of the World War II-era laker Hamilton Transfer in 1998.* | | | | | | | |
| | Canadian Transport* {2} | SU | 1979 | D | 35,100 | 730' 00" | 75' 08" | 46' 06" |
| | James Norris* | SU | 1952 | U | 18,600 | 663' 06" | 67' 00" | 35' 00" |
| | *(Converted to a self-unloader, '81)* | | | | | | | |

| Fleet #. | Fleet Name / Vessel Name | Type of Vessel | Year Built | Type of Engine | Cargo Cap. or Gross* | Overall Length | Breadth | Depth or Draft* |
|---|---|---|---|---|---|---|---|---|
| | John D. Leitch* | SU | 1967 | D | 31,600 | 730' 00" | 78' 00" | 45' 00" |
| | *(Canadian Century '67 - '02) (Rebuilt with new mid-body, widened by 3'- '02)* | | | | | | | |
| | Montrealais* | BC | 1962 | T | 27,800 | 730' 00" | 75' 00" | 39' 00" |
| | *(Launched as Montrealer)* | | | | | | | |
| | Quebecois* | BC | 1963 | T | 27,800 | 730' 00" | 75' 00" | 39' 00" |
| | Seaway Queen* | BC | 1959 | T | 24,300 | 713' 03" | 72' 00" | 37' 00" |
| | *(Last operated Dec. 12, 1999; 5 year survey expired September 2002; Laid up at Toronto, ON.)* | | | | | | | |

**ESSROC CANADA, INC., NORTH YORK, ON - VESSELS MANAGED BY UPPER LAKES GROUP, INC.**

| Fleet #. | Fleet Name / Vessel Name | Type of Vessel | Year Built | Type of Engine | Cargo Cap. or Gross* | Overall Length | Breadth | Depth or Draft* |
|---|---|---|---|---|---|---|---|---|
| | Metis | CC | 1956 | B | 5,800 | 331' 00" | 43' 09" | 26' 00" |
| | Stephen B. Roman | CC | 1965 | D | 7,600 | 488' 09" | 56' 00" | 35' 06" |
| | *(Fort William '65 - '83) (Converted to a self-unloading cement carrier, '83)* | | | | | | | |
| **U-14** | **UPPER LAKES TOWING, INC., ESCANABA, MI** | | | | | | | |
| | Joseph H. Thompson | SU | 1944 | B | 21,200 | 706' 06" | 71' 06" | 38' 06" |
| | *(USNS Marine Robin '44 - '52)* | | | | | | | |
| | *Converted from a saltwater vessel to a self-unloading bulk carrier, '52; Engine removed, converted to a self-unloading barge, '91)* | | | | | | | |
| | Joseph H. Thompson Jr. | TBA | 1990 | D | 841* | 146' 06" | 38' 00" | 35' 00" |
| **V-1** | **VAN ENKEVORT TUG & BARGE, INC., BARK RIVER, MI** | | | | | | | |
| | Great Lakes Trader | SU | 2000 | B | 39,600 | 740' 00" | 78' 00" | 45' 00" |
| | Joyce L. Van Enkevort | AT | 1998 | D | 1,179* | 135' 04" | 50' 00" | 26' 00" |
| | **[ATB Van Enkevort / Trader OA dimensions together]** | | | | | 844' 10" | 78' 00" | 45' 00" |
| | Olive L. Moore | TB | 1928 | D | 301* | 125' 00" | 27' 01" | 13' 09" |
| | *(John F. Cushing '28 - '66, James E. Skelly '66 - '66)* | | | | | | | |
| **V-2** | **VERREAULT NAVIGATION, INC., LES MECHINS, QC** | | | | | | | |
| | I.V. No. 9 | GC | 1936 | D | 320 | 110' 00" | 23' 10" | 8' 05" |
| | *(A.C.D. '36 - '69)* | | | | | | | |
| | I.V. No. 10 | GC | 1936 | D | 320 | 110' 00" | 23' 10" | 8' 05" |
| | *(G.T.D. '36 - '69)* | | | | | | | |
| | I.V. No. 14 | GC | 1937 | D | 229 | 113' 00" | 22' 05" | 8' 06" |
| | *(Kermic '37 - '74)* | | | | | | | |
| | Nindawayma | CF | 1976 | D | 6,197* | 333' 06" | 55' 00" | 36' 06" |
| | *(Monte Cruceta '76 - '76, Monte Castillo '76 - '78, Manx Viking '78 - '87, Manx '87 - '88, , Skudenes '88 - '89Ontario No.1 {2} '89 - '89) (Last operated in 1992; Laid up at Montreal, QC.)* | | | | | | | |
| | Port Mechins | DR | 1949 | R | 1,321 | 200' 00" | 40' 02" | 18' 00" |
| | Rosaire | DR | 1952 | B | 714* | 137' 07" | 44' 06" | 9' 01" |
| **V-3** | **VISTA FLEET, DULUTH, MN** | | | | | | | |
| | Vista King | ES | 1978 | D | 60* | 78' 00" | 28' 00" | 5' 02" |
| | Vista Star | ES | 1987 | D | 95* | 91' 00" | 24' 09" | 7' 08" |
| | *(Island Empress '87 - '88)* | | | | | | | |
| **V-4** | **VOIGHT'S MARINE SERVICES, ELLISON BAY, WI** | | | | | | | |
| | Bounty | ES | 1968 | D | 23* | 40' 00" | 14' 00" | 3' 03" |
| | Island Clipper {2} | ES | 1987 | D | 149* | 65' 00" | 20' 00" | 5' 00" |
| | Yankee Clipper | ES | 1971 | D | 41* | 54' 00" | 17' 00" | 5' 00" |
| **V-5** | **VOYAGEUR CRUISES, INC., CHARLEVOIX, MI** | | | | | | | |
| | Voyageur | ES | 1981 | D | 72* | 105' 00" | 21' 06" | 6' 00"* |
| **W-1** | **WAGNER CHARTER CO., INC., CAROL STREAM, IL** | | | | | | | |
| | Buccaneer | ES | 1925 | D | 98* | 100' 00" | 23' 00" | 14' 06" |
| | *(USCGC Dexter '25 - '35, USS Dexter [YP-67] '35 - '46, Kingfisher '46 - '61, Jamaica II '61 - '61, Trinidad {1} '61 - '94)* | | | | | | | |
| | Jamaica | ES | 1967 | D | 88* | 105' 00" | 25' 00" | 10' 06" |
| **W-2** | **WALSTROM MARINE, HARBOR SPRINGS, MI** | | | | | | | |
| | Ottawa | TB | 1914 | D | 74* | 57' 04" | 17' 09" | 6' 00" |
| | Lydie Rae | TB | 1945 | D | 21* | 48' 00" | 12' 01" | 7' 00" |
| | *(Ashland {2} '44 - '72, Charles F. Liscomb '72 - '94, Jason '94 - '01)* | | | | | | | |

**Buckeye loads taconite ore at Escanaba.** *(Rod Burdick)*

| Fleet #. | Fleet Name<br>Vessel Name | Type of<br>Vessel | Year<br>Built | Type of<br>Engine | Cargo Cap.<br>or Gross* | Overall<br>Length | Breadth | Depth or<br>Draft* |
|---|---|---|---|---|---|---|---|---|
| **W-3** | **WASHINGTON ISLAND FERRY LINE, INC., WASHINGTON ISLAND, WI** | | | | | | | |
| | C. G. Richter | CF | 1950 | D | 82* | 70' 06" | 25' 00" | 9' 05" |
| | Eyrarbakki | CF | 1970 | D | 95* | 87' 00" | 36' 00" | 7' 06" |
| | Robert Noble | CF | 1979 | D | 97* | 90' 04" | 36' 00" | 8' 03" |
| | Voyager | CF | 1960 | D | 98* | 65' 00" | 35' 00" | 8' 00" |
| | Washington {2} | CF | 1989 | D | 93* | 100' 00" | 37' 00" | 9' 00" |
| **W-4** | **WENDELLA BOAT TOURS., CHICAGO, IL** | | | | | | | |
| | Sunliner | ES | 1959 | D | 41* | 67' 00" | 20' 00" | 4' 00" |
| | Wendella | ES | 1961 | D | 35* | 68' 00" | 17' 00" | 6' 05" |
| | Wendella LTD | ES | 1992 | D | 66* | 68' 00" | 20' 00" | 4' 09" |
| **W-5** | **WILLIAM ROBERT PARR, PARRY SOUND, ON** | | | | | | | |
| | Mink Isle | TB | 1947 | D | 27* | 50' 00" | 13' 00" | 6' 07"* |
| **W-6** | **WINDY OF CHICAGO LTD., CHICAGO, IL** | | | | | | | |
| | Windy | ES/4S | 1996 | W | 75* | 148' 00" | 25' 00" | 8' 00" |
| | Windy II | ES/4S | 2000 | W | 99* | 150' 00" | 25' 00" | 8' 05" |
| **W-7** | **WISCONSIN DEPARTMENT OF NATURAL RESOURCES, BAYFIELD & STURGEON BAY, WI** | | | | | | | |
| | Hack Noyes | RV | 1947 | D | 50* | 56' 00" | | 4' 00" |
| | Barney Devine | RV | 1937 | D | 42* | 50' 00" | 14' 05" | 6' 00" |
| **Y-1** | **YANKEE LADY YACHT CHARTERS, TORONTO, ON** | | | | | | | |
| | Yankee Lady<br>(Peggy Vee V '65 - '88) | ES | 1965 | D | 56* | 42' 10" | 16' 06" | 9' 02" |
| | Yankee Lady II<br>(Blue Chip II '80 - '89) | ES | 1980 | D | 68* | 75' 00" | 16' 00" | 9' 08" |
| | Yankee Lady III | ES | 1995 | D | 292* | 99' 07" | 26' 09" | 11'08" |
| **Z-1** | **ZENITH TUGBOAT CO., DULUTH, MN** | | | | | | | |
| | Athena | TB | 1939 | D | 119* | 82' 00" | 22' 06" | 11" 04" |

(John E. Matton, USS Tamaque YTM-741, Athena, James A Harper '73 - '86)

**MANAGEMENT GROUP FOR THE FOLLOWING TUG:**

| | | | | | | | | |
|---|---|---|---|---|---|---|---|---|
| | Seneca | TB | 1939 | D | 132* | 94' 020" | 22' 00" | 9' 00" |

(General {1} '39 - '39, Raymond Card '39 - '40, USS Keshena '40 - '47, Mary L. McAllister '47 - '81)

**Saginaw uses her searchlights to help dock at Ferrysburg, Mich.** (Mike Modderman)

Canadian Voyager in the Welland Canal, Nov. 12, 2001, during her last season of operation. *(Jeff Cameron)*

**bhp:** brake horsepower, a measure of diesel engine output power measured at the crankshaft before entering gear box or any other power take-out device

**ihp:** indicated horsepower, based on an internal measurement of mean cylinder pressure, piston area, piston stroke and engine speed. Used for reciprocating engines

**shp:** shaft horsepower, a measure of engine output at the propeller shaft at the output of the reduction gear box. Used for steam and diesel-electric engines

**cpp:** controllable pitch propeller

| Vessel Name | Engine Manufacturer & Model # | Engine Type | Total Engines | Total Cylinders | Rated HP | Total Props | Speed MPH |
|---|---|---|---|---|---|---|---|
| Adam E. Cornelius | GM - Electro-Motive Div. - 20-645-E7B | Diesel | 2 | 20 | 7,200 bhp | 1 cpp | 16.1 |
| Agawa Canyon | Fairbanks Morse - 10-38D8-1/8 | Diesel | 4 | 10 | 6,662 bhp | 1 cpp | 13.8 |
| Algobay | Pielstick - 10PC2-3V-400 | Diesel | 2 | 10 | 10,699 bhp | 1 cpp | 13.8 |
| Algocape | Sulzer - 6RND76 | Diesel | 1 | 6 | 9,599 bhp | 1 | 17.3 |
| Algocatalyst | Pielstick - 12PC2-V-400 | Diesel | 1 | 12 | 6,000 bhp | 1 cpp | 17.3 |
| Algocen | Fairbanks Morse - 10-38D8-1/8 | Diesel | 4 | 10 | 7,999 bhp | 1 cpp | 13.8 |
| Algoeast | B&W - 6K45GF | Diesel | 1 | 6 | 5,299 bhp | 1 cpp | 15.8 |
| Algofax | M.A.N. - K5Z70/120 | Diesel | 2 | 5 | 6,410 bhp | 1 | 15.5 |
| Algoisle | M.A.N. - K6Z78/155 | Diesel | 1 | 6 | 9,000 bhp | 1 cpp | 19.3 |
| Algolake | Pielstick - 10PC2-2V-400 | Diesel | 2 | 10 | 9,000 bhp | 1 cpp | 17.3 |
| Algomarine | Sulzer - 6RND76 | Diesel | 1 | 6 | 9,599 bhp | 1 cpp | 17.0 |
| Algonorth | Werkspoor - 9TM410 | Diesel | 2 | 9 | 11,999 bhp | 1 cpp | 16.1 |
| Algonova | Fairbanks Morse - 12-38D8-1/8 | Diesel | 2 | 12 | 4,000 bhp | 1 cpp | 15.0 |
| Algontario | B&W - 7-74VTBF-160 | Diesel | 1 | 7 | 8,750 bhp | 1 cpp | 14.4 |
| Algoport | Pielstick - 10PC2-3V-400 | Diesel | 2 | 10 | 10,699 bhp | 1 cpp | 13.8 |
| Algorail | Fairbanks Morse - 10-38D8-1/8 | Diesel | 4 | 10 | 8,065 bhp | 1 cpp | 13.8 |
| Algosar | M.A.N. - K5Z70/120E | Diesel | 1 | 5 | 6,500 bhp | 1 cpp | 17.3 |
| Algosoo | Pielstick - 10PC2-V-400 | Diesel | 2 | 10 | 9,000 bhp | 1 cpp | 15.0 |
| Algosound | Canadian General Electric Co. Ltd. | Turbine | 1 | ** | 9,900 shp | 1 | 17.3 |
| Algosteel | Sulzer - 6RND76 | Diesel | 1 | 6 | 9,599 bhp | 1 | 17.0 |
| Algoville | M.A.N. - K6Z78/155 | Diesel | 1 | 6 | 9,900 bhp | 1 cpp | 17.8 |
| Algoway | Fairbanks Morse - 10-38D8-1/8 | Diesel | 4 | 10 | 8,065 bhp | 1 cpp | 13.8 |
| Algowood | MaK - 6M552AK | Diesel | 2 | 6 | 10,199 bhp | 1 cpp | 13.8 |
| Alpena | De Laval Steam Turbine Co. | Turbine | 1 | ** | 4,400 shp | 1 | 14.1 |
| Amelia Desgagnes | Allen - 12PVBCS12-F | Diesel | 2 | 12 | 4,000 bhp | 1 cpp | 16.1 |
| American Mariner | GM - Electro-Motive Div. - 20-645-E7 | Diesel | 2 | 20 | 7,200 bhp | 1 cpp | 15.0 |
| American Republic | GM - Electro-Motive Div. - 20-645-E7 | Diesel | 2 | 20 | 7,200 bhp | 2 cpp | 15.0 |
| Anna Desgagnes | M.A.N. - K5SZ70/125B | Diesel | 1 | 5 | 10,332 bhp | 1 | 17.8 |
| Armco | Westinghouse Elec. Corp. | Turbine | 1 | ** | 7,700 shp | 1 | 19.0 |
| Arthur K. Atkinson | Nordberg | Diesel | 2 | 12 | 5,610 bhp | 2 | |
| Arthur M. Anderson | Westinghouse Elec. Corp. | Turbine | 1 | ** | 7,700 shp | 1 | 16.1 |
| Atlantic Erie | Sulzer - 6RLB66 | Diesel | 1 | 6 | 11,100 bhp | 1 cpp | 16.1 |
| Atlantic Huron | Sulzer - 6RLB66 | Diesel | 1 | 6 | 11,094 bhp | 1 cpp | 17.3 |
| Badger | Skinner Engine Co. | Steeple Compound Uniflow | 2 | 4 | 8,000 ihp | 2 | 18.4 |
| Buckeye | Bethlehem Steel Co. | Turbine | 1 | ** | 7,700 shp | 1 | 17.3 |
| Buffalo | GM - Electro-Motive Div. - 20-645-E7 | Diesel | 2 | 20 | 7,200 bhp | 1 cpp | 16.1 |
| Burns Harbor | GM - Electro-Motive Div. - 20-645-E7 | Diesel | 4 | 20 | 14,400 bhp | 2 cpp | 18.4 |
| Calumet | Nordberg | Diesel | 1 | 16 | 4,234 bhp | 1 | 12.1 |
| Canadian Century | B&W - 5-74VT2BF-160 | Diesel | 1 | 5 | 7,500 bhp | 1 cpp | 16.1 |
| Canadian Enterprise | M.A.N. - 7L40/15 | Diesel | 2 | 7 | 8,804 bhp | 1 cpp | 13.8 |
| Canadian Leader | Canadian General Electric Co. Ltd. | Turbine | 1 | ** | 9,900 shp | 1 | 19.0 |
| Canadian Mariner | General Electric Co. | Turbine | 1 | ** | 9,900 shp | 1 | 19.0 |
| Canadian Miner | Fairbanks Morse - 12-38D8-1/8 | Diesel | 4 | 12 | 8,000 bhp | 1 cpp | 15.0 |
| Canadian Navigator | Doxford Engines Ltd. - 76J4 | Diesel | 1 | 4 | 9,680 bhp | 1 | 16.7 |
| Canadian Olympic | M.A.N. - 8L40/54A | Diesel | 2 | 8 | 10,001 bhp | 1 cpp | 15.0 |
| Canadian Progress | Caterpillar - 3612-TA | Diesel | 2 | 12 | 9,000 bhp | 1 cpp | 15.5 |
| Canadian Prospector | Gotaverken - 760/1500VGS6U | Diesel | 1 | 6 | 7,500 bhp | 1 | 16.1 |

| Vessel Name | Engine Manufacturer & Model # | Engine Type | Total Engines | Total Cylinders | Rated HP | Total Props | Speed MPH |
|---|---|---|---|---|---|---|---|
| Canadian Provider | John Inglis Co. Ltd. | Turbine | 1 | ** | 10,000 shp | 1 | 17.3 |
| Canadian Ranger | Sulzer - 5RND68 | Diesel | 1 | 5 | 6,100 bhp | 1 cpp | 19.6 |
| Canadian Transfer | Sulzer - 5RND68 | Diesel | 1 | 5 | 6,100 bhp | 1 cpp | 18.4 |
| Canadian Transport | M.A.N. - 8L40/45 | Diesel | 2 | 8 | 10,001 bhp | 1 cpp | 13.8 |
| Capt. Henry Jackman | MaK - 6M552AK | Diesel | 2 | 6 | 9,465 bhp | 1 cpp | 17.3 |
| Capt. Ralph Tucker | B&W - 7-50VT2BF-110 | Diesel | 1 | 7 | 5,326 bhp | 1 | 15.5 |
| Cason J. Callaway | Westinghouse Elec. Corp. | Turbine | 1 | ** | 7,700 shp | 1 | 16.1 |
| Catherine Desgagnes | Sulzer - 6SAD60 | Diesel | 1 | 6 | 3,841 bhp | 1 | 15.5 |
| Cecelia Desgagnes | B&W - 6S50LU | Diesel | 1 | 6 | 5,100 bhp | 1 cpp | 17.3 |
| Cedarglen | B&W - 7-74VTBF-160 | Diesel | 1 | 7 | 8,750 bhp | 1 cpp | 15.5 |
| Charles M. Beeghly | General Electric Co. | Turbine | 1 | ** | 9,350 shp | 1 | 17.8 |
| Chi-Cheemaun | Ruston Paxman Diesels Ltd. - 16RKCM | Diesel | 2 | 16 | 7,000 bhp | 2 | 18.7 |
| Columbia Star | GM - Electro-Motive Div. - 20-645-E7B | Diesel | 4 | 20 | 14,400 bhp | 2 cpp | 17.3 |
| Courtney Burton | General Electric Co. | Turbine | 1 | ** | 7,700 shp | 1 | 16.7 |
| CSL Laurentien | Pielstick - 10PC2-2V-400 | Diesel | 2 | 10 | 9,000 bhp | 1 cpp | 16.1 |
| CSL Niagara | Pielstick - 10PC2-2V-400 | Diesel | 2 | 10 | 9,000 bhp | 1 cpp | 15.0 |
| CSL Tadoussac | Sulzer - 6RND76 | Diesel | 1 | 6 | 9,599 bhp | 1 | 17.0 |
| Cuyahoga | Caterpillar - 3608 | Diesel | 1 | 8 | 3,000 bhp | 1 | |
| David Z. Norton | Alco - 16V251E | Diesel | 2 | 16 | 5,600 bhp | 1 | 16.1 |
| Day Peckinpaugh | GM - Detroit Diesel Allison Div. - 6-110 | Diesel | 2 | 6 | 480 bhp | 2 | 9.2 |
| Diamond Star | B&W - 6L35MC | Diesel | 1 | 6 | 5,030 bhp | 1 cpp | 14.4 |
| Dorothy Ann / | GM - Electro-Motive Div. - 20-645-E7B | Diesel | 2 | 20 | 7,200 bhp | 2 Ulstein Z Drive | 16.1 |
| Pathfinder (Articulated Tug / Barge) | | | | | | | |
| E. M. Ford | Cleveland Ship Building Co. | Quadruple Expansion | 1 | 4 | 1,500 ihp | 1 | 11.5 |
| Earl W. Oglebay | Alco - 16V251E | Diesel | 2 | 16 | 5,600 bhp | 1 | 16.1 |
| Edgar B. Speer | Pielstick - 18PC2-3V-400 | Diesel | 2 | 18 | 19,260 bhp | 2 cpp | 17.0 |
| Edward L. Ryerson | General Electric Co. | Turbine | 1 | ** | 9,900 shp | 1 | 19.0 |
| Edwin H. Gott | Enterprise - DMRV-16-4 | Diesel | 2 | 16 | 19,500 bhp | 2 cpp | 16.7 |
| Elton Hoyt 2nd | Bethlehem Steel Co. | Turbine | 1 | ** | 7,700 shp | 1 | 17.3 |
| Emerald Star | B&W - 6L35MC | Diesel | 1 | 6 | 5,030 bhp | 1 cpp | 14.4 |
| Emmet J. Carey | GM - Detroit Diesel Allison Div. - 6-71N | Diesel | 2 | 6 | 400 bhp | 2 | |
| English River | Werkspoor - TMAB-390 | Diesel | 1 | 8 | 1,850 bhp | 1 cpp | 13.8 |
| Everlast / (Articulated Tug / Barge) | | | | | | | |
| Norman McLeod | Daihatsu - 8DSM-32 | Diesel | 2 | 8 | ? bhp | 2 | 16.5 |
| F. M. Osborne | Caterpillar - D334 | Diesel | 2 | 6 | 410 bhp | 1 | |
| Ferbec | Sulzer - 6RD90 | Diesel | 1 | 6 | 14,999 bhp | 1 | 17.3 |
| Fred R. White Jr. | GM - Electro-Motive Div. - 20-645-E7 | Diesel | 2 | 20 | 7,200 bhp | 1 cpp | 16.1 |
| Frontenac | Sulzer - 6RND76 | Diesel | 1 | 6 | 9,599 bhp | 1 cpp | 17.0 |
| Gemini | Alco - 16V251E | Diesel | 2 | 16 | 5,150 bhp | 2 | 14.4 |
| George A. Stinson | Pielstick - 16PC2-2V-400 | Diesel | 2 | 16 | 16,000 bhp | 2 | 17.3 |
| Gordon C. Leitch | Sulzer - 6RND76 | Diesel | 1 | 6 | 9,599 bhp | 1 cpp | 17.3 |
| H. Lee White | GM - Electro-Motive Div. - 20-645-E7B | Diesel | 2 | 20 | 7,200 bhp | 1 cpp | 15.0 |
| Halifax | John Inglis Co. Ltd. | Turbine | 1 | ** | 10,000 shp | 1 | 19.6 |
| Herbert C. Jackson | General Electric Co. | Turbine | 1 | ** | 6,600 shp | 1 | |
| Indiana Harbor | GM - Electro-Motive Div. - 20-645-E7 | Diesel | 4 | 20 | 14,400 bhp | 2 cpp | 16.1 |
| Invincible / (Articulated Tug / Barge) | | | | | | | |
| McKee Sons | GM - Electro-Motive Div. - 16-645-E7B | Diesel | 2 | 16 | 5,750 bhp | 2 | 13.8 |
| J. A. W. Iglehart | De Laval Steam Turbine Co. | Turbine | 1 | ** | 4,400 shp | 1 | 15.0 |
| J. B. Ford | American Ship Building Co. | Triple Exp. | 1 | 3 | 1,500 ihp | 1 | |
| J. S. St. John | GM - Electro-Motive Div. - 8-567 | Diesel | 1 | 8 | 850 bhp | 1 | 11.5 |
| Jacklyn M. / (Articulated Tug / Barge) | | | | | | | |
| Integrity | Caterpillar - 3608-DITA | Diesel | 2 | 8 | 6,008 bhp | 2 | 17.3 |
| Jacques Desgagnes | Lister Blackstone Marine Ltd. | Diesel | 2 | 8 | 1,200 bhp | 2 | 12.1 |
| Jade Star | B&W - 6L35MC | Diesel | 1 | 6 | 5,030 bhp | 1 cpp | 14.4 |
| James Norris | Canadian Vickers Ltd. | Uniflow | 1 | 5 | 4,000 ihp | 1 | 16.1 |
| James R. Barker | Pielstick - 16PC2-2V-400 | Diesel | 2 | 16 | 16,000 bhp | 2 cpp | 15.5 |
| Jane Ann IV / (Articulated Tug / Barge) | | | | | | | |
| Sarah Spencer | Pielstick - 8PC2-2L-400 | Diesel | 2 | 8 | 8,000 bhp | 2 | 15.8 |
| Jean Parisien | Pielstick - 10PC2-2V-400 | Diesel | 2 | 10 | 9,000 bhp | 1 cpp | 15.0 |
| Jiimaan | Ruston Paxman Diesels Ltd. - 6RK215 | Diesel | 2 | 6 | 2,839 bhp | 2 cpp | 15.0 |
| John B. Aird | MaK - 6M552AK | Diesel | 2 | 6 | 9,459 bhp | 1 cpp | 13.8 |
| John G. Munson | General Electric Co. | Turbine | 1 | ** | 7,700 shp | 1 | 17.3 |
| John J. Boland | GM - Electro-Motive Div. - 20-645-E7B | Diesel | 2 | 20 | 7,200 bhp | 1 cpp | 15.0 |
| John R. Emery | GM - Detroit Diesel Allison Div. - 6-110 | Diesel | 2 | 6 | 550 bhp | 2 | |
| John Sherwin | De Laval Steam Turbine Co. | Turbine | 1 | ** | 9,350 shp | 1 | 16.7 |

| Vessel Name | Engine Manufacturer & Model # | Engine Type | Total Engines | Total Cylinders | Rated HP | Total Props | Speed MPH |
|---|---|---|---|---|---|---|---|
| Joseph H. Frantz | Enterprise - DMRV-12-4 | Diesel | 1 | 12 | 4,000 bhp | 1 cpp | 13.2 |
| Joseph H. Thompson Jr. / | *(Articulated Tug / Barge)* | | | | | | |
| *Joseph H. Thompson* | General Electric Co. - 7FDM16 | Diesel | 3 | 16 | 7,500 bhp | 1 | |
| Joseph L. Block | GM - Electro-Motive Div. - 20-645-E7 | Diesel | 2 | 20 | 7,200 bhp | 1 cpp | 17.3 |
| Joyce L. Van Enkevort / | *(Articulated Tug / Barge)* | | | | | | |
| *Great Lakes Trader* | Caterpillar - 3612 | Diesel | 2 | 12 | 10,200 bhp | 2 cpp | |
| Kaye E. Barker | De Laval Steam Turbine Co. | Turbine | 1 | ** | 7,700 shp | 1 | 17.3 |
| Kinsman Independent | Bethlehem Steel Co. | Turbine | 1 | ** | 4,400 shp | 1 | |
| L. E. Block | Westinghouse Elec. Corp. | Turbine | 1 | ** | 4,950 shp | 1 | |
| Lee A. Tregurtha | Bethlehem Steel Co. | Turbine | 1 | ** | 7,700 shp | 1 | 16.7 |
| M. H. Baker III | Sulzer - 6RLA66 | Diesel | 1 | 6 | 11,095 bhp | 1 cpp | 17.3 |
| Mapleglen | General Electric Co. | Turbine | 1 | ** | 9,350 shp | 1 | 17.8 |
| Maria Desgagnes | B&W - 6S42MC | Diesel | 1 | 6 | 8,361 bhp | 1 cpp | 16.1 |
| Marine Star | General Electric Co. | Turbine | 1 | ** | 10,001 shp | 1 | 21.9 |
| Mathilda Desgagnes | Fairbanks Morse - 10-38D8-1/8 | Diesel | 2 | 10 | 3,200 bhp | 2 | |
| Maumee | Nordberg - FS-1312-H5C | Diesel | 1 | 12 | 3,240 bhp | 1 | 11.5 |
| Melissa Desgagnes | Allen - 12PVBCS12-F | Diesel | 2 | 12 | 4,000 bhp | 1 cpp | 13.8 |
| Mesabi Miner | Pielstick - 16PC2-2V-400 | Diesel | 2 | 16 | 16,000 bhp | 2 cpp | 15.5 |
| Michigan  / | *(Articulated Tug / Barge)* | | | | | | |
| *Great Lakes* | GM - Electro-Motive Div. - 20-645-E6 | Diesel | 2 | 16 | 3,900 bhp | 2 | 13.2 |
| Middletown | Bethlehem Steel Co. | Turbine | 1 | ** | 7,700 shp | 1 | 16.1 |
| Mississagi | Caterpillar - 3612-TA | Diesel | 1 | 12 | 4,500 bhp | 1 cpp | |
| Montrealais | Canadian General Electric Co. Ltd. | Turbine | 1 | ** | 9,900 shp | 1 | 19.0 |
| Nanticoke | Pielstick - 10PC2-2V-400 | Diesel | 2 | 10 | 10,699 bhp | 1 cpp | 13.8 |
| Oakglen | Westinghouse Elec. Corp. | Turbine | 1 | ** | 8,500 shp | 1 | 17.3 |
| Oglebay Norton | GM - Electro-Motive Div. - 20-645-E7 | Diesel | 4 | 20 | 14,400 bhp | 2 cpp | 18.4 |
| Paul H. Townsend | Nordberg | Diesel | 1 | 6 | 2,150 bhp | 1 | 12.1 |
| Paul R. Tregurtha | Pielstick - 16PC2-3V-400 | Diesel | 2 | 16 | 17,120 bhp | 2 cpp | 15.5 |
| Peter R. Cresswell | MaK - 6M552AK | Diesel | 2 | 6 | 10,199 bhp | 1 cpp | 13.8 |
| Petrolia Desgagnes | B&W - 8K42EF | Diesel | 1 | 8 | 5,000 bhp | 1 cpp | 16.4 |
| Philip R. Clarke | Westinghouse Elec. Corp. | Turbine | 1 | ** | 7,700 shp | 1 | 16.1 |
| Pineglen | MaK - 6M601AK | Diesel | 1 | 6 | 8,158 bhp | 1 cpp | 15.5 |
| Presque Isle | Mirrlees Blackstone Ltd. - KVMR-16 | Diesel | 2 | 16 | 14,840 bhp | 2 cpp | |
| Quebecois | Canadian General Electric Co. Ltd. | Turbine | 1 | ** | 9,900 shp | 1 | 19.0 |
| Reserve | Westinghouse Elec. Corp. | Turbine | 1 | ** | 7,700 shp | 1 | 19.0 |
| Richard Reiss | GM - Electro-Motive Div. - 20-645-E6 | Diesel | 1 | 20 | 2,950 bhp | 1 | |
| Roger Blough | Pielstick - 16PC2V-400 | Diesel | 2 | 16 | 14,200 bhp | 1 cpp | 16.7 |
| Rt. Hon. Paul J. Martin | Pielstick - 10PC2-V-400 | Diesel | 2 | 10 | 9,000 bhp | 1 cpp | 15.0 |
| S. T. Crapo | GLEW | Triple Exp. | 1 | 3 | 1,800 ihp | 1 | 13.2 |
| Saginaw | De Laval Steam Turbine Co. | Turbine | 1 | ** | 7,700 shp | 1 | 16.1 |
| Sam Laud | GM - Electro-Motive Div. - 20-645-E7 | Diesel | 2 | 20 | 7,200 bhp | 1 cpp | 16.1 |
| Saturn | GM - Electro-Motive Div. - 12-645-E6 | Diesel | 2 | 12 | 3,000 bhp | 2 | 10.9 |
| Sauniere | MaK - 6M552AK | Diesel | 2 | 6 | 8,799 bhp | 1 cpp | 15.0 |
| Seaway Queen | John Inglis Co. Ltd. | Turbine | 1 | ** | 8,250 shp | 1 | 17.8 |
| Southdown Challenger | Skinner Engine Co. | Uniflow | 1 | 4 | 3,500 ihp | 1 | |
| St. Clair | GM - Electro-Motive Div. - 20-645-E7 | Diesel | 3 | 20 | 10,800 bhp | 1 cpp | 16.7 |
| Ste. Claire | Toledo Ship Building Co. | Triple Exp. | 1 | 3 | 1,083 ihp | 1 | |
| Stephen B. Roman (Total) | | Diesel | | | 5,996 bhp | 1 cpp | 18.4 |
| *Stephen B. Roman (Center)* | Fairbanks Morse - 10-38D8-1/8 | Diesel | 2 | 10 | 3,331 bhp | | |
| *Stephen B. Roman (Wing)* | Fairbanks Morse - 8-38D8-1/8 | Diesel | 2 | 8 | 2,665 bhp | | |
| Stewart J. Cort | GM - Electro-Motive Div. - 20-645-E7 | Diesel | 4 | 20 | 14,400 bhp | 2 cpp | 18.4 |
| Susan W. Hannah / | *(Articulated Tug / Barge)* | | | | | | |
| *Southdown Conquest* | GM - Electro-Motive Div. - 12-645-E5 | Diesel | 2 | 12 | 4,320 bhp | 2 | 11.5 |
| Teakglen | Fairbanks Morse - 8-38D8-1/8 | Diesel | 4 | 8 | 5,332 bhp | 1 cpp | 16.1 |
| Thalassa Desgagnes | B&W - 8K42EF | Diesel | 1 | 8 | 5,000 bhp | 1 cpp | 16.4 |
| Undaunted / | *(Articulated Tug / Barge)* | | | | | | |
| *Pere Marquette 41* | GM - Cleveland Diesel Div. - 12-278A | Diesel | 1 | 12 | 2,400 bhp | 1 | 11.5 |
| Vega Desgagnes | Wartsila - 9R32 | Diesel | 2 | 9 | 7,559 bhp | 1 cpp | 16.1 |
| Walter J. McCarthy Jr. | GM - Electro-Motive Div. - 20-645-E7B | Diesel | 4 | 20 | 14,400 bhp | 2 cpp | 16.1 |
| Wellington Kent | MaK - 9M552AK | Diesel | 1 | 9 | 7,504 bhp | 1 cpp | |
| Wilfred Sykes | Westinghouse Elec. Corp. | Turbine | 1 | ** | 7,700 shp | 1 | 16.1 |
| Wolf River | Fairbanks Morse - 10-38D8-1/8 | Diesel | 1 | 10 | 1,880 bhp | 1 | 10.4 |
| Wolverine | Alco - 16V251E | Diesel | 2 | 16 | 5,600 bhp | 1 | 17.8 |
| Yankcanuck | Cooper-Bessemer Corp. | Diesel | 1 | 8 | 1,860 bhp | 1 | 11.5 |

# Saltwater Fleets

**Marinette returns from a Lake Superior port.**
*(Roger LeLievre)*

This list reflects vessels whose primary trade routes are on saltwater, but which also regularly visit Great Lakes and St. Lawrence Seaway ports. It is not meant to be a complete listing of every saltwater vessel that could potentially visit the Great Lakes and St. Lawrence Seaway. To attempt to do so, given the sheer number of world merchant vessels, would be space prohibitive. Fleets listed may operate other vessels than those included herein.

| Fleet #. | Fleet Name / Vessel Name | Type of Vessel | Year Built | Type of Engine | Cargo Cap. or Gross* | Overall Length | Breadth | Depth or Draft* |
|---|---|---|---|---|---|---|---|---|
| IA-1 | **ADRICO SHIPPING COMPANY, ATHENS, GREECE** | | | | | | | |
| | Nobility | GC | 1981 | D | 30,900 | 617' 06" | 76' 00" | 47' 07" |
| | *Nosira Lin '81 - '89, Dan Bauta '89 - '89, Kristianiafjord '89 - '93, Federal Vibeke '93 - '00, Kalista '00 - '02)* | | | | | | | |
| IA-2 | **AHILLEOS MARITIME CO. LTD., BIRKIRKARA, MALTA** | | | | | | | |
| | Linden | BC | 1977 | D | 12,100 | 478' 07" | 64' 04" | 35' 00" |
| | *(Brunto '77 - '85, General Vargas '85 - '93, Brunto '93 - '02)* | | | | | | | |
| IA-3 | **ALBA SHIPPING LTD. A/S, AALBORG, DENMARK** | | | | | | | |
| | Kasla | TK | 1974 | D | 8,639 | 427' 07" | 57' 10" | 26' 03" |
| IA-4 | **ALUNITED MARITIME PRIVATE LTD., SINGAPORE, SINGAPORE** | | | | | | | |
| | Khaleda | GC | 1978 | D | 16,000 | 517' 03" | 75' 00" | 43' 00" |
| | *(Bondoukou '78-'88, Moslavina '88-'99 )* | | | | | | | |
| IA-5 | **AMASUS SHIPPING B.V., FARMSUM, NETHERLANDS** | | | | | | | |
| | Eemshorn | GC | 1995 | D | 4,250 | 293' 10" | 43' 03" | 23' 04" |
| | Esperance | GC | 2002 | D | 3,850 | 290' 08" | 41' 00" | 23' 00" |
| | Vega | GC | 1992 | D | 2,880 | 371' 09" | 50' 04" | 11' 06" |
| IA-6 | **ANBROS SHIPPING CO. S.A., PIRAEUS, GREECE** | | | | | | | |
| | Akrathos | BC | 1981 | D | 25,817 | 605' 08" | 75' 05" | 46' 05" |
| | Dora | BC | 1978 | D | 30,350 | 622' 07" | 76' 05" | 47' 05" |
| | *(Federal St. Laurent {1} '78 - '95, Federal Dora '95 - '99)* | | | | | | | |
| IA-7 | **AMERICAN CANADIAN CARIBBEAN LINE, INC., WARREN, RI, USA** | | | | | | | |
| | Grande Caribe | PA | 1997 | D | 94* | 183' 00" | 40' 00" | 9' 08" |
| | Grande Mariner | PA | 1998 | D | 97* | 183' 00" | 40' 00" | 9' 08" |
| | Niagara Prince | PA | 1994 | D | 99* | 175' 00" | 40' 00" | 14' 00" |
| IA- 8 | **ARKLOW SHIPPING LTD., WICKLOW, IRELAND** | | | | | | | |
| | Arklow Bridge | GC | 1995 | D | 7,182 | 327' 07" | 65' 01" | 28' 05" |
| IA-9 | **ATLANTIS MANAGEMENT, INC., PIRAEUS, GREECE** | | | | | | | |
| | Atlantis Charm | BC | 1982 | D | 22,558 | 539' 02" | 75' 02" | 44' 06" |
| | Atlantis Pride | BC | 2001 | D | 28,075 | 554' 04" | 89' 02" | 44' 06" |
| IA-10 | **ATHENA MARINE CO. LTD., LIMASSOL, CYPRUS** | | | | | | | |
| | *FOLLOWING VESSELS UNDER CHARTER TO FEDNAV LTD.* | | | | | | | |
| | Federal Ems | BC | 2002 | D | 35,200 | 655' 80" | 78' 04" | 50' 01" |
| | Federal Weser | BC | 2001 | D | 37,372 | 655' 80" | 78' 04" | 50' 01" |
| IA-11 | **ATLANTSKA PLOVIDBA D.D., DUBROVNIK, CROATIA** | | | | | | | |
| | Mljet | BC | 1982 | D | 29,643 | 622' 01" | 74' 11" | 49' 10" |
| | *FOLLOWING VESSEL CURRENTLY UNDER CHARTER TO FEDNAV LTD.* | | | | | | | |
| | Orsula | BC | 1996 | D | 34,198 | 656' 02" | 77' 01" | 48' 11" |
| | *(Federal Calumet {2} '96 - '97)* | | | | | | | |
| IA-12 | **AURORA SHIPPING, INC., MANILA, PHILIPPINES** | | | | | | | |
| | Aurora Gold | GC | 1976 | D | 10,027 | 419' 10" | 60' 02" | 32' 06" |
| | Aurora Jade | BC | 1979 | D | 13,206 | 436' 04" | 67' 08" | 37' 09" |
| | Aurora Topaz | BC | 1982 | D | 28,268 | 639' 09" | 75' 10" | 46' 11" |
| | *(Sea Fortune '82-'85, Miss Aliki '86-'93)* | | | | | | | |
| IA-13 | **AZOV SHIPPING CO., MARIUPOL, UKRAINE** | | | | | | | |
| | Avdeevka | BC | 1977 | D | 26,398 | 570' 11" | 75' 03" | 47' 07" |
| | *(Goldensari '77-'80, Bogasari Tiga '80-'86)* | | | | | | | |

| Fleet #. | Fleet Name / Vessel Name | Type of Vessel | Year Built | Type of Engine | Cargo Cap. or Gross* | Overall Length | Breadth | Depth or Draft* |
|---|---|---|---|---|---|---|---|---|
| | General Blazhevich | GC | 1981 | D | 7,805 | 399' 09" | 67' 00" | 27' 03" |
| | *FOLLOWING VESSELS UNDER CHARTER TO CANADIAN FOREST NAVIGATION LTD.* | | | | | | | |
| | Dobrush | BC | 1982 | D | 28,160 | 644' 06" | 75' 10" | 46' 11" |
| | *(World Goodwill '82-'85)* | | | | | | | |
| | Makeevka | BC | 1982 | D | 28,136 | 644' 06" | 75' 07" | 46' 11" |
| | *(World Shanghai '82-'85)* | | | | | | | |
| **IB-1** | **B & N, BYLOCK & NORDSJOFRAKT AS, OSLO, NORWAY** | | | | | | | |
| | Andromeda | GC | 1999 | D | 6,715 | 388' 09" | 49' 08" | 27' 02" |
| | Bergon | GC | 1978 | D | 5,449 | 330' 10" | 54' 02" | 26' 03" |
| | Bremon | GC | 1976 | D | 8,650 | 393' 10" | 54' 06" | 33' 04" |
| | Capricorn | GC | 2000 | D | 6,715 | 388' 09" | 49' 08" | 27' 02" |
| | Nordon | GC | 2002 | D | 17,600 | 467' 05" | 72' 00" | 41' 00" |
| | Swallow | GC | 1996 | D | 4,251 | 296' 09" | 43' 04" | 23' 11" |
| | Swan | GC | 1999 | D | 4,304 | 297' 03" | 44' 06" | 23' 06" |
| | Swing | GC | 1999 | D | 4,134 | 297' 07" | 43' 03" | 27' 09" |
| | Tofton | GC | 1980 | D | 14,883 | 522' 02" | 70' 03" | 41' 04" |
| **IB-2** | **BAY OCEAN MANAGEMENT, INC., ENGLEWOOD CLIFFS, NEW JERSEY, USA** | | | | | | | |
| | Lake Champlain | BC | 1992 | D | 26,264 | 591' 01" | 75' 09" | 45' 07" |
| | *(Ziemia Lodzka '92-'92)* | | | | | | | |
| | *FOLLOWING VESSELS UNDER CHARTER TO FEDNAV LTD.* | | | | | | | |
| | Lake Carling | BC | 1993 | D | 26,264 | 591' 01" | 75' 09" | 45' 07" |
| | *(Ziemia Cieszynska '93-'93)* | | | | | | | |
| | Lake Charles | BC | 1990 | D | 26,209 | 591' 01" | 75' 09" | 45' 07" |
| | *(Ziemia Gornoslaska '88-'91)* | | | | | | | |
| | Lake Erie | BC | 1980 | D | 35,630 | 737' 06" | 76' 02" | 47' 01" |
| | *(Federal Ottawa '80 - '95)* | | | | | | | |
| | Lake Michigan | BC | 1981 | D | 38,294 | 729' 11" | 76' 03" | 47' 01" |
| | *(Federal Maas {1} '81 - '95)* | | | | | | | |
| | Lake Ontario | BC | 1980 | D | 35,630 | 729' 11" | 76' 03" | 47' 01" |
| | *(Federal Danube '80 - '95)* | | | | | | | |
| | Lake Superior | BC | 1981 | D | 35,630 | 729' 11" | 76' 03" | 47' 01" |
| | *(Federal Thames '81 - '95)* | | | | | | | |
| **IB-3** | **BELUGA SHIPPING GMBH, BREMEN, GERMANY** | | | | | | | |
| | Beluga Obsession | GC | 1982 | D | 5,327 | 270' 03" | 51' 11" | 29' 06" |
| | *(Lindeborg '82-'96, Linden '96-'99)* | | | | | | | |
| | Beluga Performer | GC | 1982 | D | 6,081 | 303' 04" | 53' 02" | 33' 06" |
| | *(Samsun Carrier '82-'86, Frisian Carrier '86-'86, Haskerland '86-'91, Inara '91-'92, Haskerland '92-'98)* | | | | | | | |
| **IB-4** | **BIGLIFT SHIPPING BV, ROOSENDAAL, NETHERLANDS** | | | | | | | |
| | Enchanter | HL | 1998 | D | 16,069 | 452' 09" | 74' 10" | 31' 03" |
| | Happy Buccaneer | HL | 1984 | D | 13,740 | 478' 06" | 93' 01" | 48' 08" |
| | Project Europa | HL | 1983 | D | 13,493 | 456' 02" | 75' 02" | 42' 08" |
| | Thor Scan | HL | 1982 | D | 9,800 | 404' 08" | 67' 09" | 33' 10" |
| | Titan Scan | HL | 1982 | D | 9,864 | 404' 08" | 67' 11" | 33' 10" |
| **IB-5** | **BRIESE SCHIFFAHRTS GMBH & CO. KG, LEER, GERMANY** | | | | | | | |
| | Bavaria | GC | 1996 | D | 3,500 | 288' 09" | 42' 00" | 23' 04" |
| | BBC America | GC | 1999 | D | 4,806 | 330' 01" | 54' 06" | 26' 07" |
| | BBC Brazil | GC | 1997 | D | 4,900 | 330' 01" | 54' 06" | 26' 07" |
| | *(Launched as Torum Industrial Harmony '97 '00)* | | | | | | | |
| | BBC Canada | GC | 1999 | D | 4,798 | 330' 01" | 54' 06" | 26' 07" |
| | BBC Chile | GC | 2001 | D | 7,616 | 353' 05" | 59' 07" | 33' 01" |
| | BBC Denmark | GC | 1999 | D | 4,806 | 330' 01" | 54' 06" | 26' 07" |
| | BBC Finland | GC | 2000 | D | 8,760 | 353' 06" | 59' 09" | 33' 02" |
| | BBC Holland | GC | 2002 | D | 4,303 | 330' 00" | 54' 06" | 26' 07" |
| | BBC Iceland | GC | 1999 | D | 4,806 | 330' 01" | 54' 06" | 26' 07" |
| | *(Industrial Accord '99-'02)* | | | | | | | |

| Fleet #. | Fleet Name / Vessel Name | Type of Vessel | Year Built | Type of Engine | Cargo Cap. or Gross* | Overall Length | Breadth | Depth or Draft* |
|---|---|---|---|---|---|---|---|---|
| | BBC Japan | GC | 2001 | D | 4,900 | 330' 01" | 54' 06" | 26' 07" |
| | *(Juister Riff '01-'01)* | | | | | | | |
| | BBC Norway | GC | 2000 | D | 7,800 | 353' 06" | 59' 09" | 33' 02" |
| | BBC Scotland | GC | 2002 | D | 4,713 | 330' 01" | 54' 06" | 26' 07" |
| | Bremer Flagge | GC | 1985 | D | 3,840 | 326' 01" | 46' 05" | 23' 06" |
| | *(Santa Helena '85-'97)* | | | | | | | |
| | Santiago | GC | 1997 | D | 3,525 | 280' 10" | 42' 00" | 23' 04" |

**IC-1 CANADA MARITIME LTD., HAMILTON, BERMUDA**

| | Fleet Name / Vessel Name | Type of Vessel | Year Built | Type of Engine | Cargo Cap. or Gross* | Overall Length | Breadth | Depth or Draft* |
|---|---|---|---|---|---|---|---|---|
| | Canmar Courage | CO | 1996 | D | 34,330 | 709' 01" | 105' 10" | 62' 04" |
| | Canmar Fortune | CO | 1995 | D | 34,330 | 709' 01" | 105' 10" | 62' 04" |
| | Canmar Glory | CO | 1979 | D | 18,964 | 580' 10" | 88' 09" | 44' 04" |
| | *(Seatrain Saratoga '79-'80, TFL Jefferson '80-'87, Asian Senator '87-'90, CMB Mover '90-'90, CMB Monarch '90-'91, Sea Falcon '91-'94)* | | | | | | | |
| | Canmar Honour | CO | 1998 | D | 40,879 | 803' 10" | 105' 08" | 35' 05" |
| | Canmar Pride | CO | 1998 | D | 40,879 | 803' 10" | 105' 08" | 35' 05"* |
| | Canmar Triumph | CO | 1978 | D | 18,606 | 580' 10" | 88' 10" | 44' 04" |
| | *(Seatrain Independence '78-'81, Dart Americana '81-'87, American Senator '87-'89, CMB Marque '89-'90)* | | | | | | | |
| | Canmar Valour | C0 | 1979 | D | 18,800 | 580' 07" | 88' 09" | 44' 04" |
| | *(Seatrain Oriskany '79-'81, Dart Britain '81-'87, Taiwan Senator '87-'90, OOCL Assurance '90-'97)* | | | | | | | |
| | Canmar Venture | CO | 2003 | D | | Under Construction | | |
| | Canmar Victory | CO | 1979 | D | 18,381 | 580' 09" | 88' 10" | 44' 04" |
| | *(Seatrain Chesapeake '79-'81, Dart Atlantica '81-'87, Singapore Senator '87-'89, American Senator '89-'90)* | | | | | | | |
| | Cast Performance | CO | 1983 | D | 32,424 | 727' 02" | 105' 08" | 49' 03" |
| | *Tokyo Maru '83-'90, Alligator Joy '90-'95, Canmar Endeavour -'96-'98, Contship Endeavour '98-'99)* | | | | | | | |
| | Cast Power | CO | 1982 | D | 32.207 | | | |
| | *(America Maru '82-'90, Alligator Excellence '90-'95, Canmar Success '98-98, Contship Success '98-'99)* | | | | | | | |
| | Cast Progress | CO | 1986 | D | 40,009 | 796' 02" | 105' 09" | 69' 02" |
| | *(Astro Prosperity '86-'96, Alligator Reliance '96-'01)* | | | | | | | |

**IC-2 CANFORNAV LTD., MONTREAL, QUEBEC, CANADA**

| | Fleet Name / Vessel Name | Type of Vessel | Year Built | Type of Engine | Cargo Cap. or Gross* | Overall Length | Breadth | Depth or Draft* |
|---|---|---|---|---|---|---|---|---|
| | Bluewing | BC | 2002 | D | 27,000 | 581' 00" | 77' 07" | 31' 08" |
| | Cinnamon | BC | 2002 | D | 27,000 | 581' 00" | 77' 07" | 31' 08" |
| | Freewing | BC | 2003 | D | 27,000 | 581' 00" | 77' 07" | 31' 08" |
| | Greenwing | BC | 2002 | D | 27,000 | 581' 00" | 77' 07" | 31' 08" |
| | Mandarin | BC | 2003 | D | 27,000 | 581' 00" | 77' 07" | 31' 08" |
| | Porchard | BC | 2003 | D | 35,200 | 629' 09" | 77' 05" | 50' 00" |
| | Puffin | BC | 2003 | D | 35,200 | 629' 09" | 77' 05" | 50' 00" |

**At press time, Canadian Forest Navigation Co., Ltd. had the following vessels under long-term charter. Please consult their respective fleets for details:** Dobrush, Goldeneye, Makeevka, Malyovitza, Milo, Pintail, Peonia, Pytheas, Toro

**IC-3 CARISBROOKE SHIPPING PLC, COWES, ISLE OF WIGHT, UNITED KINGDOM**

| | Fleet Name / Vessel Name | Type of Vessel | Year Built | Type of Engine | Cargo Cap. or Gross* | Overall Length | Breadth | Depth or Draft* |
|---|---|---|---|---|---|---|---|---|
| | Anja-C | GC | 1991 | D | 3,222 | 327' 03" | 41' 00" | 20' 10" |
| | Anna-C | GC | 2002 | D | 4,900 | 312' 00" | 49' 07" | 23' 02" |
| | Catharina-C | CG | 1999 | D | 5,057 | 312' 00" | 49' 07" | 23' 02" |
| | Emily-C | GC | 1996 | D | 4,650 | 294' 07" | 43' 02" | 23' 05" |
| | Greta-C | GC | 2002 | D | 18,800 | 419' 02" | 52' 01" | 33' 07" |
| | Hanna-C | GC | 2002 | D | 10,450 | 457' 00" | 59' 07" | 33' 07" |
| | Janet-C | GC | 1998 | D | 4,570 | 294' 11" | 43' 04" | 23' 06" |
| | Jannie-C | GC | 2002 | D | 9,300 | 434' 03" | 52' 01" | 33' 07" |
| | Johanna-C | GC | 1998 | D | 4,570 | 294' 11" | 43' 04" | 23' 06" |
| | Klazina-C | GC | 1983 | D | 2,554 | 266' 09" | 39' 04" | 17' 09" |
| | Lia-C | GC | 2001 | D | 4,928 | 312' 00" | 49' 07" | 23' 02" |
| | Mark-C | GC | 1996 | D | 4,620 | 294' 11" | 43' 04" | 23' 06" |
| | Nordstrand | GC | 1991 | D | 2,800 | 289' 08" | 41' 00" | 21' 04" |
| | Vectis Falcon | GC | 1978 | D | 3,564 | 285' 06" | 45' 01" | 22' 04" |
| | *(Clarknes '78-'83, Fribourg '83-'93)* | | | | | | | |
| | Vectis Isle | GC | 1990 | D | 3,222 | 327' 02" | 41' 00" | 20' 1 |

**Federal Weser off Grosse Ile in the Detroit River, Dec. 10. 2002.** *(George Haynes)*

| Fleet #. | Fleet Name<br>Vessel Name | Type of<br>Vessel | Year<br>Built | Type of<br>Engine | Cargo Cap.<br>or Gross* | Overall<br>Length | Breadth | Depth or<br>Draft* |
|---|---|---|---|---|---|---|---|---|
| **IC-4** | **CATSAMBIS SHIPPING LTD., PIRAEUS, GREECE** | | | | | | | |
| | Adimon | BC | 1977 | D | 30,880 | 644' 11" | 75' 04" | 47' 06" |
| | *(Hercegovonia '77-'98)* | | | | | | | |
| **IC-5** | **CEBU SEALINK CORPORATION,MANILA, PHILIPPINES** | | | | | | | |
| | Rubin Falcon | BC | 1996 | D | 18,315 | 446' 00" | 74' 10" | 40' 00" |
| **IC-6** | **CHARTWORLD SHIPPING CORP., PIRAEUS, GREECE** | | | | | | | |
| | Golden Sun | BC | 1977 | D | 22,647 | 539' 03" | 75' 01" | 44' 06" |
| | *(Zuiho '77-'88, Miramar '88-'93)* | | | | | | | |
| **IC-7** | **CHEKKA SHIPPING S.A., ATHENS, GREECE** | | | | | | | |
| | Alexander K. | BC | 1978 | D | 30,353 | 622' 07" | 76' 05" | 47' 05" |
| | *(Federal Saguenay {1} '78 - '95, Federal Calliope '95 - '99, Calliope '99 - 2000)* | | | | | | | |
| **IC-8** | **CHINA OCEAN SHIPPING (GROUP) CO., BEIJING, PEOPLE'S REPUBLIC OF CHINA** | | | | | | | |
| | An Guang Jiang | GC | 1987 | D | 14,913 | 491'02" | 71' 06" | 41' 00" |
| | An Kang Jiang | GC | 1985 | D | 15,852 | 487' 02" | 74' 07" | 43' 04" |
| | An Qing Jiang | GC | 1985 | D | 14,913 | 491' 02" | 71' 06" | 41' 00" |
| | An Ze Jiang | GC | 1987 | D | 14,913 | 491' 02" | 71' 06" | 41' 00" |
| | Da Hua | GC | 1998 | D | 16,957 | 502' 00" | 75' 08" | 46' 03" |
| | Hui Fu | BC | 1978 | D | 35,887 | 734' 02" | 76' 08" | 47' 05" |
| | *(Federal Clyde '78 - '81, President Quezon '81 - '87, Federal St. Clair '87 - '94)* | | | | | | | |
| | Hun Jiang | GC | 1981 | D | 15,265 | 474' 11" | 67' 01" | 38' 07" |
| | Ocean Priti | BC | 1982 | D | 27,019 | 599' 05" | 75' 04" | 46' 08" |
| | Tong Fu | BC | 1977 | D | 35,887 | 729'11" | 76' 00" | 47' 00" |
| | *(Federal Calumet {1} '77 - '94)* | | | | | | | |
| | Yick Hua | BC | 1984 | D | 28,086 | 584' 08" | 75' 11" | 48' 05" |
| **IC-9** | **CLARKE INC., MONTREAL, QUEBEC, CANADA** | | | | | | | |
| | Cabot {2} | RR | 1979 | D | 7,132 | 564' 09" | 73' 11" | 45' 09" |
| | Cicero | RR | 1978 | D | 6,985 | 482' 10" | 73' 11" | 45' 09" |
| | Trans-St.-Laurent | RR | 1963 | D | 645 | 261' 11" | 62' 04" | 18' 00" |
| **IC-10** | **CLIPPER CRUISE LINE, ST. LOUIS, MISSOURI, USA** | | | | | | | |
| | Clipper Adventurer | PA | 1975 | D | 4,364* | 328' 01" | 53' 03" | 23' 00" |
| | Clipper Odyssey | PA | 1989 | D | 5,200* | 337' 10" | 50'07" | 20'04" |
| | Nantucket Clipper | PA | 1984 | D | 96* | 207' 00" | 37' 00" | 11' 06" |
| | Yorktown Clipper | PA | 1988 | D | 97* | 257' 00" | 43' 00" | 12' 05" |
| **IC-11** | **COMMERCIAL TRADING & DISCOUNT CO. LTD., ATHENS, GREECE** | | | | | | | |
| | Ira | BC | 1979 | D | 26,697 | 591' 02" | 75' 10" | 45' 08" |
| | Ivi | BC | 1979 | D | 26,697 | 591' 04" | 75' 10" | 45' 08" |
| **IC-12** | **COMMON PROGRESS COMPANIA NAVIERA S.A., PIRAEUS, GREECE** | | | | | | | |
| | Kastor P | BC | 1983 | D | 22,713 | 528' 03" | 75' 07" | 45' 07" |
| | *(Sea Augusta '83-'85, Jovian Lily '85-'91)* | | | | | | | |
| | Polydefkis P | BC | 1982 | D | 22,713 | 528' 03" | 75' 07" | 45' 07" |
| | *(Sea Astrea '82-'85, Jovian Luzon '85-'91)* | | | | | | | |
| **IC-13** | **COMPAGNIE DES ILES DU PONANT, NANTES, FRANCE** | | | | | | | |
| | Le Levant | PA | 1998 | D | 3,504* | 326' 09" | 45' 11" | 11' 06"* |
| **IC-14** | **CORNER SHIPPING CO. LTD., PIRAEUS, GREECE** | | | | | | | |
| | Sylvia | BC | 1981 | D | 22,525 | 539' 02" | 75' 02" | 44' 06" |
| | *(Chimo '81-'89, Bergen Pride '89-'93, China Power '93-'96)* | | | | | | | |
| **IC-15** | **CSL INTERNATIONAL, INC., BEVERLY, MASSACHUSETTS, USA** | | | | | | | |
| | CSL Asia | BC | 1999 | D | 45,729 | 609'05" | 99'09" | 54'02" |
| | CSL Atlas | SU | 1990 | D | 67,308 | 746'01" | 105'02" | 63'00" |
| | CSL Cabo | SU | 1971 | D | 31,364 | 596'02" | 84'04" | 49'10" |
| | CSL Spirit | SU | 2000 | D | 70,037 | 737'10" | 105'07" | 64'00" |
| | CSL Trailblazer | SU | 1978 | D | 26,608 | 583'11" | 85'02" | 46'03" |

**Chios Sailor assisted by the tug Missouri at the Soo Locks.** *(Roger LeLievre)*

| Fleet #. | Fleet Name<br>Vessel Name | Type of<br>Vessel | Year<br>Built | Type of<br>Engine | Cargo Cap.<br>or Gross* | Overall<br>Length | Breadth | Depth or<br>Draft* |
|---|---|---|---|---|---|---|---|---|
| | M. H. Baker III | SU | 1982 | D | 38,900 | 730' 00" | 75' 10" | 50' 00" |
| | *(Atlantic Superior '82 - '97)* | | | | | | | |
| | Shelia Ann | SU | 1999 | D | 70,037 | 737' 10" | 105' 07" | 64' 00" |
| | **MARBULK SHIPPING, INC. - MANAGED BY CSL INTERNATIONAL, INC.** | | | | | | | |
| | **PARTNERSHIP BETWEEN CSL INTERNATIONAL, INC. AND ALGOMA CENTRAL CORP.** | | | | | | | |
| | Ambassador | SU | 1983 | D | 37,263 | 730' 00" | 75' 10" | 50' 00" |
| | *(Canadian Ambassador '83 - '85, Ambassador '85 - 2000, Algosea {2} 2000 - 2000)* | | | | | | | |
| | Antwerpen | BC | 1979 | D | 41,100 | 652' 11" | 96' 04" | 50' 05" |
| | Bahamaspirit | BC | 1995 | D | 46,606 | 615' 02" | 105' 09" | 52' 10" |
| | Eastern Power | SU | 1989 | D | 69,808 | 738' 02" | 105' 09" | 60' 01" |
| | Nelvana | SU | 1983 | D | 74,973 | 797' 05" | 105' 11" | 66' 04" |
| | Pioneer | SU | 1981 | D | 37,448 | 730' 00" | 75' 10" | 50' 00" |
| | *(Canadian Pioneer '81 - '86)* | | | | | | | |
| | Thornhill | SU | 1981 | D | 35,463 | 635' 11" | 90' 08" | 48' 07" |
| | Weser Stahl | SU | 1999 | D | 47,257 | 630' 07" | 105' 10" | 51' 06" |
| | **CSL AUSTRALIA PTY. LTD., - A SUBSIDIARY OF CSL INTERNATIONAL, INC.** | | | | | | | |
| | CSL Pacific | SU | 1977 | D | 31,921 | 596' 05" | 81' 07" | 47' 06" |
| | River Boyne | SU | 1982 | T | 76,308 | 836' 08" | 116' 02" | 60' 00" |
| | River Embley | SU | 1983 | T | 76,358 | 836' 07" | 116' 02" | 60' 00" |
| | Stadacona {2} | SU | 1984 | D | 32,452 | 599' 11" | 90' 10" | 49' 07" |
| | *(CSL Yarra '84-'02)* | | | | | | | |
| IC-16 | **CYPRUS MARITIME CO. LTD., ATHENS GREECE** | | | | | | | |
| | Lake Superior | BC | 1982 | D | 30,670 | 617' 04" | 76' 00" | 47' 07" |
| | *(Broompark '82-'99, Millenum Raptor '02, Cardinal '02-'02)* | | | | | | | |
| ID-1 | **DENSAN SHIPPING CO. LTD., ISTANBUL, TURKEY** | | | | | | | |
| | Gunay A | BC | 1981 | D | 30,900 | 617' 04" | 76' 00" | 47' 07" |
| | *(Nosira Sharon '81-'89, Berta Dan '89-'93)* | | | | | | | |
| ID-2 | **DET NORDENFJELDSKE D/S AS, TRONDHEIM, NORWAY** | | | | | | | |
| | Consensus Reefer | GC | 1991 | D | 9,157 | 452' 04" | 60' 08" | 41' 03" |

| Fleet #. | Fleet Name<br>Vessel Name | Type of<br>Vessel | Year<br>Built | Type of<br>Engine | Cargo Cap.<br>or Gross* | Overall<br>Length | Breadth | Depth or<br>Draft* |
|---|---|---|---|---|---|---|---|---|
| ID-3 | **DIANA SHIPPING AGENCIES S.A., PIRAEUS, GREECE** | | | | | | | |
| | Cedar | BC | 2000 | D | 16,360 | 576' 02" | 76' 01" | 44' 25" |
| | Elm | BC | 1984 | D | 21,978 | 509' 02" | 75' 01" | 44' 07" |
| | *(Polarqueen '85-'96)* | | | | | | | |
| | Pine | BC | 2002 | D | 24,765 | 576' 02" | 76' 01" | 44' 25 |
| ID-4 | **DYNASTY SHIPPING CO. LTD., ATHENS, GREECE** | | | | | | | |
| | Plamer | BC | 1978 | D | 29,212 | 593' 03" | 75' 11" | 47' 07" |
| | *(Doric Javelin '78 - '89, Federal Inger '89 - '96, Inger '96 - '96, Flame '00-'02)* | | | | | | | |
| IE-1 | **EGON OLDENDORFF LTD., LUEBECK, GERMANY** | | | | | | | |
| | Anna Oldendorff | BC | 1994 | D | 18,297 | 604' 07" | 74' 09" | 40' 00" |
| | Elise Oldendorff | BC | 1998 | D | 20,100 | 488' 10" | 75' 11" | 44' 03" |
| | Helena Oldendorff | BC | 1984 | D | 28,354 | 644' 06" | 75' 10" | 46' 11" |
| | *(Noble River '84-'86)* | | | | | | | |
| | Johann Oldendorff | GC | 1999 | D | 20,567 | 502' 07" | 77' 05" | 44' 03" |
| | Maria Oldendorff | GC | 1988 | D | 20,586 | 595' 06" | 77' 01" | 44' 00" |
| | Mathilde Oldendorff | BC | 1999 | D | 20,427 | 488' 10" | 75' 11" | 44' 03" |
| | Regina Oldendorff | BC | 1986 | D | 28,031 | 639' 09" | 75' 10" | 46' 11" |
| | Rixta Oldendorff | BC | 1986 | D | 28,031 | 639' 09" | 75' 10" | 46' 11" |
| IE-2 | **ELMIRA SHIPPING & TRADING S.A., ATHENS, GREECE**<br>*FOLLOWING VESSELS UNDER CHARTER TO FEDNAV LTD.* | | | | | | | |
| | Aegean Sea | BC | 1983 | D | 31,431 | 598' 09" | 77' 06" | 50' 06" |
| | *(Southern Pacific '83-'91, Consensus Pacific '91-'94, Aegean Clipper '94-'98)* | | | | | | | |
| | Mecta Sea | BC | 1984 | D | 28,166 | 584' 08" | 75' 11" | 48' 05" |
| | *(Socrates '84-'92, Union '92-'97)* | | | | | | | |
| | Tecam Sea | BC | 1984 | D | 28,166 | 584' 08" | 75' 11" | 48' 05" |
| | *(Rich Alliance '84-'89, Monte Bonita '89-'93, University '93-'95, Alam University '95-'97)* | | | | | | | |
| IE-3 | **ENZIAN SHIPPING AG, BERNE, SWITZERLAND** | | | | | | | |
| | Alessia | GC | 1999 | D | 5,647 | 311' 03" | 42' 09" | 23' 02" |
| | Celene | GC | 2001 | D | 8,600 | 424' 05" | 52' 000" | 31 09" |
| | Claudia | GC | 1999 | D | 5,647 | 311' 06" | 42' 09" | 23 02" |
| | Kathrin | GC | 1999 | D | 2,999 | 311' 00" | 42' 09" | 23 02" |
| | Marie Jeanne | GC | 1999 | D | 5,049 | 311'11" | 43' 04" | 23' 05" |
| | Sabina | GC | 2000 | D | 9,231 | 419' 06" | 52' 05" | 32' 00" |
| IE-4 | **ER DENIZCILIK SANAYI NAKLIYAT VE TICARET A.S., ISTANBUL, TURKEY** | | | | | | | |
| | Balaban I | BC | 1979 | D | 24,747 | 562' 06" | 75' 00" | 46' 00" |
| | *(Ocean Glory '79-'83, Serafim '83-'91)* | | | | | | | |
| IE-5 | **ESTONIAN SHIPPING CO., TALLINN, ESTONIA** | | | | | | | |
| | Aleksander Kolmpere | BC | 1987 | D | 24,105 | 605' 09" | 74' 10" | 46' 06" |
| | *(Skulptor Matveyev '87-'92)* | | | | | | | |
| | Gustav Sule | BC | 1987 | D | 24,105 | 605' 09" | 74' 10" | 46' 06" |
| IE-6 | **EURUS MARITIME S.A., PANAMA CITY, PANAMA** | | | | | | | |
| | Fairchem Vanguard | TK | 1999 | D | 9,149* | 436' 04" | 74' 06" | 39' 08" |
| IF-1 | **FAR-EASTERN SHIPPING CO. (FESCO), VLADIVOSTOK, RUSSIA** | | | | | | | |
| | Khudozhnik Kraynev | BC | 1986 | D | 24,105 | 605' 00" | 75' 01" | 46' 03" |
| IF-2 | **FEDNAV LTD., MONTREAL, QUEBEC, CANADA**<br>*CANARCTIC SHIPPING CO. LTD. - A DIVISION OF FEDNAV LTD.* | | | | | | | |
| | Arctic | BC | 1978 | D | 26,440 | 692' 04" | 75' 05" | 49' 05" |
| | Arctic Kalvik | SB | 1983 | D | 4,391 | 288' 09" | 57' 05" | 32' 10" |
| | *(Kalvik '84-'97)* | | | | | | | |
| | Federal Baffin | BC | 1995 | D | 43,732 | 623' 04" | 100' 00" | 54' 06" |
| | Federal Franklin | BC | 1995 | D | 43,706 | 623' 04" | 100' 00" | 54' 06" |
| | *FEDNAV INTERNATIONAL LTD. - A DIVISION OF FEDNAV LTD.* | | | | | | | |
| | Federal Hudson {3} | BC | 2000 | D | 35,750 | 656' 02" | 77' 11" | 48' 08" |

| Fleet #. | Fleet Name<br>Vessel Name | Type of<br>Vessel | Year<br>Built | Type of<br>Engine | Cargo Cap.<br>or Gross* | Overall<br>Length | Breadth | Depth or<br>Draft* |
|---|---|---|---|---|---|---|---|---|
| | Federal Hunter {2} | BC | 2001 | D | 36,563 | 656' 02" | 77' 11" | 48' 08" |
| | Federal Kivalina | BC | 2000 | D | 36,563 | 656' 02" | 77' 11" | 48' 08" |
| | Federal Maas {2} | BC | 1997 | D | 34,372 | 656' 02" | 77' 11" | 48' 08" |
| | Federal Oshima | BC | 1999 | D | 35,700 | 656' 02" | 77' 11" | 48' 08" |
| | Federal Progress<br>(*Northern Progress '89-'02*) | BC | 1989 | D | 38,130 | 580' 07" | 86' 07" | 48' 08" |
| | Federal Rhine {2} | BC | 1997 | D | 34,372 | 656' 02" | 77' 11" | 48' 08" |
| | Federal Rideau | BC | 2000 | D | 36,563 | 656' 02" | 77' 11" | 48' 08" |
| | Federal Saguenay {2} | BC | 1996 | D | 34,372 | 656' 02" | 77' 11" | 48' 08" |
| | Federal Schelde {3} | BC | 1997 | D | 34,372 | 656' 02" | 77' 11" | 48' 08" |
| | Federal St. Laurent {3} | BC | 1996 | D | 34,372 | 656' 02" | 77' 11" | 48' 08" |
| | Federal Venture<br>(*Northern Venture '89-'02*) | BC | 1989 | D | 38,130 | 580' 07" | 86' 07" | 48' 08" |
| | Federal Welland | BC | 2000 | D | 35,750 | 656' 02" | 77' 11" | 48' 08" |
| | Federal Yukon | BC | 2000 | D | 35,750 | 656' 02" | 77' 11" | 48' 08" |

**At press time, FedNav Ltd. had the following vessels under charter. Please consult their respective fleets for details:** Aegean Sea, Daviken, Federal Agno, Federal Asahi, Federal Elbe, Federal Ems, Federal Fuji, Federal Polaris, Federal Shimanto, Federal Sumida, Federal Weser, Federal Yoshino, Goviken, Inviken, Lake Carling, Lake Charles, Lake Erie, Lake Michigan, Lake Ontario, Lake Superior, Mecta Sea, Orsula, Sandviken, Spar Garnet, Spar Jade, Spar Opal, Spar Ruby, Tecam Sea, Utviken, Yarmouth

| Fleet #. | Fleet Name<br>Vessel Name | Type of<br>Vessel | Year<br>Built | Type of<br>Engine | Cargo Cap.<br>or Gross* | Overall<br>Length | Breadth | Depth or<br>Draft* |
|---|---|---|---|---|---|---|---|---|
| **IF-3** | **FLINTER GRONINGEN B.V. (ANCORA AFS MGRS.), GRONINGEN, THE NETHERLANDS** | | | | | | | |
| | Flinterborg | GC | 1990 | D | 3,020 | 269' 00" | 41' 03" | 21' 06" |
| | Flinterdam | GC | 1996 | D | 4,506 | 325' 07" | 44' 06" | 23' 06" |
| | Flinterdijk | GC | 2000 | D | 6,250 | 366' 07" | 48' 08" | 26' 09" |
| | Flinterduin | GC | 2000 | D | 6,359 | 364' 01" | 49' 02" | 26' 09" |
| | Flintereems | GC | 2000 | D | 6,200 | 366' 07" | 48' 08" | 26' 09" |
| | Flinterhaven | GC | 1997 | D | 6,067 | 366' 07" | 48' 08" | 26' 09" |
| | Flinterland | GC | 1995 | D | 4,216 | 300' 01" | 44' 08" | 23' 07" |
| | Flintermaas | GC | 2000 | D | 6,200 | 366' 07" | 48' 08" | 26' 09" |
| | Flintermar | GC | 1995 | D | 4,170 | 300' 01" | 44' 09" | 23' 07" |
| | Flintersky | GC | 2001 | D | 9,200 | 424' 06" | 55' 05" | 32' 10" |
| | Flinterspirit | GC | 2001 | D | 6,358 | 366' 07" | 48' 08" | 26' 09" |
| | Flinterstar | GC | 2002 | D | 9,200 | 424' 06" | 55' 05" | 32' 10" |
| | Flinterzee | GC | 1997 | D | 6,075 | 366' 07" | 48' 08" | 26' 09" |
| | Flinterzijl | GC | 1996 | D | 4,540 | 325' 09" | 44' 09" | 23' 07" |
| **IF-4** | **FORTUM OIL AND GAS OY, FORTUM, FINLAND** | | | | | | | |
| | Kihu | TK | 1984 | D | 160,507 | 527' 11" | 76' 00" | 46' 08" |
| | Sirri | TK | 1981 | D | 47,502 | 351' 01" | 59' 00" | 30' 01" |
| | Sotka | TK | 1976 | D | 101,991 | 539' 07" | 73' 00" | 39' 05" |
| | Tavi | TK | 1985 | D | 160,507 | 527' 11" | 76' 00" | 58' 05" |
| | Uikku | TK | 1977 | D | 108,231 | 539' 07" | 73' 00" | 39' 05" |
| | Vikla | TK | 1982 | D | 53,490 | 437' 04" | 63' 02" | 31' 03" |
| **IF-5** | **FRANCO COMPANIA NAVIERA S.A., ATHENS, GREECE** | | | | | | | |
| | Stefania I<br>(*Astral Ocean '85-'95, Sea Crystal '95-'97*) | BC | 1985 | D | 28,269 | 584' 08" | 75' 11" | 48' 05" |
| **IF-6** | **FUKUJIN KISEN CO. LTD., OCHI EHIME, JAPAN**<br>***FOLLOWING VESSELS UNDER CHARTER TO FEDNAV LTD.*** | | | | | | | |
| | Federal Shimanto | BC | 2001 | D | 32,787 | 624' 08" | 77' 05" | 49' 10" |
| | Federal Yoshino | BC | 2001 | D | 32,787 | 624' 08" | 77' 05" | 49' 10" |
| **IG-1** | **GEARBULK HOLDING LTD., HAMILTON, BERMUDA** | | | | | | | |
| | Alouette Arrow<br>(*Finnarctis '91-'94, Chimo '91-'94*) | GC | 1980 | D | 14,241 | 522' 04" | 70' 03" | 36' 10" |
| | Rathrowan | TK | 1991 | D | 24,046 | 315' 00" | 47' 08" | 27' 03" |

Hope 1 at Hamilton May 26, 2002. *(Roger LeLievre)*

| Fleet #. | Fleet Name / Vessel Name | Type of Vessel | Year Built | Type of Engine | Cargo Cap. or Gross* | Overall Length | Breadth | Depth or Draft* |
|---|---|---|---|---|---|---|---|---|
| **IG-2** | **GENESIS SEATRADING CORP., PIRAEUS, GREECE** | | | | | | | |
| | Rio Glory | BC | 1981 | D | 30,900 | 617' 04" | 76' 00" | 47' 07" |
| | *(Darya Kamal '81-'01)* | | | | | | | |
| **IG-3** | **GRAIG SHIP MANAGEMENT, CARDIFF, ENGLAND, UNITED KINGDOM** | | | | | | | |
| | CEC Blue | GC | 1992 | D | 4,110 | 290' 01" | 49' 08" | 24' 07" |
| | *(Arktis Blue '92-'99)* | | | | | | | |
| | CEC Faith | GC | 1994 | D | 7,225 | 331' 08" | 63' 00" | 30' 06" |
| | *(Arktis Faith '99-'00)* | | | | | | | |
| | CEC Fantasy | GC | 1994 | D | 7,120 | 331' 08" | 63' 00" | 30' 06" |
| | *(Arktis Fantasy '94-'99)* | | | | | | | |
| | CEC Force | GC | 1995 | D | 7,121 | 331' 08" | 63' 00" | 30' 06" |
| | *(Arktis Force '99-'00)* | | | | | | | |
| | CEC Future | GC | 1994 | D | 7,120 | 331' 08" | 63' 00" | 30' 06" |
| | *(Arktis Future '01-'01)* | | | | | | | |
| | CEC Hunter | GC | 1995 | D | 5,401 | 319' 07" | 53' 08" | 27' 11" |
| | *(Arktis Hunter '95-'00)* | | | | | | | |
| | CEC Light | GC | 1993 | D | 5,401 | 319' 07" | 53' 08" | 27' 11" |
| | *(CIC Light '99-'02)* | | | | | | | |
| | CEC Vision | GC | 1994 | D | 5,401 | 319' 07" | 53' 08" | 27' 11" |
| | *(Arctis Vision '94-'99, CIC Vision '99-'02)* | | | | | | | |
| | Tracer | HL | 2000 | D | 8,874 | 329' 09" | 73' 06" | 26' 11" |
| | Tramper | HL | 2000 | D | 8,874 | 329' 09" | 73' 06" | 26' 11" |
| | Transporter | HL | 1999 | D | 8,874 | 329' 09" | 73' 06" | 26' 11" |
| | Traveller | HL | 2000 | D | 8,874 | 329' 09" | 73' 06" | 26' 11" |
| **IG-4** | **GREAT LAKES EUROPEAN SHIPPING AS, ORNSKOLDSVIK, SWEDEN** | | | | | | | |
| | **WILSON SHIP MANAGEMENT, MGR.** | | | | | | | |
| | Marinette | GC | 1967 | D | 12,497 | 503' 03" | 66' 07" | 36' 09" |
| | *(Tunadal '75-'97, Abitibi John Cabot '97-'98)* | | | | | | | |
| | Menominee | GC | 1967 | D | 12,497 | 503' 03" | 66' 07" | 36' 09" |
| | *(Holmsund '67-'97)* | | | | | | | |
| **IG-5** | **GREEN MANAGEMENT AS, MINDE, NORWAY** | | | | | | | |
| | Nomadic Patria | GC | 1978 | D | 17,160 | 511' 09" | 73' 11" | 45' 10" |
| | *(Patria '78-'88, Ukrania '88-'89, Patria '89-'90)* | | | | | | | |
| | Nomadic Pollux | GC | 1977 | D | 17,161 | 511' 10" | 73' 11" | 46' 00" |
| | *(Pollux '77-'88, Baltikum '88-'89, Pollux '89-'90)* | | | | | | | |
| **IH-1** | **H. S. S. HOLLAND SHIP SERVICE B.V., ROTTERDAM, THE NETHERLANDS** | | | | | | | |
| | Makiri Green | GC | 1999 | D | 17,539 | 468' 07" | 70' 07" | 43' 08" |
| | Margaretha Green | GC | 1999 | D | 17,539 | 468' 07" | 70' 07" | 43' 08" |
| | Maria Green | GC | 1998 | D | 17,539 | 468' 07" | 70' 07" | 43' 08" |
| | Marinus Green | GC | 2000 | D | 16,000 | 468' 07" | 70' 07" | 43' 08" |
| | Marion Green | GC | 1999 | D | 17,538 | 468' 07" | 70' 07" | 43' 08" |
| **IH-2** | **HAPAG-LLOYD SEETOURISTIK (CRUISES) GMBH, HAMBURG, GERMANY** | | | | | | | |
| | c. Columbus | PA | 1997 | D | 14,903* | 475' 09" | 70' 06" | 43' 06" |
| **IH-3** | **HARBOR SHIPPING & TRADING CO. S.A., CHIOS, GREECE** | | | | | | | |
| | Chios Charity | BC | 1981 | D | 29,002 | 589' 11" | 76' 01" | 47' 07" |
| | *(Violetta '81 - '86, Capetan Yiannis '86 - '88, Federal Nord '88 - '96, Nordic Moor '96 - '98)* | | | | | | | |
| | Chios Harmony | BC | 1977 | D | 29,337 | 594' 01" | 75' 11" | 47' 07" |
| | *(Golden Dolphin '77-'90, Romanea '90-'91)* | | | | | | | |
| | Chios Pride | BC | 1981 | D | 28,500 | 627' 07" | 75' 03" | 44' 04" |
| | *(Regent Palm '81-'87, Protoporos III '87-'89, Crystal B. '89-'95, Ocean Leader '95-'97)* | | | | | | | |
| | Chios Sailor | BC | 1984 | D | 30,850 | 617' 04" | 75' 11" | 47' 07" |
| | *(Radnik '77-'96, Grant Carrier '96-'01)* | | | | | | | |
| | Chios Sky | BC | 1977 | D | 27,541 | 600' 06" | 74' 08" | 47' 01" |
| | *(London Baron '77-'83, Olympic Phoenix '83-'92, Jeannie '92-'99, St.George A. '99-'00, St.George '00-'01)* | | | | | | | |

| --- | --- | --- | --- | --- | --- | --- | --- | --- |
| **IH-4** | **HARREN & PARTNER SCHIFFAHRTS GMBH, EMS, GERMANY** | | | | | | | |
| | Pampero | GC | 1995 | D | 5,660 | 371' 11" | 53' 10" | 25' 09" |
| | Pancaldo | HL | 2000 | D | 7,000 | 387' 01" | 64' 03" | 30' 08" |
| | Paramar | GC | 1999 | D | 4,023 | 294' 04" | 44' 07" | 23' 07" |
| | Patria | HL | 1999 | D | 5,300 | 331' 00" | 61' 00" | 33' 01" |
| | Rhein Master | GC | 1994 | D | 4,766 | 330' 00" | 54' 02" | 24' 07" |
| | Solymar | GC | 1998 | D | 4,023 | 294' 04" | 44' 07" | 23' 07" |
| | Transmar | GC | 1998 | D | 4,023 | 294' 04" | 44' 07" | 23' 07" |
| | Ultramar | GC | 1997 | D | 4,023 | 294' 04" | 44' 07" | 23' 07" |
| **IH-5** | **HELIKON SHIPPING ENTERPRISES LTD., LONDON, ENGLAND, UNITED KINGDOM** | | | | | | | |
| | Elikon | BC | 1980 | D | 16,106 | 582' 00" | 75' 02" | 44' 04" |
| | *(Bailey '80-'89)* | | | | | | | |
| **IH-6** | **HILAL SHIPPING TRADING & INDUSTRY CO., ISTANBUL, TURKEY** | | | | | | | |
| | Hilal II | BC | 1981 | D | 25,845 | 585' 00" | 75' 09" | 45' 11" |
| | *(Yin Kim '81-'94)* | | | | | | | |
| **II -1** | **INDOCHINA SHIPMANAGEMENT (HK) LTD., HONG KONG, HONG KONG** | | | | | | | |
| | Cashin | BC | 1984 | D | 28,791 | 606' 11" | 75' 11" | 48' 01" |
| | *(LT Argosy '84-'98, Millenium Hawk '98-'02)* | | | | | | | |
| | Giant | BC | 1981 | D | 27,048 | 627' 07" | 75' 03" | 44' 03" |
| | *(Oak Star '81-'82, Soren Toubro '82-'98, Millenium Falcon '02)* | | | | | | | |
| | Harstad | BC | 1981 | D | 27,036 | 627' 07" | 75' 03" | 44' 03" |
| | *(Eggarlock '81-'82, Holck-Larson '82-'98, Millenium Condor "98-02)* | | | | | | | |
| | Jamaica | BC | 1979 | D | 17,686 | 481' 03" | 75' 01" | 40' 01" |
| | *(Baltic Confidence '84-'89, Baltic '89-'91, Baltic Confidence '91-'01, Millenium Baltic '01-'02)* | | | | | | | |
| | Kent | BC | 1984 | D | 28,786 | 606' 11" | 75' 11" | 48' 01" |
| | *(LT Odyssey '84-'98, Millenium Osprey '98-'02)* | | | | | | | |
| | Moor Laker | BC | 1984 | D | 27,915 | 584' 08" | 69' 03" | 48' 05" |
| | *(St. Catheriness4-'90, Asian Erie '90-'92, Handy Laker '92-'98)* | | | | | | | |
| | Stokmarnes | BC | 1983 | D | 28,788 | 606' 11" | 75' 11" | 48' 01" |
| | *(Mangal Desai '83-'98, Millenium Eagle '98-'02)* | | | | | | | |
| **II-2** | **INTERSCAN SCHIFFAHRTSGESELLSCHAFT MBH, HAMBURG, GERMANY** | | | | | | | |
| | Patriot | GC | 1994 | D | 3,086 | 270' 06" | 41' 03" | 21' 08" |
| | Patria | GC | 1996 | D | 3,519 | 270' 03" | 41' 02" | 23' 07" |
| | Pinta | GC | 1993 | D | 2,795 | 270' 00" | 41' 02" | 21' 08" |
| **II-3** | **INTERSHIP NAVIGATION CO. LTD., LIMASSOL, CYPRUS** | | | | | | | |
| | ***FOLLOWING VESSELS UNDER CHARTER TO FEDNAV LTD.*** | | | | | | | |
| | Federal Elbe | GC | 2003 | D | 35,200 | 655' 80" | 78' 04" | 50' 01" |
| | Federal Leda | GC | 2003 | D | 35,200 | 655' 80" | 78' 04" | 50' 01" |
| **IJ-1** | **J. G. GOUMAS (SHIPPING) CO. S.A., PIRAEUS, GREECE** | | | | | | | |
| | Alaska Rainbow | BC | 1985 | D | 22,782 | 515' 11" | 75' 07" | 44' 08" |
| | Washington Rainbow II | BC | 1984 | D | 22,828 | 515' 11" | 75' 07" | 44' 08" |
| **IJ-2** | **JADROPLOV DD, SPLIT, CROATIA** | | | | | | | |
| | Hope | BC | 1982 | D | 30,900 | 617' 03" | 76' 00" | 47' 07" |
| | *(Nosira Madeleine '82-'89, Bella Dan '89-'93, Hope 1 '93-'02)* | | | | | | | |
| **IJ-3** | **JARDINE SHIP MANAGEMENT LTD., HONG KONG, PEOPLE'S REPUBLIC OF CHINA** | | | | | | | |
| | Golden Laker | BC | 1996 | D | 30,838 | 607' 01" | 77' 05" | 48' 11" |
| **IJ-4** | **JO TANKERS B.V., SPIJKENISSE, NETHERLANDS** | | | | | | | |
| | Jo Hassel | TK | 1986 | D | 8,139 | 356' 00" | 58' 05" | 32' 02" |
| | Jo Spirit | TK | 1998 | D | 33,205 | 352' 02" | 52' 02" | 30' 02" |
| **IJ-5** | **JUMBO SHIPPING CO. S.A., ROTTERDAM, NETHERLANDS** | | | | | | | |
| | Daniella | HL | 1989 | D | 7,600 | 322' 09" | 68' 06" | 37' 02" |
| | *(Stellaprima '89-'90)* | | | | | | | |

**Thorsimba visits the lakes from Denmark.** *(Jimmy Sprunt)*

**Virginiaborg loads at the General Mills elevator in Duluth.** *(Glenn Blaszkiewicz)*

| Fleet #. | Fleet Name / Vessel Name | Type of Vessel | Year Built | Type of Engine | Cargo Cap. or Gross* | Overall Length | Breadth | Depth or Draft* |
|---|---|---|---|---|---|---|---|---|
| | Fairlane | HL | 2000 | D | 7,300 | 361' 03" | 68' 05" | 44' 02" |
| | Fairlift | HL | 1990 | D | 7,780 | 329' 02" | 68' 10" | 43' 08" |
| | Fairload | HL | 1995 | D | 7,500 | 313' 11" | 60' 03" | 37' 02" |
| | Fairmast | HL | 1983 | D | 6,833 | 360' 07" | 63' 07" | 34' 05" |
| | Gajah Borneo | HL | 1978 | D | 5,076 | 327' 05" | 59' 02" | 32' 00" |
| | Jumbo Challenger | HL | 1983 | D | 6,375 | 360' 11" | 63' 00" | 34' 05" |
| | Jumbo Spirit | HL | 1995 | D | 5,200 | 313' 11" | 60' 03" | 37' 02" |
| | Jumbo Vision | HL | 2000 | D | 7,300 | 361' 03" | 68' 05" | 44' 02" |
| | Stellamare | HL | 1982 | D | 2,850 | 289' 04" | 51' 02" | 24' 00" |
| | Stellanova | HL | 1996 | D | 5,198 | 313' 08" | 60' 03" | 37' 02" |
| | Stellaprima | HL | 1991 | D | 7,600 | 329' 02" | 68' 10" | 43' 08" |

**IK-1  K.C. MARITIME LTD., HONG KONG, PEOPLE'S REPUBLIC OF CHINA**

| | | | | | | | | |
|---|---|---|---|---|---|---|---|---|
| | Darya Devi | BC | 1985 | D | 28,019 | 584' 08" | 75' 11" | 48' 05" |
| | *(Astral Mariner '85-'90, Lake Challenge '90-'97, Manila Angus '97-'98)* | | | | | | | |
| | Darya Ma | BC | 1983 | D | 30,750 | 617' 04" | 76' 00" | 47' 07" |

**IK-2  KEISHIN KAIUN K.K., HAKATA, JAPAN**

| | | | | | | | | |
|---|---|---|---|---|---|---|---|---|
| | Rubin Lark | BC | 1997 | D | 18,315 | 486' 01" | 74' 10" | 40' 00" |

**IK-3  KNUTSEN O.A.S. SHIPPING A/S, HAUGESUND, NORWAY**

| | | | | | | | | |
|---|---|---|---|---|---|---|---|---|
| | Ellen Knutsen | TK | 1992 | D | 105,193 | 464' 03" | 75' 07" | 38' 09" |
| | Sidsel Knutsen | TK | 1993 | D | 163,463 | 533' 02" | 75' 05" | 48' 07" |
| | Synnove Knutsen | TK | 1992 | D | 105,193 | 464' 03" | 75' 07" | 38' 09" |
| | Torill Knutsen | TK | 1990 | D | 112,275 | 464' 08" | 75' 07" | 38' 09" |
| | Turid Knutsen | TK | 1993 | D | 163,463 | 533' 03" | 75' 07" | 48' 07" |

**IK- 4  KOMA SHIPPING SERVICE LTD., MURMANSK, RUSSIA**

| | | | | | | | | |
|---|---|---|---|---|---|---|---|---|
| | Tuloma | BC | 1984 | D | 29,785 | 622' 00" | 74' 11" | 49' 10" |
| | *(Split '84-'02)* | | | | | | | |

**IK-5  KREY SCHIFFAHRTS GMBH & CO. KG, SIMONSWOLDE, GERMANY**

| | | | | | | | | |
|---|---|---|---|---|---|---|---|---|
| | Nordcap | GC | 2000 | D | 8,760 | 353' 06" | 59' 09" | 33' 02" |
| | Ostkap | GC | 2000 | D | 8,760 | 353' 06" | 59' 09" | 33' 02" |
| | Westkap | GC | 2000 | D | 8,760 | 353' 06" | 59' 09" | 33' 02" |

**IL-1  LAURIN MARITIME (AMERICA), INC., HOUSTON, TEXAS, USA**

| | | | | | | | | |
|---|---|---|---|---|---|---|---|---|
| | Mountain Blossom | TK | 1986 | D | 70,020 | 527' 07" | 74' 11" | 39' 04" |
| | Nordic Blossom | TK | 1981 | D | 152,216 | 505' 03" | 74' 07" | 45' 04" |
| | *(Nordic Sun '81 - '89, Nordic '89 - '94)* | | | | | | | |
| | Sunny Blossom | TK | 1986 | D | 92,326 | 527' 07" | 74' 11" | 39' 05" |

**IL-2  LISCO BALTIC SERVICE, KLAIPEDA, LITHUANIA**

| | | | | | | | | |
|---|---|---|---|---|---|---|---|---|
| | Kapitonas A. Lucka | BC | 1980 | D | 14,550 | 479' 08" | 67' 09" | 42' 04" |
| | *(Ivan Nesterov '80 - '91)* | | | | | | | |
| | Kapitonas Andzejauskas | BC | 1978 | D | 14,550 | 479' 08" | 67' 09" | 42' 04" |
| | *(Kapitan Meshcheryakove '78 - '92, Kapitonas Mesceriakov '92 - '96)* | | | | | | | |
| | Kapitonas Domeika | BC | 1979 | D | 14,550 | 479' 08" | 67' 09" | 42' 04" |
| | *(Kapitan Valvilov '79 - '92, Kapitonas Valvilov '92 - '95)* | | | | | | | |
| | Kapitonas Kaminskas | BC | 1978 | D | 14,550 | 479' 08" | 67' 09" | 42' 04" |
| | *(Kapitan Gudin '78 - '92, Kapitonas Gudin '92 - '95)* | | | | | | | |
| | Kapitonas Marcinkus | BC | 1977 | D | 14,550 | 479' 08" | 67' 09" | 42' 04" |
| | *(Kapitan Ismiakov '77 - '92, Kapitonas Ismiakov 92 - '96)* | | | | | | | |
| | Kapitonas Serafinas | BC | 1980 | D | 14,550 | 479' 08" | 67' 09" | 42' 04" |
| | *(Kapitan Stulov '80 - '91, Kapitonas Stulov '91 - '97)* | | | | | | | |
| | Kapitonas Stulpinas | BC | 1981 | D | 14,550 | 479' 08" | 67' 09" | 42' 04" |
| | *(Yustas Paleckis '81 - '92)* | | | | | | | |

**IM-1  MALAYSIA INTERNATIONAL SHIPPING CORP., SELANGOR, SINGAPORE**

| | | | | | | | | |
|---|---|---|---|---|---|---|---|---|
| | Federal Bergen | BC | 1984 | D | 29,159 | 593' 00" | 76' 00" | 47' 00" |
| | *(High Peak '84 - '90, Federal Bergen '90 - '92, Thunder Bay '92 - '93)* | | | | | | | |

| Fleet #. | Fleet Name / Vessel Name | Type of Vessel | Year Built | Type of Engine | Cargo Cap. or Gross* | Overall Length | Breadth | Depth or Draft* |
|---|---|---|---|---|---|---|---|---|
| **IM-2** | **MAYFLOWER SHIP MANAGEMENT CO., PIRAUES, GREECE** | | | | | | | |
| | Yellowknife | BC | 1984 | D | 29,651 | 622' 00" | 74' 08" | 49' 08" |
| | *(Bihac '84-'93, La Boheme '93-'95, Lindsey M. '98-'99, Med Pride '99-'01)* | | | | | | | |
| | ***FOLLOWING VESSEL CURRENTLY UNDER CHARTER TO FEDNAV LTD.*** | | | | | | | |
| | Yarmouth | BC | 1985 | D | 29,462 | 601' 00" | 76' 00" | 48' 11" |
| | *(Paolo Pittaluga '85 - '91, Federal Oslo '91 - 2000)* | | | | | | | |
| **IM-3** | **METRON SHIPPING & AGENCIES S.A., PIRAEUS, GREECE** | | | | | | | |
| | Pontokratis | BC | 1981 | D | 28,738 | 590' 02" | 75' 11" | 47' 07" |
| | Pontoporos | BC | 1984 | D | 29,155 | 590' 02" | 75' 11" | 47' 07" |
| **IM-4** | **MURMANSK SHIPPING CO., MURMANSK, RUSSIA** | | | | | | | |
| | Admiral Ushakov | BC | 1979 | D | 19,885 | 531' 07" | 75' 01" | 44' 05" |
| | Aleksandr Nevskiy | BC | 1978 | D | 19,590 | 532' 02" | 75' 02" | 44' 05" |
| | Ivan Bogun | BC | 1981 | D | 19,885 | 531' 10" | 75' 02" | 44' 05" |
| | Ivan Susanin | BC | 1981 | D | 19,885 | 531' 10" | 75' 02" | 44' 05" |
| | Kapitan Chukhchin | BC | 1981 | D | 19,240 | 531' 10" | 75' 02" | 44' 05" |
| | Mikhail Kutuzov | BC | 1979 | D | 19,590 | 531' 10" | 75' 01" | 44' 05" |
| | Mikhail Strekalovskiy | BC | 1981 | D | 19,252 | 531' 10" | 75' 02" | 44' 05" |
| | Pavel Vavilov | BC | 1981 | D | 19,252 | 531' 10" | 75' 02" | 44' 05" |
| **IN1** | **NAVARONE S.A. MARINE ENTERPRISES, LIMASSOL, CYPRUS** | | | | | | | |
| | ***FOLLOWING VESSEL UNDER CHARTER TO CANADIAN FOREST NAVIGATION LTD.*** | | | | | | | |
| | Pintail | BC | 1983 | D | 28,035 | 647' 08" | 75' 10" | 46' 11" |
| | *(Punica '83-'95)* | | | | | | | |
| **IN-2** | **NAVIGATION MARITIME BULGARE LTD., VARNA, BULGARIA** | | | | | | | |
| | Bogdan | BC | 1997 | D | 14,011 | 466' 02" | 72' 08" | 36' 04" |
| | Kamenitza | BC | 1980 | D | 24,150 | 605' 08" | 75' 00" | 46' 05" |
| | Kapitan Georgi Georgiev | BC | 1980 | D | 24,150 | 605' 08" | 75' 00" | 46' 05" |
| | Kom | BC | 1997 | D | 13,971 | 466' 02" | 72' 10" | 36' 05" |
| | Koznitsa | BC | 1984 | D | 24,100 | 605' 08" | 75' 02" | 46' 07" |
| | Milin Kamak | BC | 1979 | D | 25,857 | 607' 07" | 75' 02" | 46' 07" |
| | Okoltchitza | BC | 1982 | D | 24,148 | 605' 08" | 75' 05" | 46' 06" |
| | Perelik | BC | 1998 | D | 13,887 | 466' 02" | 72' 10" | 36' 05" |
| | Persenk | BC | 1998 | D | 13,900 | 466' 02" | 72' 08" | 36' 04" |
| | Shipka | BC | 1978 | D | 24,385 | 607' 07" | 75' 02" | 46' 07" |
| | ***FOLLOWING VESSEL UNDER CHARTER TO CANADIAN FOREST NAVIGATION LTD.*** | | | | | | | |
| | Malyovitza | BC | 1983 | D | 24,456 | 605' 00" | 75' 05" | 46' 06" |
| **IN-3** | **NB MARITIME MANAGEMENT (CYPRUS) LTD., LIMASSOL, CYPRUS** | | | | | | | |
| | Kapitan Vakula | BC | 1982 | D | 19,240 | 531' 10" | 75' 00" | 44' 00" |
| | Kapitan Vodenko | BC | 1982 | D | 19,240 | 531' 10" | 75' 00" | 44' 00" |
| **IN-4** | **NISSEN KAIUN K.K., HAKATA, JAPAN** | | | | | | | |
| | Rubin Eagle | BC | 1995 | D | 18,315 | 447' 10" | 74' 10" | 40' 00" |
| | Rubin Halcyon | BC | 1997 | D | 18,315 | 486' 01" | 74' 10" | 40' 00" |
| | Rubin Stork | BC | 1996 | D | 18,315 | 446' 00" | 74' 10" | 40' 00" |
| **IN-5** | **NORTHERN SHIPPING CO., ARKHANGELSK, RUSSIA** | | | | | | | |
| | Fedor Varaksin | BC | 1977 | D | 14,200 | 498' 00" | 68' 11" | 38' 01" |
| | Kapitan Glazachev | BC | 1976 | D | 14,200 | 498' 00" | 68' 11" | 38' 01" |
| | Petr Strelkov | BC | 1977 | D | 14,200 | 498' 00" | 68' 11" | 38' 01" |
| | Vladimir Timofeev | BC | 1973 | D | 13,995 | 493' 01" | 69' 03" | 38' 01" |
| **IN-6** | **NOVOROSSIYSK SHIPPING CO. (NOVOSHIP), NOVOROSSIYSK, RUSSIA** | | | | | | | |
| | Alioth | TK | 1999 | D | 146,870 | 489' 10" | 77' 11" | 41' 06" |
| | Almak | TK | 1999 | D | 146,870 | 489' 10" | 77' 11" | 41' 06" |
| | Altair | TK | 2000 | D | 146,870 | 489' 10" | 77' 11" | 41' 06" |
| | Arcturus | TK | 2000 | D | 146,870 | 489' 10" | 77' 11" | 41' 06" |
| | Boris Livanov | BC | 1986 | D | 23,920 | 605' 09" | 75' 00" | 46' 05" |

| Fleet #. | Fleet Name / Vessel Name | Type of Vessel | Year Built | Type of Engine | Cargo Cap. or Gross* | Overall Length | Breadth | Depth or Draft* |
|---|---|---|---|---|---|---|---|---|
| | Khirurg Vishnevskiy | TK | 1988 | D | 126,377 | 497' 01" | 73' 07" | 39' 10" |
| | Leonid Utesov | TK | 1989 | D | 125,799 | 497' 01" | 73' 07" | 39' 10" |
| | Sergey Lemeshev | BC | 1983 | D | 24,110 | 605' 08" | 74' 10" | 46' 05" |
| | Vladimir Vysotskiy | TK | 1988 | D | 128,315 | 497' 01" | 73' 07" | 39' 10" |
| **IO-1** | **OCEANBULK MARITIME S.A., ATHENS, GREECE** | | | | | | | |
| | Lykes Energizer | RR | 1992 | D | 17,510 | 569' 03" | 75' 07" | 45' 01" |
| | *(Kovrov '92-'97, Elan Vital '97-'97, Thorsriver '97-'00)* | | | | | | | |
| | Lykes Inspirer | GC | 1990 | D | 17,565 | 569' 03" | 75' 11" | 45' 01" |
| | *(Krasnodon '00-'96, Elena K. '96-'98, Res Cogitans '98-'99, Thorslake '99-'00)* | | | | | | | |
| | Lykes Raider | GC | 1990 | D | 17,420 | 569' 02" | 75' 04" | 44.09" |
| | *(Kislovodsk '90-'96, Barbara L. '96-'97, Bremer Voyager '97-'98, Nordana Successor '98-'99, Seaboard Venezuela '99-'00, Global Brasil '00-'01)* | | | | | | | |
| | Lykes Runner | RR | 1991 | D | 17,420 | 569' 02" | 75' 04" | 44.09" |
| | *(Krasnograd '91-'92, Beloostrov '92-'98, Nordana Kitale '98-'98, Nordana Kigoma '98-'99, Nordana Surveyor '99-'01)* | | | | | | | |
| | Lykes Winner | RR | 1990 | D | 17,565 | 569' 02" | 75' 09" | 45' 01" |
| | *(Evgeniy Mravinskiy '90-'96, Alioth Star '96-'97, Global Hawk '97-'98, Nordana Kampala '98-'99, Cobra '99-'99, Thorshope '99-'00)* | | | | | | | |
| | Strange Attractor | BC | 1978 | D | 28,873 | 593' 02" | 76' 00" | 47' 07" |
| | *(Launched as Graiglwyd. Lantau Trader '79-'95)* | | | | | | | |
| **IO-2** | **OLYMPIC SHIPPING AND MANAGEMENT S.A., ATHENS, GREECE** | | | | | | | |
| | Calliroe Patronicola | BC | 1985 | D | 29,608 | 599' 09" | 75' 11" | 48' 07" |
| | Olympic Melody | BC | 1984 | D | 29,640 | 599' 09" | 75' 11" | 48' 07" |
| | Olympic Mentor | BC | 1984 | D | 29,693 | 599' 09" | 75' 11" | 48' 07" |
| | *(Calliroe Patronicola '84-'84, Patricia-R. '84-'88)* | | | | | | | |
| | Olympic Merit | BC | 1985 | D | 29,611 | 599' 09" | 75' 11" | 48' 07" |
| | Olympic Miracle | BC | 1984 | D | 29,670 | 599' 09" | 75' 11" | 48' 07" |
| **IO-3** | **ORION SCHIFFAHRTS-GESELLSCHAFT REITH & CO., HAMBURG, GERMANY** | | | | | | | |
| | Concordia | GC | 1985 | D | 8,881 | 378' 00" | 61' 01" | 32' 02" |
| | Crio | BC | 1984 | D | 19,483 | 485' 07" | 75' 09" | 41' 08" |
| | Fortuna | GC | 1984 | D | 8,875 | 378' 00" | 61' 01" | 32' 02" |
| | Gotia | GC | 1985 | D | 12,349 | 399' 07" | 65' 07" | 36' 01" |
| | Ida | BC | 1995 | D | 18,172 | 486' 01" | 74' 10" | 40' 00" |
| | Lita | BC | 1995 | D | 18,173 | 486' 01" | 74' 10" | 40' 00" |
| | Meta | BC | 1987 | D | 18,612 | 477' 04" | 75' 11" | 40' 08" |
| | Olga | BC | 1996 | D | 18,319 | 486' 01" | 74' 10" | 40' 00" |
| | Patria | GC | 1985 | D | 8,880 | 377' 11" | 61' 01" | 32' 02" |
| **IP-1** | **PACIFIC CARRIERS LTD., SINGAPORE, SINGAPORE** | | | | | | | |
| | Alam Sejahtera | BC | 1985 | D | 29,692 | 599' 09" | 75' 10" | 48' 07" |
| | *(Olympic Dignity '85-'92)* | | | | | | | |
| | Alam Sempurna | BC | 1984 | D | 28,094 | 584' 08" | 75' 11" | 48' 05" |
| | Alam Senang | BC | 1984 | D | 28,098 | 584' 08" | 75' 11" | 48' 05" |
| | *(Goldean Alliance '84-'88, Atlantic '88-'93)* | | | | | | | |
| | Ikan Selar | BC | 1978 | D | 21,652 | 539' 02" | 75' 02" | 44' 06" |
| | Ikan Sepat | BC | 1984 | D | 28,503 | 590' 03" | 75' 04" | 47' 07" |
| | *(Trident Venture '84-'90)* | | | | | | | |
| **IP-2** | **PAN OCEAN SHIPPING CO. LTD., SEOUL, SOUTH KOREA** | | | | | | | |
| | Pan Hope | BC | 1976 | D | 22,646 | 593' 00" | 75' 02" | 44' 07" |
| | Pan Voyager | BC | 1985 | D | 29,432 | 589' 11" | 75' 09" | 47' 07" |
| **IP-3** | **POLCLIP (LUXEMBOURG) S.A., LUXEMBOURG, LUXEMBOURG** | | | | | | | |
| | Clipper Eagle | BC | 1994 | D | 16,900 | 490' 04" | 76' 00" | 39' 08" |
| | Clipper Falcon | BC | 1994 | D | 16,900 | 490' 04" | 76' 00" | 39' 08" |
| **IP-4** | **POLISH STEAMSHIP CO., SZCZECIN, POLAND** | | | | | | | |
| | Irma | BC | 2000 | D | 34,948 | 655' 10" | 77' 05" | 50' 02" |

| Fleet #. | Fleet Name<br>Vessel Name | Type of<br>Vessel | Year<br>Built | Type of<br>Engine | Cargo Cap.<br>or Gross* | Overall<br>Length | Breadth | Depth or<br>Draft* |
|---|---|---|---|---|---|---|---|---|
| | Iryda | BC | 1999 | D | 34,946 | 655' 10" | 77' 07" | 50' 02" |
| | Isa | BC | 1999 | D | 34,939 | 655' 10" | 77' 07" | 50' 02" |
| | Isadora | BC | 1999 | D | 34,948 | 655' 10" | 77' 05" | 50' 02" |
| | Isolda | BC | 1999 | D | 34,949 | 655' 10" | 77' 07" | 50' 02" |
| | Kopalnia Halemba | BC | 1990 | D | 11,715 | 471' 01" | 63' 08" | 36' 05" |
| | Kopalnia Borynia | BC | 1989 | D | 11.898 | 471' 07" | 63' 06" | 36' 04" |
| | Nogat | BC | 1999 | D | 11,542 | 498' 01" | 75' 04" | 40' 01" |
| | Odra | BC | 1992 | D | 13,790 | 471' 05" | 68' 08" | 37' 02" |
| | (Odranes '92-'99) | | | | | | | |
| | Orla | BC | 1999 | D | 17,064 | 490' 02" | 76' 00" | 39' 08" |
| | Pilica | BC | 1999 | D | 17,064 | 490' 02" | 76' 00" | 39' 08" |
| | Pomorze Zachodnie | BC | 1985 | D | 26,696 | 591' 04" | 75' 11" | 45' 08" |
| | (Launched as Ziemia Tarnowska) | | | | | | | |
| | Rega | BC | 1995 | D | 16,880 | 490' 03" | 76' 00" | 39' 08" |
| | (Fossnes '95-'02) | | | | | | | |
| | Warta | BC | 1992 | D | 13,790 | 471' 05" | 68' 08" | 37' 02" |
| | (Wartanes '92-'99) | | | | | | | |
| | Wisla | BC | 1992 | D | 13,770 | 471' 05" | 68' 08" | 37' 02" |
| | (Wislanes '92-'99) | | | | | | | |
| | Ziemia Chelminska | BC | 1984 | D | 26,700 | 591' 04" | 75' 11" | 45' 08" |
| | Ziemia Gnieznienska | BC | 1985 | D | 26,696 | 591' 04" | 75' 11" | 45' 08" |
| | Ziemia Suwalska | BC | 1984 | D | 26,706 | 591' 04" | 75' 11" | 45' 08" |
| | Ziemia Tarnowska | BC | 1985 | D | 26,700 | 591' 04" | 75' 11" | 45' 08" |
| | (Launched as Pomorze Zachodnie) | | | | | | | |
| | Ziemia Zamojska | BC | 1984 | D | 26,600 | 591' 04" | 75' 11" | 45' 08" |
| **IP-5** | **PRECIOUS SHIPPING LINES, BANGKOK, THAILAND** | | | | | | | |
| | Chada Naree | BC | 1981 | D | 18,668 | 479' 03" | 75' 01" | 41' 04" |
| | Wana Naree | BC | 1980 | D | 26,977 | 566' 00" | 75' 11" | 48' 05" |
| **IP-6** | **PRIMAL SHIPMANAGEMENT, INC., ATHENS, GREECE** | | | | | | | |
| | Arizona Dream | BC | 1980 | D | 27,311 | 627' 07" | 75' 03 | 44' 00" |
| | (El General '83-'83, Protector '83-'88, Loretta V '88-'91, G. Dost '91-'95, Mina Cebi '95-'01) | | | | | | | |
| **IP-7** | **PRISCO (UK) LTD., LONDON, ENGLAND, UNITED KINGDOM** | | | | | | | |
| | Jakov Sverdlov | TK | 1989 | D | 128,956 | 496' 01" | 73' 05" | 39' 10" |
| | Kapitan Korotaev | TK | 1988 | D | 128,956 | 496' 06" | 73' 08" | 40' 00" |
| | Kapitan Rudnev | TK | 1988 | D | 128,956 | 496' 01" | 73' 05" | 41' 01" |
| **IR-1** | **REEDEREI HANS-PETER ECKHOFF GMBH CO. HG, HOLLENSTEDT, GERMANY** | | | | | | | |
| | Kamilla | GC | 1985 | D | 2,785 | 322' 06" | 44' 07" | 23' 00" |
| | Skagen | GC | 1999 | D | 3,490 | 283' 04" | 41' 09" | 23' 02" |
| | (Launched as Ile de France '99) | | | | | | | |
| **IR-2** | **RIGEL SCHIFFAHRTS GMBH, BREMEN, GERMANY** | | | | | | | |
| | Alsterstern | TK | 1994 | D | 125,327 | 529' 05" | 75' 05" | 38' 05" |
| | Havelstern | TK | 1994 | D | 126,264 | 529' 05" | 75' 05" | 38' 05" |
| | Ledastern | TK | 1993 | D | 76,737 | 405' 11" | 58' 01" | 34' 09" |
| | Rheinstern | TK | 1993 | D | 127,937 | 529' 05" | 75' 05" | 38' 05" |
| | Travestern | TK | 1993 | D | 123,346 | 529' 05" | 75' 05" | 38' 05" |
| **IS-1** | **SCANDIA SHIPPING HELLAS, INC., ATHENS, GREECE** | | | | | | | |
| | Armonikos | BC | 1979 | D | 30,689 | 674' 03" | 75' 08" | 47' 07" |
| | (Docegult '79-'98) | | | | | | | |
| | Taxideftis | BC | 1984 | D | 28,503 | 590' 03" | 75' 04" | 47' 07" |
| | (Trident Mariner '84-'01) | | | | | | | |
| **IS-2** | **SCANSCOT SHIPPING SERVICES (DEUTSCHLAND) GMBH, HAMBURG, GERMANY** | | | | | | | |
| | Scan Arctic | RR | 1998 | D | 7,331 | 415' 01" | 66' 07" | 33' 02" |
| | Scan Atlantic | RR | 1999 | D | 7,100 | 416' 02" | 67' 07" | 37' 09" |
| | Scan Bothnia | RR | 1998 | D | 7,493 | 415' 01" | 65' 07" | 37' 09" |

**Mecta Sea at Iroquois on the St. Lawrence Seaway, July 24, 2002.** *(Peter Jobe)*

| Fleet #. | Fleet Name / Vessel Name | Type of Vessel | Year Built | Type of Engine | Cargo Cap. or Gross* | Overall Length | Breadth | Depth or Draft* |
|---|---|---|---|---|---|---|---|---|
| | Scan Finlandia | RR | 2000 | D | 7,172 | 415' 01" | 65' 07" | 37' 09" |
| | Scan Germania | RR | 2000 | D | 7,172 | 415' 01" | 65' 07" | 37' 09" |
| | Scan Hansa | RR | 1999 | D | 7,228 | 416' 02" | 67' 07" | 37' 09" |
| | Scan Oceanic | RR | 1997 | D | 5,085 | 331' 00" | 61' 00" | 31' 10" |
| | Scan Partner | RR | 1997 | D | 5,085 | 331' 00" | 61' 00" | 31' 10" |
| | Scan Pacific | RR | 1997 | D | 5,085 | 331' 00" | 61' 00" | 31' 10" |
| | Scan Polaris | RR | 1996 | D | 5,100 | 331' 00" | 61' 00" | 31' 10" |

**IS- 3    SEAARLAND SHIPPING MANAGEMENT, VILLACH, AUSTRIA**
  *THE FOLLWING VESSEL UNDER CHARTER TO CANADIAN FOREST NAVIGATION LTD.*

| | Peonia | BC` | 1983 | D | 27,995 | 647' 06" | 75' 07" | 46' 09" |
|---|---|---|---|---|---|---|---|---|

**IS-4    SEASTAR NAVIGATION CO. LTD., ATHENS, GREECE**

| | Polydefkis | BC | 1976 | D | 30,244 | 621' 06" | 75' 00" | 47' 11" |
|---|---|---|---|---|---|---|---|---|

  *(Peter '76-'81, Philippe L.D. '81-'85, La Richardais '85-'93)*
  *THE FOLLWING VESSELS UNDER CHARTER TO CANADIAN FOREST NAVIGATION LTD.*

| | Goldeneye | BC | 1986 | D | 26,706 | 591' 06" | 75' 10" | 48' 07" |
|---|---|---|---|---|---|---|---|---|

  *(Sun Ocean '86-'93, Luna Verde '93-'00)*

| | Pytheas | BC | 1981 | D | 29,514 | 590' 01" | 76' 00" | 47' 07" |
|---|---|---|---|---|---|---|---|---|

  *(Yannis C. '81-'86, Pindos '86-'87, Ikan Selayang '97-'98, Kakawi '98-'00)*

| | Toro | BC | 1983 | D | 28,126 | 584' 06" | 75' 07" | 46' 09" |
|---|---|---|---|---|---|---|---|---|

  *(La Liberte '83-'87, Libert '87-'88, Astart '88-'93, Ulloa '93-'00)*

**IS-5    SHIH WEI NAVIGATION CO. LTD., TAIPEI, TAIWAN**

| | Royal Pescadores | BC | 1997 | D | 18,369 | 486' 01" | 74' 10" | 40' 00" |
|---|---|---|---|---|---|---|---|---|

**IS-6    (THE) SHIPPING CORP. OF INDIA LTD., MUMBAI, INDIA**

| | Lok Maheshwari | BC | 1986 | D | 26,728 | 605' 03" | 75' 03" | 47' 03" |
|---|---|---|---|---|---|---|---|---|
| | Lok Prakash | BC | 1989 | D | 26,790 | 606' 11" | 75' 04" | 47' 03" |
| | Lok Pratap | BC | 1993 | D | 26,718 | 605' 09" | 75' 04" | 47' 04" |
| | Lok Pratima | BC | 1989 | D | 26,925 | 565' 00" | 74' 11" | 48' 03" |
| | Lok Prem | BC | 1990 | D | 26,714 | 605' 08" | 75' 04" | 47' 03" |
| | Lok Rajeshwari | BC | 1988 | D | 26,639 | 605' 08" | 75' 04" | 47' 03" |

**IS-7    SHUNZAN KAIUN CO. LTD., EHIME, JAPAN**

| | Spring Laker | BC | 1996 | D | 30,855 | 606' 09" | 77' 04" | 48' 08" |
|---|---|---|---|---|---|---|---|---|

**IS-8    SIDEMAR SERVIZI ACCESSORI S.P.A., GENOA, ITALY**

| | Cygnus | BC | 1987 | D | 28,500 | 610' 03" | 75' 11" | 46' 11" |
|---|---|---|---|---|---|---|---|---|
| | Gemini | BC | 1986 | D | 28,500 | 610' 03" | 75' 11" | 46' 11" |
| | Sagittarius | BC | 1987 | D | 29,365 | 610' 03" | 75' 10" | 46' 11" |
| | Sideracrux | GC | 1983 | D | 7,988 | 328' 09" | 57' 10" | 29' 07" |
| | Siderpollux | GC | 1982 | D | 8,010 | 328' 09" | 57' 10" | 29' 07" |

**IS-9    SINGA STAR PTE. LTD., SINGAPORE, SINGAPORE**

| | Changi Hope | BC | 2000 | D | 18,320 | 486' 01" | 74' 10" | 40' 00" |
|---|---|---|---|---|---|---|---|---|

**IS-10    SIOMAR ENTERPRISES LTD., PIRAEUS, GREECE**

| | Island Gem | BC | 1984 | D | 28,005 | 584' 08" | 76' 02" | 48' 05" |
|---|---|---|---|---|---|---|---|---|
| | Island Skipper | BC | 1984 | D | 28,031 | 584' 08" | 76' 02" | 48' 05" |

**IS-11    SPAR SHIPPING A.S., BERGEN, NORWAY**
  *FOLLOWING VESSELS UNDER CHARTER TO FEDNAV LTD.*

| | Spar Garnet | BC | 1984 | D | 30,686 | 589' 11" | 75' 10" | 50' 11" |
|---|---|---|---|---|---|---|---|---|

  *(Mary Anne '84 - '93, Federal Vigra '93 - '97)*

| | Spar Jade | BC | 1984 | D | 30,674 | 589' 11" | 75' 10" | 50' 11" |
|---|---|---|---|---|---|---|---|---|

  *(Fiona Mary '84 - '93, Federal Aalesund '93 - '97)*

| | Spar Opal | BC | 1984 | D | 28,214 | 585' 00" | 75' 10" | 48' 05" |
|---|---|---|---|---|---|---|---|---|

  *(Lake Shidaka '84 - '91, Consensus Atlantic '91 - '92, Federal Matane '92 - '97, Matane '97 - '97)*

| | Spar Ruby | BC | 1985 | D | 28,259 | 584' 08" | 75' 11" | 48' 05" |
|---|---|---|---|---|---|---|---|---|

  *(Astral Neptune '85-'92, Liberty Sky '92-'98, Manila Bellona '98-'98, Solveig '98-'00)*

| Fleet #.<br>Fleet Name<br>Vessel Name | Type of<br>Vessel | Year<br>Built | Type of<br>Engine | Cargo Cap.<br>or Gross* | Overall<br>Length | Breadth | Depth or<br>Draft* |
|---|---|---|---|---|---|---|---|
| **IS-12**   **SPLIETHOFF'S BEVRACHTINGSKANTOOR LTD., AMSTERDAM, NETHERLANDS** | | | | | | | |
| Aalsmeergracht | GC | 1992 | D | 12,150 | 425' 10" | 62' 05" | 38' 03" |
| Achtergracht | GC | 1990 | D | 12,150 | 425' 10" | 62' 05" | 38' 03" |
| Admiralengracht | GC | 1990 | D | 12,150 | 425' 10" | 62' 05" | 38' 03" |
| Alblasgracht | GC | 1991 | D | 12,150 | 425' 10" | 62' 05" | 38' 03" |
| Alexandergracht | GC | 1991 | D | 12,150 | 425' 10" | 62' 05" | 38' 03" |
| Amstelgracht | GC | 1990 | D | 12,150 | 425' 10" | 62' 05" | 38' 03" |
| Anjeliersgracht | GC | 1990 | D | 12,150 | 425' 10" | 62' 05" | 38' 03" |
| Ankergracht | GC | 1991 | D | 12,150 | 425' 10" | 62' 05" | 38' 03" |
| Apollogracht | GC | 1991 | D | 12,150 | 425' 10" | 62' 05" | 38' 03" |
| Archangelgracht | GC | 1990 | D | 12,150 | 425' 10" | 62' 05" | 38' 03" |
| Artisgracht | GC | 1990 | D | 12,150 | 425' 10" | 62' 05" | 38' 03" |
| Atlasgracht | GC | 1991 | D | 12,150 | 425' 10" | 62' 05" | 38' 03" |
| Edamgracht | GC | 1995 | D | 12,754 | 447' 04" | 62' 05" | 38' 03" |
| Edisongracht | GC | 1994 | D | 12,760 | 447' 04" | 62' 05" | 38' 03" |
| Eemsgracht | GC | 1995 | D | 12,754 | 447' 04" | 62' 05" | 38' 03" |
| Egelantiersgracht | GC | 1994 | D | 12,760 | 447' 10" | 62' 05" | 38' 03" |
| Egmondgracht | GC | 1994 | D | 12,760 | 447' 04" | 62' 05" | 38' 03" |
| Elandsgracht | GC | 1995 | D | 12,754 | 447' 04" | 62' 05" | 38' 03" |
| Emmagracht | GC | 1995 | D | 12,760 | 447' 04" | 62' 05" | 38' 03" |
| Erasmusgracht | GC | 1994 | D | 13,000 | 447' 04" | 62' 05" | 38' 03" |
| Eurogracht | GC | 1995 | D | 12,754 | 447' 04" | 62' 05" | 38' 03" |
| Happy Ranger | HL | 1998 | D | 15,065 | 452' 09" | 74' 10" | 31' 03" |
| Happy River | HL | 1998 | D | 15,700 | 452' 09" | 74' 10" | 31' 03" |
| Happy Rover | HL | 1997 | D | 15,700 | 452' 09" | 74' 10" | 31' 03" |
| Kaapgracht | GC | 1984 | D | 8,038 | 348' 09" | 52' 11" | 34' 05" |
| Kielgracht | GC | 1984 | D | 5,022 | 348' 09" | 52' 11" | 34' 05" |
| Lauriergracht | GC | 1988 | D | 9,656 | 371' 02" | 63' 07" | 37' 01" |
| Leliegracht | GC | 1987 | D | 9,601 | 371' 02" | 63' 01" | 37' 01" |
| Lemmergracht | GC | 1988 | D | 9,682 | 371' 02" | 63' 01" | 37' 00" |
| Levantgracht | GC | 1988 | D | 9,595 | 371' 03" | 63' 01" | 37' 00" |
| Lijnbaansgracht | GC | 1988 | D | 9,606 | 371' 02" | 63' 07" | 37' 01" |
| Lootsgracht | GC | 1989 | D | 9,682 | 371' 03" | 63' 01" | 37' 00" |
| Paleisgracht | GC | 1985 | D | 9,498 | 370' 09" | 62' 05" | 36' 05" |
| Palmgracht | GC | 1985 | D | 9,536 | 370' 09" | 62' 05" | 36' 05" |
| Parkgracht | GC | 1986 | D | 9,656 | 371' 02" | 62' 03" | 37' 01" |
| Pauwgracht | GC | 1986 | D | 9,340 | 370' 09" | 62' 05" | 36' 05" |
| Pietersgracht | GC | 1986 | D | 9,340 | 370' 09" | 62' 05" | 37' 01" |
| Pijlgracht | GC | 1985 | D | 9,650 | 370' 09" | 62' 05" | 36' 05" |
| Poolgracht | GC | 1986 | D | 9,672 | 371' 02" | 62' 03" | 37' 01" |
| Prinsengracht | GC | 1985 | D | 9,498 | 370' 09" | 62' 05" | 36' 05" |
| Scheldegracht | GC | 2000 | D | 21,250 | 564'03" | 83'03" | 47'09" |
| Schippersgracht | GC | 2000 | D | 21,402 | 551'05" | 83'03" | 47'09" |
| Singelgracht | GC | 2000 | D | 21,402 | 551'05" | 83'03" | 47'09" |
| Slotergracht | GC | 2000 | D | 21,000 | 551'05" | 83'03" | 47'09" |
| Sluisgracht | GC | 2001 | D | 21,250 | 564'03" | 83'03" | 47'09" |
| Snoekgracht | GC | 2000 | D | 21,400 | 551'05" | 83'03" | 47'09" |
| Spaarnegracht | GC | 2000 | D | 18,900 | 551'05" | 83'03" | 47'09" |
| Spiegelgracht | GC | 2000 | D | 21,349 | 551'05" | 83'03" | 47'09" |
| Spuigracht | GC | 2001 | D | 21,349 | 564'03" | 83'03" | 47'09" |
| **IS-13**   **STOLT PARCEL TANKERS, INC., GREENWICH, CONNECTICUT, USA** | | | | | | | |
| Stolt Accord | TK | 1982 | D | 87,650 | 433' 01" | 66' 04" | 37' 09" |
| Stolt Alliance<br>  *(Shoun Trader '85-'89)* | TK | 1985 | D | 88,147 | 404' 06" | 65' 08" | 36' 09" |
| Stolt Aspiration | TK | 1987 | D | 90,305 | 422' 11" | 66' 04" | 36' 01" |
| Stolt Kent | TK | 1998 | D | 122,025 | 487' 00" | 75'06" | 42' 06" |
| Stolt Taurus | TK | 1985 | D | 89,248 | 404' 06" | 67' 04" | 36' 09" |

| Fleet #. | Fleet Name / Vessel Name | Type of Vessel | Year Built | Type of Engine | Cargo Cap. or Gross* | Overall Length | Breadth | Depth or Draft* |
|---|---|---|---|---|---|---|---|---|
| | Stolt Titan | TK | 1985 | D | 89,248 | 404' 06" | 67' 04" | 36' 09" |
| | *(Shoun Titan '85-'88)* | | | | | | | |
| **IS-14** | **SURRENDRA OVERSEAS LTD., CALCUTTA, INDIA** | | | | | | | |
| | APJ Anjli | BC | 1982 | D | 27,192 | 577' 05" | 75' 11" | 47' 11" |
| | APJ Sushma | BC | 1983 | D | 27,213 | 577' 05" | 75' 11" | 47' 11" |
| **IT-1** | **TEO SHIPPING CORP., PIRAEUS, GREECE** | | | | | | | |
| | Antalina | BC | 1984 | D | 28,082 | 584' 08" | 75' 11" | 48' 05" |
| | *(Union Pioneer '84-'88, Manila Prosperity- '88-'89, Consensus Sea '89-'92, Wiltrader '92-'94)* | | | | | | | |
| | Erikousa Wave | BC | 1986 | D | 26,858 | 600' 08" | 73' 08" | 46' 08" |
| | Marilis T. | BC | 1984 | D | 28,097 | 584' 08" | 75' 11" | 47' 10" |
| | *(Union Peace '84-'88, Manila Peace- '88-'89, Consensus Sun '89-'92, Wilrider '92-'94)* | | | | | | | |
| | Sevilla Wave | BC | 1986 | D | 26,858 | 600' 08" | 73' 08" | 46' 08" |
| | Vamand Wave | BC | 1985 | D | 28,303 | 580' 08" | 75' 11" | 47' 07" |
| **IT- 2** | **TECHNOMAR SHIPPING INC., ATHENS, GREECE** | | | | | | | |
| | Dimitris Y | BC | 1983 | D | 28,192 | 584' 06" | 75' 08" | 48' 05" |
| | *(Kalliopi II '83-'88, Cineraria '88-'90, Consensus Star '90-'91, Federal Manitou '91-'95, Consensus Manitou '95-'99)* | | | | | | | |
| **IT-3** | **THENAMARIS (SHIPS MANAGEMENT), INC., ATHENS, GREECE** | | | | | | | |
| | Seaguardian II | BC | 1984 | D | 28,251 | 639' 09" | 75' 10" | 46' 11" |
| | *(Sea Master II '84 – '88, Sea Monarch '88 – '97, Sealuck V '97 – '00, Seaharmony II '00 – '01, Seamonarch II '01 – '02)* | | | | | | | |
| | Sealink | BC | 1983 | D | 28,234 | 639' 09" | 75' 10" | 46' 11" |
| | Sealuck | BC | 1976 | D | 29,300 | 594' 01" | 76' 00" | 47' 07" |
| **IT-4** | **THOR CHARTERING (T & C) A/S, SVENDBORG, DENMARK** | | | | | | | |
| | Thor Alice | GC | 1987 | D | 1,218 | 221' 01" | 37' 06" | 18' 02" |
| | Thor Amalie | GC | 1984 | D | 4,145 | 290' 09" | 52' 01" | 27' 03" |
| | Thor Inger | GC | 1988 | D | 1,210 | 221' 02" | 37' 10" | 18' 02" |
| | Thor Kirsten | GC | 1987 | D | 1,720 | 221' 00" | 37' 06" | 18' 02" |
| | Thor Kis | GC | 1984 | D | 4,281 | 290' 08" | 51' 06" | 29' 02" |
| | Thor Marie | GC | 1987 | D | 1,218 | 221' 00" | 37' 06" | 18' 02" |

**Marilis T. docked along the Welland Canal in 2001.** *(Brian Jaeschke)*

| Fleet #. | Fleet Name / Vessel Name | Type of Vessel | Year Built | Type of Engine | Cargo Cap. or Gross* | Overall Length | Breadth | Depth or Draft* |
|---|---|---|---|---|---|---|---|---|
| | Thor Mette | GC | 1986 | D | 1,200 | 221' 00" | 37' 05" | 18' 01" |
| | Thor Simba | GC | 1984 | D | 5,900 | 327' 09" | 58' 06" | 29' 07" |
| | Thor Sofia | GC | 1984 | D | 4,281 | 290' 08" | 51' 06" | 29' 02" |
| **IT- 5** | **TOMASOS BROTHERS INC., PIRAUES, GREECE** | | | | | | | |
| | Alexis | BC | 1984 | D | 27,048 | 599' 07" | 75' 04" | 46' 05" |
| | *Ocean Crony '84-'88, Linda K '89-'91, Bold Champion '91-'91)* | | | | | | | |
| **IT-6** | **TOP GLORY SHIPPING CO., LTD., PANAMA** | | | | | | | |
| | NST Challenge | BC | 1984 | D | 25,166 | 593' 01" | 75' 04" | 35' 01" |
| | *(High Light '84-'90, Scan Trader '90-'95)* | | | | | | | |
| **IT-7** | **TORKEL ALENDAL REDERI AS, KARMSUND, NORWAY** | | | | | | | |
| | Caribbean Trader | TK | 1980 | D | 48,514 | 366' 00" | 54' 02" | 27' 11" |
| | Coral Trader | TK | 1974 | D | 36.878 | 365'10" | 54'02" | 28'10" |
| | Moon Trader | TK | 1969 | D | 33,878 | 324' 10" | 41' 04" | 24' 11" |
| | South Trader | TK | 1974 | D | 41,262 | 339' 02" | 52' 00" | 27' 03" |
| | Spirit Trader | TK | 1975 | D | 18,819 | 317' 08" | 39' 06" | 23' 11" |
| **IT-8** | **TRITON BEREEDERUNGS GMBH & CO. KG, LEER, GERMANY** | | | | | | | |
| | Lebasse | GC | 1996 | D | 3,526 | 290' 08" | 42' 00" | 23' 04" |
| **IT-9** | **TSCHUDI & EITZEN AS, LYSAKER, NORWAY** | | | | | | | |
| | *FOLLOWING VESSEL UNDER CHARTER TO FEDNAV LTD.* | | | | | | | |
| | Federal Asahi {2} | BC | 2000 | D | 36,563 | 656' 02" | 77' 11" | 48' 08" |
| **IU-1** | **UNION MARINE ENTERPRISES S.A. OF PANAMA, PIRAEUS, GREECE** | | | | | | | |
| | Capetan Michalis | BC | 1981 | D | 28,600 | 593' 03" | 75' 11" | 47' 07" |
| | *(Vasiliki '81-'85)* | | | | | | | |
| **IU-2** | **UNIVAN SHIP MANAGEMENT LTD., HONG KONG, PEOPLES REPUBLIC OF CHINA** | | | | | | | |
| | Lady Hamilton {2} | BC | 1983 | D | 34,500 | 730' 01" | 75' 09" | 48' 00" |
| | *(Saskatchewan Pioneer '83 - '95)* | | | | | | | |
| **IV-1** | **V. SHIPS MANAGEMENT, INC., NICOSIA, CYPRUS** | | | | | | | |
| | Tolmi | BC | 1980 | D | 27,000 | 584' 08" | 75' 10" | 48' 05" |
| | *(O Sole Mio '80-'85, Mount Etna '85-'86, Luckyman '86-'02)* | | | | | | | |
| **IV-2** | **VERGOS MARINE MANAGEMENT, PIRAEUS, GREECE** | | | | | | | |
| | Verdon | BC | 1981 | D | 26,350 | 594' 09" | 75' 00" | 47' 01" |
| | Verily | BC | 1982 | D | 26,450 | 594' 09" | 75' 00" | 47' 01" |
| **IV-3** | **VIKEN SHIPPING AS, BERGEN, NORWAY** | | | | | | | |
| | *FOLLOWING VESSELS UNDER CHARTER TO FEDNAV LTD.* | | | | | | | |
| | Daviken | BC | 1987 | D | 34,752 | 729' 00" | 75' 11" | 48' 05" |
| | *(Malinska '87-'97)* | | | | | | | |
| | Goviken | BC | 1987 | D | 34,752 | 729' 00" | 75' 11" | 48' 05" |
| | *(Omisalj '87-'97)* | | | | | | | |
| | Inviken | BC | 1984 | D | 30,052 | 621' 05" | 75' 01" | 47' 11" |
| | *(Bar '86-'97)* | | | | | | | |
| | Sandviken | BC | 1986 | D | 34,685 | 728' 09" | 75' 11" | 48' 05" |
| | *(Petka '86-'00)* | | | | | | | |
| | Utviken | BC | 1985 | D | 30,052 | 621' 05" | 75' 01" | 47' 11" |
| | *(Bijelo Polje '87-'92, C.Blanco '92-'95)* | | | | | | | |
| | Federal Fuji | BC | 1986 | D | 29,536 | 599' 09" | 75' 11" | 48' 07" |
| | Federal Polaris | BC | 1985 | D | 29,536 | 599' 09" | 75' 11" | 48' 07" |
| **IW-1** | **W. BOCKSTIEGEL REEDEREI KG, EMDEN, GERMANY** | | | | | | | |
| | Buccaneer | GC | 2001 | D | 7,612 | 353' 00" | 60' 00" | 33' 00" |
| | *(BBC Italy '99-'01)* | | | | | | | |
| | Malte B. | GC | 1998 | D | 3,440 | 283' 06" | 42' 00" | 23' 04" |
| | Nils B. | GC | 1998 | D | 3,440 | 283' 06" | 42' 00" | 23' 04" |

# MONTROSE, PRINS WILLEM V

**Montrose visits the lakes not long before her accident.** *(Peter J. VanderLinden)*

## Saltie Spotlight

The British freighter **Montrose** was on her second visit of the year to the Great Lakes when she was struck by a barge pushed by the tug **B.H. Becker** in the Detroit River July 30, 1962. The **Montrose** rolled over on her side directly below the Ambassador Bridge until only a small part of her hull remained visible. No lives were lost, and after salvage she lived to sail the world's waterways until 1982.

The Dutch motor vessel **Prins Willem V** wasn't as lucky when she came to grief Oct. 14, 1954. Bound to Europe from Milwaukee with a load of freight, she went to the bottom of Lake Michigan after a collision with an oil barge towed behind the tanker **Sinclair Chicago**. No lives were lost, but the "Willie" quickly sank, thanks to a 20-foot gash in her side. She sits upright in 90 feet of water and is a popular site for divers.

**Prins Willem V on the Great Lakes.** *(Peter J. VanderLinden)*

| Fleet #. Fleet Name Vessel Name | Type of Vessel | Year Built | Type of Engine | Cargo Cap. or Gross* | Overall Length | Breadth | Depth or Draft* |
|---|---|---|---|---|---|---|---|
| **IW-2**   **WAGENBORG SHIPPING B.V., DELFZIJL, NETHERLANDS** | | | | | | | |
| Arion | GC | 1997 | D | 9,100 | 441' 04" | 54' 02" | 32' 02" |
| Dongeborg | GC | 1999 | D | 9,000 | 437' 08" | 52' 02" | 32' 02" |
| Drechtborg | GC | 1998 | D | 9,100 | 441' 04" | 54' 02" | 32' 02" |
| *(Drechtborg '98-'00, MSC Skaw '00-'02))* | | | | | | | |
| Kasteelborg | GC | 1998 | D | 9,025 | 428' 08" | 52' 01" | 33' 06" |
| Keizersborg | GC | 1996 | D | 9,025 | 428' 08" | 52' 01" | 33' 06" |
| Koningsborg | GC | 1999 | D | 9,067 | 428' 08" | 52' 01" | 33' 06" |
| Kwintebank | GC | 2002 | D | 9,900 | 433' 07" | 52' 01" | 31' 04" |
| Maineborg | GC | 2001 | D | 9,100 | 441' 04" | 54' 02" | 32' 02" |
| Merweborg | GC | 1997 | D | 9,400 | 441' 02" | 54' 01" | 32' 01" |
| *Merweborg '97-'00, MSC Bothnia '00-'2)* | | | | | | | |
| Metsaborg | GC | 2002 | D | 9,100 | 441' 04" | 54' 02" | 32' 02" |
| Michiganborg | GC | 1999 | D | 9,200 | 441' 03" | 54' 02" | 32' 02" |
| Missouriborg | GC | 2000 | D | 9,100 | 441' 04" | 54' 02" | 32' 02" |
| Moezelborg | GC | 1999 | D | 9,100 | 441' 04" | 54' 02" | 32' 02" |
| Morraborg | GC | 1999 | D | 8,800 | 441' 05" | 54' 06" | 32' 02" |
| MSC Baltic | GC | 1998 | D | 9,100 | 441' 04" | 54' 02" | 32' 02" |
| *(Munteborg '98-'00)* | | | | | | | |
| MSC Bothnia | GC | 1998 | D | 9,100 | 441' 04" | 54' 02" | 32' 02" |
| *(Maasborg '98-'98, Egbert Wagenborg '98-'02)* | | | | | | | |
| MSC Dardanelles | GC | 1999 | D | 8,865 | 437' 08" | 52' 02" | 32' 02" |
| *(Dintelborg '97-'01)* | | | | | | | |
| MSC Poland | GC | 2000 | D | 9,200 | 441' 03" | 54' 02" | 32' 02" |
| *(Mississippiborg '00-'01)* | | | | | | | |
| MSC Suomi | GC | 1997 | D | 9,100 | 441' 04" | 54' 02" | 32' 02" |
| *(Markborg '97-'02)* | | | | | | | |
| Vaasaborg | GC | 1999 | D | 8,300 | 434' 00" | 52' 01" | 31' 07" |
| Vancouverborg | GC | 2000 | D | 8,300 | 433' 08" | 52' 01" | 31' 07" |
| Vechtborg | GC | 1998 | D | 8,300 | 434' 00" | 52' 01" | 31' 07" |
| Veerseborg | GC | 1998 | D | 8,300 | 433' 09" | 52' 01" | 31' 07" |
| Vermontborg | GC | 2003 | D | 9,600 | 433' 09" | 52' 01" | 31' 07" |
| Victoriaborg | GC | 2001 | D | 9,000 | 437' 08" | 52' 02" | 32' 02" |
| Virginiaborg | GC | 2001 | D | 9,000 | 437' 08" | 52' 02" | 32' 02" |
| Vlieborg | GC | 1999 | D | 8,300 | 434' 00" | 52' 01" | 31' 07" |
| Vlistborg | GC | 1999 | D | 8,300 | 434' 00" | 52' 01" | 31' 07" |
| Volmeborg | GC | 2001 | D | 9,000 | 437' 08" | 52' 02" | 37' 07" |
| Voorneborg | GC | 1999 | D | 8,300 | 434' 00" | 52' 01" | 31' 07" |
| Zeus | GC | 2000 | D | 9,100 | 428' 08" | 52' 01" | 33' 06" |
| **IW-3**   **WEALTH OCEAN SERVICES, HONG KONG, HONG KONG** | | | | | | | |
| *FOLLOWING VESSEL UNDER CHARTER TO FEDNAV LTD.* | | | | | | | |
| Federal Agno | BC | 1985 | D | 29,643 | 599' 09" | 75' 09" | 48' 07" |
| *(Federal Asahi {1} '85 - '89)* | | | | | | | |
| **IY-1**   **YAOKI SHIPPING S.A., JAPAN** | | | | | | | |
| North Challenge | TK | 1998 | D | 85,141 | 406' 11" | 67' 07" | 36' 09" |
| North Defiance | TK | 2001 | D | | 443' 09" | 74' 08" | 41' 00" |
| **IZ-1**   **Z. & G. HALCOUSSIS CO. LTD., PIRAEUS, GREECE** | | | | | | | |
| Akti | BC | 1977 | D | 28,935 | 593' 10" | 76' 00" | 47' 07" |
| Alexandria | BC | 1981 | D | 29,372 | 589' 11" | 76' 00" | 47' 00" |

References for "Know Your Ships" include The St. Lawrence Seaway Authority,
The Lake Carriers' Association, The Institute for Great Lakes Research, Lloyd's Register of Shipping,
Transport Canada, U.S. Army Corps of Engineers, United States Coast Guard, "Seaway Ships 2002,"
"Shipfax," Fairplay, www.boatnerd.com, www.wellandcanal.ca and publications of the Toronto
Marine Historical Society, the Marine Historical Society of Detroit and the World Ship Society.

# Marine Museums

Former Corps of Engineers'
tug Ludington is open to
the public at Kewaunee.
*(Roger LeLievre)*

| Fleet #. | Fleet Name / Vessel Name | Type of Vessel | Year Built | Type of Engine | Cargo Cap. or Gross* | Overall Length | Breadth | Depth or Draft* |
|---|---|---|---|---|---|---|---|---|

**Information can change without notice. Call ahead to verify location and hours.**

**MU-1 — BERNIER MARITIME MUSEUM, L' ISLET-SUR-MER, QC – (418) 247-5001**

| | | | | | | | | |
|---|---|---|---|---|---|---|---|---|
| | Daniel McAllister | TB | 1907 | D | 268* | 115' 00" | 23' 02" | 12' 00" |

*(Helena '07 - '57, Helen M. B. '57 - '66) (Former McAllister Towing & Salvage, Inc. vessel)*

| | | | | | | | | |
|---|---|---|---|---|---|---|---|---|
| | Detector | SV | 1915 | R | 584* | 147' 00" | 35' 00" | 10' 00"* |

*(Former Canadian Coast Guard survey vessel)*

| | | | | | | | | |
|---|---|---|---|---|---|---|---|---|
| | Ernest Lapointe | IB | 1941 | R | 1,179* | 185' 00" | 36' 00" | 22' 06" |

*(Former Canadian Coast Guard icebreaker)*

| | | | | | | | | |
|---|---|---|---|---|---|---|---|---|
| | Jean Yvan | GC | 1958 | D | 200 | 84' 00" | 24' 00" | 8' 00" |

*(Former Louis Gascon "Goelette" type cargo vessel)*

**MU-2 — BUFFALO AND ERIE COUNTY NAVAL AND MILITARY PARK, BUFFALO, NY – (716) 847-1773**

| | | | | | | | | |
|---|---|---|---|---|---|---|---|---|
| | Croaker [IXSS-246] | | 1944 | D | 1,526* | 311' 07" | 27' 02" | 33' 09" |

*(Former U. S. Navy "Emergency Program (Gato)" class submarine [SS / SSK / AGSS / IXSS-246])*

| | | | | | | | | |
|---|---|---|---|---|---|---|---|---|
| | Little Rock [CLG-4] | | 1945 | T | 10,670* | 610' 01" | 66' 04" | 25' 00"* |

*(Former U. S. Navy "Cleveland / Little Rock" class guided missile cruiser [CL-92 / CLG-4])*

| | | | | | | | | |
|---|---|---|---|---|---|---|---|---|
| | PTF-17 [PTF-17] | | 1968 | D | 69* | 80' 04" | 24' 07" | 6' 10"* |

*(Former U. S. Navy "Trumpy" class fast patrol/torpedo boat)*

| | | | | | | | | |
|---|---|---|---|---|---|---|---|---|
| | The Sullivans [DD-537] | | 1943 | T | 2,500* | 376' 06" | 39' 08" | 22' 08" |

*(Launched as USS Putnam [DD-537]) (Former U. S. Navy "Fletcher" class destroyer)*

**MU-3 — CANAL PARK MARINE MUSEUM, DULUTH, MN – (218) 727-2497**

| | | | | | | | | |
|---|---|---|---|---|---|---|---|---|
| | Bayfield | TB | 1953 | D | 23* | 45' 00" | 13' 00" | 7' 00"* |

*(Former U. S. Army Corps of Engineers tug is an on-shore exhibit not open for tours)*

**MU-4 — CAPTAIN NORMAN'S RIVERBOAT INN LTD., TORONTO, ON – (416) 363-6062**

| | | | | | | | | |
|---|---|---|---|---|---|---|---|---|
| | Jadran | GC | 1957 | D | 2,520* | 295' 06" | 42' 08" | 24' 08" |

*(Former Jadranska Plovidba vessel last operated in 1975)*

**MU-5 — CITY OF KEWAUNEE, KEWAUNEE, WI – (920) 388-5000**

| | | | | | | | | |
|---|---|---|---|---|---|---|---|---|
| | Ludington | TB | 1943 | D | 249* | 115' 00" | 26' 00" | 13' 08" |

*(Major Wilbur F. Browder [LT-4] '43 - '47) (Former U. S. Army Corps of Engineers vessel)*

**MU-6 — COLUMBIA YACHT CLUB, CHICAGO, IL – (312) 938-3625**

| | | | | | | | | |
|---|---|---|---|---|---|---|---|---|
| | Abegweit {1} | CF | 1947 | D | 6,694* | 372' 06" | 61' 00" | 24' 09" |

*(Abegweit {1} '47 - '81, Abby '81 - '97) (Former CN Marine, Inc. vessel, which last operated in 1981, is now in use as a private, floating clubhouse.)*

**MU-7 — ERIE MARITIME MUSEUM, ERIE, PA – (814) 452-2744**

| | | | | | | | | |
|---|---|---|---|---|---|---|---|---|
| | Niagara | 2B | 1988 | W | 295* | 198' 00" | 32' 00" | 10' 06" |

*(Reconstruction of Oliver Hazard Perry's U. S. Navy brigantine from the War of 1812)*

**MU-8 — GREAT LAKES CENTER FOR MARINE HISTORY, ST. IGNACE, MI**

| | | | | | | | | |
|---|---|---|---|---|---|---|---|---|
| | Maple [WAGL-234] | | 1939 | D | 350* | 122' 03" | 27' 00" | 7' 06"* |

*(USCGC Maple [WLI / WAGL-234] '39 - '73, Roger R. Simons '73 - '94)*
*(Former U. S. Coast Guard "122-Foot" class lighthouse tender [WLI / WAGL-234] / EPA vessel)*

**MU-9 — GREAT LAKES CLIPPER PRESERVATION ASSOCIATION, MUSKEGON, MI – (231) 755-0990**

| | | | | | | | | |
|---|---|---|---|---|---|---|---|---|
| | Milwaukee Clipper | PA | 1905 | Q | 4,272 | 361' 00" | 45' 00" | 28' 00" |

*(Juniata '04 - '41) (Former Wisconsin & Michigan Steamship Co. vessel last operated in 1970)*

**MU-10 — GREAT LAKES HISTORICAL SOCIETY, CLEVELAND, OH – (800) 893-1485**

| | | | | | | | | |
|---|---|---|---|---|---|---|---|---|
| | Cod [IXSS-224] | | 1943 | D/V | 1,525* | 311' 08" | 27' 02" | 33' 09" |

*(Former U.S. Navy "Albacore (Gato)" class submarine [SS / AGSS / IXSS-224])*

**MU-11 — GREAT LAKES NAVAL MEMORIAL AND MUSEUM, MUSKEGON, MI – (231) 755-1230**

| | | | | | | | | |
|---|---|---|---|---|---|---|---|---|
| | Hammond Bay | TB | 1953 | D | 23* | 45' 00" | 13' 00" | 7' 00"* |

*(Former U.S. Army Corps of Engineers tugboat)*

| | | | | | | | | |
|---|---|---|---|---|---|---|---|---|
| | LST-393 | | 1942 | D | 2,100 | 328' 00" | 50' 00" | 25' 00" |

*(USS LST-393 '42 - '47, Highway 16 '47 - '99)*
*(Former U. S. Navy / Wisconsin & Michigan Steamship Co. vessel last operated July 31, 1973)*

**Brig Niagara, War of 1812 veteran, pays a visit to Put-In-Bay.** *(Roger LeLievre)*

| Fleet #. | Fleet Name<br>Vessel Name | Type of<br>Vessel | Year<br>Built | Type of<br>Engine | Cargo Cap.<br>or Gross* | Overall<br>Length | Breadth | Depth or<br>Draft* |
|---|---|---|---|---|---|---|---|---|
| | McLane  **[WMEC-146]** | | 1927 | D | 289* | 125' 00" | 24' 00" | 12' 06" |
| | *(USCGC McLane [WSC / WMEC-146] '27 - '70, Manatra II '70 - '93)* | | | | | | | |
| | *(Former U. S. Coast Guard "Buck & A Quarter" class medium endurance cutter)* | | | | | | | |
| | Michigan | CS | 1971 | B | | 120' 00" | 33' 00" | 3' 06"* |
| | *(Former U.S. Army Corps of Engineers barge)* | | | | | | | |
| | Silversides  **[AGSS-236]** | | 1941 | D/V | 1,526* | 311' 08" | 27' 03" | 33' 09" |
| | *(Former U. S. Navy "Albacore (Gato)" class submarine)* | | | | | | | |

**MU-12  H. LEE WHITE MARINE MUSEUM, OSWEGO, NY – 315) 342-0480**

| Fleet #. | Fleet Name<br>Vessel Name | Type of<br>Vessel | Year<br>Built | Type of<br>Engine | Cargo Cap.<br>or Gross* | Overall<br>Length | Breadth | Depth or<br>Draft* |
|---|---|---|---|---|---|---|---|---|
| | LT-5 | TB | 1943 | D | 305* | 115' 00" | 28' 00" | 14' 00" |
| | *(Major Elisha K. Henson '43 - '47, U. S. Army LT-5 '47 - '47, Nash '47 - '95)* | | | | | | | |
| | *(Former U. S. Army Corps of Engineers vessel last operated in 1989)* | | | | | | | |

**MU-13  HARBOR HERITAGE SOCIETY, CLEVELAND, OH – (216) 574-6262**

| | William G. Mather {2} | BC | 1925 | T | 13,950 | 618' 00" | 62' 00" | 32' 00" |
|---|---|---|---|---|---|---|---|---|
| | *(Former Cleveland-Cliffs Steamship Co. vessel last operated Dec. 21, 1980)* | | | | | | | |

**MU-14  HMCS FRASER, BRIDGEWATER, NS - (902) 543-1169**

| | Fraser  **[DDH-233]** | | 1957 | T | 2,858* | 366' 00" | 42' 00" | 19' 08"* |
|---|---|---|---|---|---|---|---|---|
| | *(Former Royal Canadian Navy "St. Laurent (River)" class helicopter-carrying frigate)* | | | | | | | |

**MU-15  IRVIN ORE BOAT TOURS, DULUTH, MN – (218) 722-7876**

| | Lake Superior | TB | 1943 | D | 248* | 114' 00" | 26' 00" | 13' 08" |
|---|---|---|---|---|---|---|---|---|
| | *(Major Emil H. Block '43 - '47, U. S. Army LT-18 '47 - '50)* | | | | | | | |
| | *(Former U. S. Army Corps of Engineers vessel last operated in 1995)* | | | | | | | |
| | William A. Irvin | BC | 1938 | T | 14,050 | 610' 09" | 60' 00" | 32' 06" |
| | *(Former United States Steel Corp. vessel last operated Dec. 16, 1978)* | | | | | | | |

**MU-16  LAKE COUNTY HISTORICAL SOCIETY, TWO HARBORS, MN – (218) 834-4898**

| | Edna G. | TB | 1896 | R | 154* | 102' 00" | 23' 00" | 14' 06" |
|---|---|---|---|---|---|---|---|---|
| | *(Former Duluth, Missabe & Iron Range Railroad tug last operated in 1981)* | | | | | | | |

**MU-17  LE SAULT DE SAINTE MARIE HISTORIC SITES, INC., SAULT STE. MARIE, MI – (906) 632-3658**

| | Valley Camp {2} | BC | 1917 | R | 12,000 | 550' 00" | 58' 00" | 31' 00" |
|---|---|---|---|---|---|---|---|---|
| | *(Louis W. Hill '17 - '55)  (Former Republic Steel Corp. vessel last operated in 1966)* | | | | | | | |

**MU-18  MARINE MUSEUM OF THE GREAT LAKES AT KINGSTON, KINGSTON, ON – (613) 542-2261**

| | Alexander Henry | IB | 1959 | D | 1,674* | 210' 00" | 44' 00" | 17' 09" |
|---|---|---|---|---|---|---|---|---|
| | *(Former Canadian Coast Guard vessel was retired in 1985)* | | | | | | | |

**MU-19  MARINE MUSEUM OF UPPER CANADA, TORONTO, ON – (416) 392-1765**

| | Ned Hanlan | TB | 1932 | R | 105* | 79' 06" | 19' 00" | 9' 09" |
|---|---|---|---|---|---|---|---|---|
| | *(Former Municipality of Toronto vessel last operated in 1965)* | | | | | | | |

**MU-20  MARITIME MUSEUM OF THE ATLANTIC, HALIFAX, NS - (902) 424-7490**

| | Acadia | RV | 1913 | R | 846* | 170' 00" | 33' 06" | 12' 00"* |
|---|---|---|---|---|---|---|---|---|
| | *(Former Royal Canadian Navy research vessel)* | | | | | | | |

**MU-21  MUSEUM OF SCIENCE AND INDUSTRY, CHICAGO, IL – (773) 684-1414**

| | U-505 | | 1941 | D/V | 1,178* | 252' 00" | 22' 04" | 15' 05"* |
|---|---|---|---|---|---|---|---|---|
| | *(Former German Type IX-C submarine, captured by the U. S. Navy Task Group 22.3 in the Atlantic* | | | | | | | |
| | *Ocean off Africa on June 4, 1944)* | | | | | | | |

**MU-22  MUSEUM SHIP WILLIS B. BOYER, TOLEDO, OH –  (419) 936-3070**

| | Willis B. Boyer | BC | 1911 | T | 15,000 | 617' 00" | 64' 00" | 33' 01" |
|---|---|---|---|---|---|---|---|---|
| | *(Col. James M. Schoonmaker '11 - '69)* | | | | | | | |
| | *(Former Cleveland-Cliffs Steamship Co. vessel last operated in 1980)* | | | | | | | |

**MU-23  NORISLE: TOWNSHIP OF ASSIGINACK, MANITOWANING, ON – (705) 859-3905**

| | Norisle | PA | 1946 | R | 1,668* | 215' 09" | 36' 03" | 16' 00" |
|---|---|---|---|---|---|---|---|---|
| | *(Former Ontario Northland Transportation Commission vessel last operated in 1974)* | | | | | | | |

**MU-24  PARKS CANADA, OTTAWA, ON** *(Vessel is scheduled to become a museum in Hamilton in 2003)*

| | Haida  **[G-63]** | | 1943 | T | 2,744* | 377' 00" | 37' 06" | 15' 02" |
|---|---|---|---|---|---|---|---|---|
| | *(Former Royal Canadian Navy "Tribal" class destroyer [G-63 / DDE-215].* | | | | | | | |

| Fleet #. | Fleet Name<br>Vessel Name | Type of<br>Vessel | Year<br>Built | Type of<br>Engine | Cargo Cap.<br>or Gross* | Overall<br>Length | Breadth | Depth or<br>Draft* |
|---|---|---|---|---|---|---|---|---|
| MU-25 | **PETERSEN STEAMSHIP CO., DOUGLAS, MI – (616) 857-2464** | | | | | | | |
| | Keewatin {2} | PA | 1907 | Q | 3,856* | 346' 00" | 43' 08" | 26' 06" |
| | *(Former Canadian Pacific Railway Co. vessel last operated Nov. 29, 1965)* | | | | | | | |
| | Reiss | TB | 1913 | R | 99* | 80' 00" | 20' 00" | 12' 06" |
| | *(Q. A. Gillmore '13 - '32)  (Former Reiss Steamship Co. tug last operated in 1969)* | | | | | | | |
| MU-26 | **PORT HURON MUSEUM OF ARTS & HISTORY, PORT HURON, MI – (810) 982-0891** | | | | | | | |
| | WLV-526   **[HURON]** | | 1920 | D | 392* | 96' 05" | 24' 00" | 10' 00"* |
| | *(Former U. S. Coast Guard 96-foot-class lightship was retired Aug. 25, 1970)* | | | | | | | |
| MU-27 | **S. S. CITY OF MILWAUKEE - NATIONAL HISTORIC LANDMARK, MANISTEE, MI – (231) 398-0328** | | | | | | | |
| | City of Milwaukee | TF | 1931 | R | 26 rail cars | 360' 00" | 56' 03" | 21' 06" |
| | *(Former Ann Arbor Railroad System vessel last operated in 1981)* | | | | | | | |
| MU-28 | **S. S. METEOR MARITIME MUSEUM, SUPERIOR, WI – (715) 392-5742** | | | | | | | |
| | Meteor {2} | TK | 1896 | R | 40,100 | 380' 00" | 45' 00" | 26' 00" |
| | *(Frank Rockefeller 1896 - '28, South Park '28 - '43)* | | | | | | | |
| | *(Former Cleveland Tankers, Inc. vessel last operated in 1969)* | | | | | | | |
| MU-29 | **ST. MARYS RIVER MARINE CENTRE, SAULT STE. MARIE, ON – (705) 256-7447** | | | | | | | |
| | Norgoma | PA | 1950 | D | 1,477* | 188' 00" | 37' 06" | 22' 06" |
| | *(Former Ontario Northland Transportation Commission vessel last operated in 1974)* | | | | | | | |
| MU-30 | **STE. CLAIRE FOUNDATION, CLEVELAND, OH** | | | | | | | |
| | Ste. Claire | PA | 1910 | R | 870* | 197' 00" | 65' 00" | 14' 00" |
| | *(Last operated Sept.2, 1991;  Undergoing restoration at Toledo, OH)* | | | | | | | |
| MU-31 | **STEAMER COLUMBIA FOUNDATION, DETROIT, MI** | | | | | | | |
| | Columbia {2} | PA | 1902 | R | 968* | 216' 00" | 60' 00" | 13' 06" |
| | *(Last operated Sept. 2, 1991 – Laid up at Ecorse, MI. At press time indications were that the vessel has been sold to an East Coast preservation group and will leave the lakes in 2003)* | | | | | | | |
| MU-32 | **THE CANADIAN NAVAL MEMORIAL TRUST, HALIFAX, NS - (902) 429-2132** | | | | | | | |
| | Sackville   **[K-181]** | | 1941 | T | 1,170* | 208' 00" | 33' 00" | 17' 06" |
| | *(Former Royal Canadian Navy "Flower" class corvette)* | | | | | | | |
| MU-33 | **WISCONSIN MARITIME MUSEUM, MANITOWOC, WI – (920) 684-0218** | | | | | | | |
| | Cobia   **[AGSS-245]** | | 1944 | D/V | 1,500* | 311' 09" | 27' 03" | 33' 09" |
| | *(Former U. S. Navy "Emergency Program (Gato)" class submarine)* | | | | | | | |

# MARINE MUSEUMS ASHORE

### Information can change without notice. Call ahead to verify location and hours.

**ANTIQUE BOAT MUSEUM, 750 MARY ST., CLAYTON, NY – (315) 686-4104 –** A large collection of fresh-water boats and engines. Annual show is the first weekend of August.  Open May 15-October 15.

**ASHTABULA MARINE & U.S. COAST GUARD MEMORIAL MUSEUM, 1071 WALNUT BLVD., ASHTABULA, OH – (440) 964-6847:** Housed in the 1898-built former lighthouse-keeper's residence, the museum includes models, paintings, artifacts, photos, the world's only working scale model of a Hulett ore unloading machine and the pilothouse from the steamer **Thomas Walters**. Open April-October.

**BAYFIELD MARITIME MUSEUM, FIRST STREET, BAYFIELD, WI – (715) 779-9919:** Exhibits explore com-mercial fishing, boatbuilding, lighthouses and shipwrecks.  Memorial Day-early October.

**CANAL PARK MARINE MUSEUM, ALONGSIDE THE SHIP CANAL, DULUTH, MN – (218) 727-2497:** Museum provides displays, historic artifacts and programs that explain the roles of Duluth and Superior in Great Lakes shipping as well as the job of the U.S. Army Corps of Engineers in maintaining the nation's waterways. Many excellent models and other artifacts are on display. Open all year.

**COLLINGWOOD MUSEUM, MEMORIAL PARK, COLLINGWOOD, ON – (705) 445-4811:** More than 100 years of shipbuilding, illustrated with models, photos and videos. Open all year.

**DOOR COUNTY MARITIME MUSEUM, 120 N. MADISON AVE., STURGEON BAY, WI – (920) 743-5958:** Many excellent models help portray the role shipbuilding has played in the Door Peninsula. Refurbished pilothouse on display. Open all year.

**DOSSIN GREAT LAKES MUSEUM, 100 THE STRAND, BELLE ISLE, DETROIT, MI – (313) 852-4051:** Models, photographs, interpretive displays, the smoking room from the 1912 passenger steamer **City of Detroit III**, an anchor from the **Edmund Fitzgerald** and the pilothouse from the steamer **William Clay Ford** are on display. Open all year.

**FAIRPORT HARBOR MUSEUM, 129 SECOND ST., FAIRPORT, OH – (440) 354-4825:** Located in the Fairport Lighthouse, displays include the pilothouse from the lake carrier **Frontenac** and the mainmast of the first **U.S.S. Michigan**. Open late May-Labor Day.

**GREAT LAKES HISTORICAL SOCIETY, 480 MAIN ST., VERMILION, OH – (800) 893-1485:** Museum tells the story of the Great Lakes through ship models, paintings, exhibits and artifacts, including engines and other machinery. Pilothouse of retired laker **Canopus** and a replica of the Vermilion lighthouse are on display. Museum open all year. An affiliated operation is the **U.S.S. Cod**, on display in Cleveland.

**GREAT LAKES SHIPWRECK MUSEUM, WHITEFISH POINT, MI – (906) 635-1742 or (800)-635-1742:** Located next to the Whitefish Point lighthouse, the museum includes lighthouse and shipwreck artifacts, a shipwreck video theater, the restored lighthouse-keeper's quarters and an **Edmund Fitzgerald** display that includes the ship's bell. Open May 15-October 15.

**LE SAULT DE SAINTE MARIE HISTORIC SITES, INC., 501 EAST WATER ST., SAULT STE. MARIE, MI – (906)-632-3658:** The 1917-built steamer **Valley Camp**, which once sailed for the Republic Steel Co., is the centerpiece of this extensive museum. Dedicated in 1968, the Valley Camp's three vast cargo holds house artifacts, ship models, aquariums, photos and other memorabilia, as well as a tribute to the **Edmund Fitzgerald** that includes the ill-fated vessel's lifeboats. Extensive gift shop offers a large selection of nautical books and other items. Tours available. Open May 15-October 15.

**MARITIME MUSEUM OF SANDUSKY, 125 MEIGS ST., SANDUSKY, OHIO – (419) 624-0274:** Exhibits explore local maritime history. Open all year.

**MARQUETTE MARINE MUSEUM, EAST RIDGE & LAKESHORE DR., MARQUETTE, MI – (906) 226-2006:** Located in an 1890s waterworks building, the museum re-creates the offices of the first commercial fishing and passenger freight companies. Displays also include charts, photos, models and maritime artifacts. Open May 31-September 30.

**MICHIGAN MARITIME MUSEUM, 260 DYCKMAN AVE., SOUTH HAVEN, MI – (616) 637-8078:** Exhibits dedicated to the U.S. Lifesaving Service and U.S. Coast Guard. Displays tell the story of various kinds of boats and their uses on the Great Lakes. Open all year.

**OWEN SOUND MARINE – RAIL MUSEUM, 1165 FIRST AVE., OWEN SOUND, ON – (519) 371-3333:** Museum depicts the history of each industry (but leans more toward the marine end) through displays, models and photos. Seasonal.

**PORT COLBORNE MARINE & HISTORICAL MUSEUM, 280 KING ST., PORT COLBORNE, ON – (905) 834-7604:** Wheelhouse from the steam tug **Yvonne Dupre Jr.**, an anchor from the propeller ship **Raleigh** and a lifeboat from the steamer **Hochelaga** are among the museum's displays. Open May-December.

**U.S. ARMY CORPS OF ENGINEERS MUSEUM, SOO LOCKS VISITOR CENTER, E. PORTAGE AVE., SAULT STE. MARIE, MI – (906) 632-3311:** Exhibits include a working model of the Soo Locks, historic photos and a 25-minute film. Also, three observation decks adjacent to the MacArthur Lock provide an up-close view of ships locking through. No admission; open May-November. Check at the Visitor Center information desk for a list of vessels expected at the locks.

**WELLAND CANAL VISITOR CENTRE, AT LOCK 3, THOROLD, ON – (905) 984-8880:** Museum traces the development of the Welland Canal. Museum and adjacent gift shop open year 'round. Observation deck open during the navigation season. Check at the information desk for vessels expected at Lock 3.

**WISCONSIN MARITIME MUSEUM, 75 MARITIME DRIVE, MANITOWOC, WI – (920) 684-0218:** Displays explore the history of area shipbuilding and also honor submariners and submarines built in Manitowoc. The World War II submarine Cobia is adjacent to the museum and open for tours. Open all year.

# Extra Tonnage

A shipyard worker stands beneath the 1,000-footer Edgar B. Speer's propeller.
(Roger LeLievre)

## MEANINGS OF BOAT WHISTLES

**1 SHORT:** I intend to leave you on my port side (answered by same if agreed upon)

**2 SHORT:** I intend to leave you on my starboard side (answered by same if agreed upon)

   (Passing arrangements may be agreed upon by radio. If so, no whistle signal is required.)

**5 OR MORE SHORT BLASTS SOUNDED RAPIDLY:** Danger.

**1 PROLONGED:** Vessel leaving dock

**3 SHORT:** Operating astern propulsion

**1 PROLONGED, SOUNDED AT INTERVALS OF NOT MORE THAN 2 MINUTES:** Vessel moving in restricted visibility

**1 SHORT, 1 PROLONGED, 1 SHORT:** Vessel at anchor in restricted visibility (optional). May be accompanied by the ringing of a bell on the forward part of the ship and a gong on the after end.

**3 PROLONGED and 2 SHORT:** Salute (formal)

**1 PROLONGED and 2 SHORT:** Salute (commonly used)

**3 PROLONGED and 1 SHORT:** International Shipmasters' Association member's salute

*Some of the above signals are listed in the pilot rules. Others have been adopted through common use.*

## MAJOR GREAT LAKES LOADING PORTS

| Iron Ore | Limestone | Coal | Grain | Cement |
|---|---|---|---|---|
| Duluth, MN | Port Inland, MI | Superior, WI | Thunder Bay, ON | Charlevoix, MI |
| Superior, WI | Cedarville, MI | Chicago, IL | Duluth, MN | Alpena, MI |
| Two Harbors, MN | Drummond | Toledo, OH | Milwaukee, WI | |
| Marquette, MI |   Island, MI | Sandusky, OH | Chicago, IL | **Petroleum** |
| Escanaba, MI | Calcite, MI | Ashtabula, OH | Sarnia, ON | Sarnia, ON |
| | Stoneport, MI | Conneaut, OH | Toledo, OH | E. Chicago, IL. |
| | Marblehead, OH | | | |

## MAJOR UNLOADING PORTS

The primary iron ore and limestone receiving ports are Cleveland, Chicago, Gary, Burns Harbor, Indiana Harbor, Detroit, Toledo, Ashtabula and Conneaut. Coal is carried by self-unloaders to power plants in the U.S. and Canada. Most grain loaded on the lakes is destined for export via the St. Lawrence Seaway. Cement is delivered to terminals from Lake Superior to Lake Ontario. Tankers bring petroleum products to cities as diverse in size as Cleveland, Detroit, Escanaba and Muskegon. Self-unloaders carry limestone, road salt and sand to cities throughout the region.

**Charles M. Beeghly unloads coal at Marquette. The ore dock is at left.** *(Rod Burdick)*

# THE SOO LOCKS

## American Locks

### MacArthur Lock

Named after World War II Gen. Douglas MacArthur, the MacArthur Lock is 800-feet long (243.8 meters) between inner gates, 80-feet wide (24.4 meters) and 31-feet deep (9.4 meters) over the sills. The lock was built by the U.S. in the war years 1942-'43 and opened to traffic July 11, 1943. The maximum-sized vessel that can transit the MacArthur Lock is 730-feet long (222.5 meters) by 76-feet wide (23 meters). In emergencies, this limit may be exceeded for vessels up to 767-feet in length (233.8 meters).

### Poe Lock

The Poe Lock is 1,200-feet long (365.8 meters), 110-feet wide (33.5 meters) and has a depth over the sills of 32-feet (9.8 meters). Named after Col. Orlando M. Poe, it was built by the U.S. in the years 1961-'68. The lock's vessel limit is 1,100 feet long (335.3 meters) by 105 feet wide (32 meters). There are currently more than 30 vessels sailing the lakes restricted by size to the Poe Lock.

### Davis Lock

Named after Col. Charles E.L.B. Davis, the Davis Lock measures 1,350-feet long (411.5 meters) between inner gates, 80 feet-wide (24.4 meters) and 23-feet deep (7 meters) over the sills. It was built in the years 1908-'14 and now sees limited use due to its shallow depth.

### Sabin Lock

Measuring the same as the Davis Lock, the Sabin Lock was built from 1913-'19. Named after L.C. Sabin, the lock is currently inactive.

## St. Marys River

Connecting Lake Superior with Lake Huron, the 80-mile (128.7 km) long St. Marys River includes breathtaking scenery, picturesque islands and its share of hazardous twists and turns.

Remote Isle Parisienne marks the river's beginning; the equally-lonely DeTour Reef Light marks its end. Between are two marvels of engineering, the West Neebish Cut, a channel literally dynamited out of solid rock, and the Soo Locks, which stand where Native Americans in dugout canoes once challenged the St. Marys Rapids.

Vessels in the St. Marys River system are under control of the U.S. Coast Guard at Sault Ste. Marie, MI, and are required to check in with Soo Traffic on VHF Ch.12 (156.600 Mhz) at various locations in the river. In the vicinity of the locks, they fall under jurisdiction of the Lockmaster, who must be contacted on VHF Ch. 14 (156.700 Mhz) for lock assignments. Many vessels are also equipped with Automated Information System (AIS) transponders which electronically transmit their positions and other data.

The first lock was built on the Canadian side of the river by the Northwest Fur Co. in 1797-98. That lock was 38-feet (11.6 meters) long and barely 9-feet (2.7 meters) wide.

The first ship canal on the American side, known as the State Canal, was built from 1853-55 by engineer Charles T. Harvey. There were two tandem locks on masonry, each 350-feet (106.7 meters) long by 70 feet (21.3 meters) wide, with a lift of about 9-feet (2.7 meters).

The canal was destroyed in 1888 by workers making way for newer and bigger locks. ▶

**Aerial view of the Soo Locks shows, from left, the MacArthur and Poe locks, and the inactive Davis and Sabin locks.** *(Roger LeLievre)*

## A New Soo Lock?

Discussion continues about building a new lock in the space now occupied by the Davis and Sabin locks. It would relieve the pressure on the Poe, the only lock now able to handle vessels more than 730-feet (222.5 meters) long and/or 76-feet (23 meters) wide.

Cost of such a lock was estimated at $225 million in 1999. If built, it would be paid for by the U.S. federal government and the states surrounding the Great Lakes.

Although it looked like construction might start on a new lock in 2002, an economic downturn and other factors have led to further postponement of the project.

### The Canadian Canal

The present Canadian Lock has its origins in a canal constructed during the years 1887-'95 through the red sandstone rock of St. Marys Island on the north side of the St. Marys Rapids. The most westerly canal on the Seaway route, the waterway measures 7,294-feet (2,223.4 meters), or about 1.4 miles (2.2 km) long, from end to end of upper and lower piers. A 900-foot (274.3 meters) long lock served vessels until the collapse of a lock wall in 1987 closed the waterway.

In 1998, after $10.3 million in repairs, a much smaller lock opened, built inside the old lock chamber. Operated by Parks Canada, it is used mainly by pleasure craft, tugs and tour boats.

All traffic through the Soo Locks passes toll-free.
Locks in the Seaway system operate on gravity – no pumps are used.

# THE WELLAND CANAL

The 27-mile long (43.7 km) Welland Canal, which was built to bypass nearby Niagara Falls, overcomes a difference in water level of 326.5 feet (99.5 meters) between lakes Erie and Ontario.

The first Welland Canal opened in 1829; the present (fourth) canal opened officially on Aug. 6, 1932 with the passage of the steamer Lemoyne. Each of the seven Welland Canal locks has an average lift of 46.5 feet (14.2 meters). All locks (except Lock 8) are 859-feet (261.8 meters) long, 80-feet (24.4 meters) wide and 30-feet (9.1 meters) deep. Lock 8, at 1,380 feet (420.6 km), is the longest lock in the world.

The maximum sized vessel that may transit the canal is 740-feet (225.5 meters) long, 78-feet (23.8 meters) wide and 26-feet (7.9 meters) in draft. Connecting channels are kept dredged to a minimum of 27-feet (8.2 meters).

**Locks 1, 2** and **3** are at St. Catharines, on the Lake Ontario end of the waterway. At Lock 3, the Welland Canal Viewing Center and Museum houses an

**Two saltwater vessels pass at Lock 6 in the Welland Canal.** *(Peter Jobe)*

information desk (which posts a list of vessels expected at the lock), a gift shop and restaurant. At Thorold, **locks 4, 5** and **6**, twinned to help speed passage of vessels, are controlled with an elaborate interlocking system for safety. These locks (positioned end to end, they resemble a short flight of stairs) have an aggregate lift of 139.5 feet (42.5 meters) and are similar to the Gatun Locks on the Panama Canal. Just south of locks 4, 5 and 6 is **Lock 7**. **Lock 8**, seven miles (11.2 km) upstream at Port Colborne, completes the process, making the final adjustment to Lake Erie's level.

In 1973, a new channel was constructed to replace the section of the canal that bisected the city of Welland. The Welland bypass eliminated long delays for ship navigation, road and rail traffic.

The average passage time for the Welland Canal is about 12 hours, with the majority spent transiting locks 4-7. Vessels passing through the Welland Canal and St. Lawrence Seaway must also carry a qualified pilot.

There are also 11 railway and highway bridges crossing the Welland Canal. The most significant are the landmark vertical-lift bridges that provide a clearance of 126 feet (36.6 meters) for vessels passing underneath. Tunnels at Thorold and South Welland allow vehicle traffic to pass beneath the waterway.

All vessel traffic though the Welland Canal is regulated by a control center. Upbound vessels must call Seaway Welland off Port Weller, on VHF Ch. 14 (156.700 Mhz), while downbound vessels are required to make contact off Port Colborne. Cameras keep vessels under constant observation, and individual locks (and most bridges over the canal) are controlled from the center.

# THE ST. LAWRENCE SEAWAY

The St. Lawrence Seaway is a deep waterway extending some 2,038 miles (3,701.4 km) from the Atlantic Ocean to the head of the Great Lakes at Duluth, including Montreal harbor and the Welland Canal. More specifically, it is a system of locks and canals (U.S. and Canadian), built between 1954 and 1958 at a cost of $474 million and opened in 1959, that allow vessels to pass from Montreal to the Welland Canal at the western end of Lake Ontario. The vessel size limit within this system is 740-feet (225.6 meters) long, 78-feet (23.8 meters) wide and 26-feet (7.9 meters) draft.

Closest to the ocean is the **St. Lambert Lock**, which lifts ships some 15 feet (4.6 meters) from Montreal harbor to the level of the Laprairie Basin, through which the channel sweeps in a great arc 8.5 miles (13.7 km) long, to the second lock. The **Cote St. Catherine Lock**, like the other six St. Lawrence Seaway locks, is built to the dimensions shown in the table at left. The Cote St. Catherine lifts ships from the level of the Laprairie Basin, 30 feet (9.1 meters) to the level of Lake St. Louis, bypassing the Lachine Rapids. Beyond it, the channel runs 7.5 miles (12.1 km) before reaching Lake St. Louis.

### LOCK DIMENSIONS

| | |
|---|---|
| Length | 766' (233.5 meters) |
| Width | 80' (24 meters) |
| Depth | 30' (24.4 meters) |

The **Lower Beauharnois Lock**, bypassing the Beauharnois Power House, lifts ships 41 feet (12.5 meters) and sends them through a short canal to the **Upper Beauharnois Lock**, where they are lifted 41 feet (12.5 meters) to reach the Beauharnois Canal. After a 13 mile (20.9 km) trip in the canal, and a 30-mile (48.3 km) passage through Lake St. Francis, vessels reach the U.S. border and the **Snell Lock**, which has a lift of 45 feet (13.7 meters) and empties into the 10-mile (16.1 km) Wiley-Dondero Canal.

After passing through the Wiley-Dondero, ships are raised another 38 feet (11.6 meters) by the **Dwight D. Eisenhower Lock**, after which they enter Lake St. Lawrence, the pool upon which nearby power-generating stations draw for their turbines located a mile to the north.

At the Western end of Lake St. Lawrence, the **Iroquois Lock** allows ships to bypass the Iroquois Control Dam. The lift here is only about one foot (.3 meters). Once in the waters west of Iroquois, the channel meanders through the Thousand Islands to Lake Ontario and beyond.

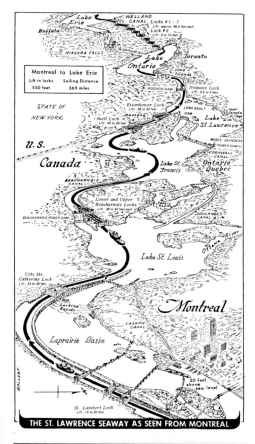

**THE ST. LAWRENCE SEAWAY AS SEEN FROM MONTREAL**

# FOLLOWING THE FLEET

**These prerecorded messages help track vessel arrivals and departures.**

| | | |
|---|---|---|
| Algoma Central Marine .................. | **(905) 708-3873** | ACM vessel movements |
| Boatwatcher's Hotline ..................... | **(218) 722-6489** | Superior, Duluth, Two Harbors, Taconite Harbor and Silver Bay traffic |
| CSX Coal Docks/Torco Dock ......... | **(419) 697-2304** | Toledo, OH, vessel information |
| DMIR Ore Dock ............................ | **(218) 628-4590** | Duluth, MN, vessel information |
| Eisenhower Lock ........................... | **(315) 769-2422** | Eisenhower Lock vessel movements |
| Inland Lakes Management ............ | **(989) 354-4400** | ILM vessel movements |
| Michigan Limestone docks ............ | **(989) 734-2117** | Calcite, MI vessel information |
| Michigan Limestone docks ............ | **(906) 484-2201** | Ext. 503 - Cedarville, MI vessel info. |
| Oglebay Norton Co. ....................... | **(800) 861-8760** | O-N Vessel movements |
| Presque Isle Corp. ....................... | **(989) 595-6611** | Stoneport, MI, vessel information |
| Sarnia Traffic ............................... | **(519) 337-5861** | Vessel traffic, St. Clair, Detroit rivers |
| Soo Traffic .................................... | **(906) 635-3224** | Previous day's traffic – St. Marys River |
| Superior Midwest Energy Terminal | **(715) 395-3559** | Superior, WI, vessel information |
| Thunder Bay Port Authority .......... | **(807) 345-1256** | Thunder Bay, ON, vessel information |
| USS Great Lakes Fleet ................. | **(218) 628-4389** | USS vessel movements |
| Upper Lakes Group ...................... | **(905) 688-5878** | ULG vessel movements |
| Welland Canal .............................. | **(905) 688-6462** | Welland Canal traffic update |

**With a VHF scanner, boatwatchers can tune to ship-to-ship and ship-to-shore traffic, using the following frequency guide.**

| | | |
|---|---|---|
| Commercial vessels only | **Ch. 13** (156.650 Mhz) | Bridge-to-Bridge Communications |
| **Calling / Distress  ONLY** | **Ch. 16** (156.800 Mhz) | **Calling / Distress ONLY** |
| Commercial vessels only | **Ch. 06** (156.300 Mhz) | Working Channel |
| Commercial vessels only | **Ch. 08** (156.400 Mhz) | Working Channel |
| Supply boat at Sault Ste. Marie, MI | **Ch. 08** (156.400 Mhz) | Supply boat Ojibway |
| Detour Reef to Lake St. Clair Light | **Ch. 11** (156.550 Mhz) | Sarnia Traffic - Sector 1 |
| Long Point Light to Lake St. Clair Light | **Ch. 12** (156.600 Mhz) | Sarnia Traffic - Sector 2 |
| Montreal to about mid-Lake St. Francis | **Ch. 14** (156.700 Mhz) | Seaway Beauharnois - Sector 1 |
| Mid-Lake St. Francis to Bradford Island | **Ch. 12** (156.600 Mhz) | Seaway Eisenhower - Sector 2 |
| Bradford Island to Crossover Island | **Ch. 11** (156.550 Mhz) | Seaway Iroquois - Sector 3 |
| Crossover Island to Cape Vincent | **Ch. 13** (156.650 Mhz) | Seaway Clayton - Sector 4 |
| | | St. Lawrence River portion |
| Cape Vincent to mid-Lake Ontario | **Ch. 13** (156.650 Mhz) | Seaway Sodus - Sector 4 |
| | | Lake Ontario portion |
| Mid-Lake Ontario to Welland Canal | **Ch. 11** (156.550 Mhz) | Seaway Newcastle - Sector 5 |
| Welland Canal | **Ch. 14** (156.700 Mhz) | Seaway Welland - Sector 6 |
| Welland Canal to Long Point Light | **Ch. 11** (156.550 Mhz) | Seaway Long Point - Sector 7 |
| St. Marys River Traffic Service | **Ch. 12** (156.600 Mhz) | Soo Traffic, Sault Ste. Marie, MI |
| Lockmaster, Soo Locks | **Ch. 14** (156.700 Mhz) | Soo Lockmaster (call WUE-21) |
| Coast Guard traffic | **Ch. 21** (157.050 Mhz) | United States Coast Guard |
| Coast Guard traffic | **Ch. 22** (157.100 Mhz) | United States Coast Guard |
| U.S. Mailboat, Detroit, MI | **Ch. 10** (156.500 Mhz) | Mailboat J. W. Westcott II |

# Colors of the Great Lakes & Seaway Smokestacks

**A.B.M. Marine**
Thunder Bay, ON

**Algoma Central Marine Group**
Div. of Algoma Central Corp.
St. Catharines, ON

**Algoma Tankers Ltd.**
Div. of Algoma Central Corp.
Dartmouth, NS

**American Canadian Caribbean Line, Inc.**
Warren, RI

**American Marine Construction**
Benton Harbor, MI

**American Steamship Co.**
Williamsville, NY

**Andrie, Inc.**
Muskegon, MI

**Apostle Island Cruise Service**
Bayfield, WI

**Arnold Transit Co.**
Mackinac Island, MI

**Atlantic Towing Ltd.**
St. John, NB

**Basic Towing, Inc.**
Escanaba, MI

**Bay City Boat Lines**
Bay City, MI

**Bay Shipbuilding Co.**
Sturgeon Bay, WI

**Beaver Island Boat Co.**
Charlevoix, MI

**Bethlehem Steel Corp.**
Chesterton, IN

**Bigane Vessel Fueling Co.**
Chicago, IL

**Billington Contracting Inc.**
Duluth, MN

**Blue Circle Cement Co.**
Detroit, MI
Toronto, ON

**Blue Heron Co.**
Tobermory, ON

**Buffalo Public Works Dept.**
Buffalo, NY

**Busch Marine, Inc.**
Carrollton, MI

**Canada Steamship Lines, Inc.**
Montreal, QC

**Canadian Coast Guard**
Ottawa, ON

**Central Marine Logistics, Inc.**
Highland, IN

**Chicago Fire Department**
Chicago, IL

**City of Toronto**
**Park & Recreation Dept.**
Toronto, ON

**Cleveland Fire Department**
Cleveland, OH

**Cleveland Tankers (1991), Inc.**
Algoma Tankers, Ltd. Mgr.
Cleveland, OH

**Clipper Cruise Line**
St. Louis, MO

**Columbia Yacht Club**
Chicago, IL

**Croisieres AML Inc.**
Quebec, QC

**Croisieres Marjolaine, Inc.**
Chicoutimi, QC

**Croisieres Nordik, Inc.**
Div. of Transport Desgagnes, Inc.
Quebec, QC

**C.A. Crosbie Shipping Ltd.**
Montreal, QC

**Dan Minor & Sons, Inc.**
Port Colborne, ON

**Dean Construction Co.**
Belle River, ON

**Detroit City Fire Department**
Detroit, MI

**Diamond Jack's River Tours**
Grosse Ile, MI

**Duc D'Orleans Cruise Boat**
Corunna, ON

**Eastern Canada Towing Ltd.**
Halifax, NS

**Eastern Upper Peninsula Transportation Authority**
Sault Ste. Marie, MI

**Edward E. Gillen Co.**
Milwaukee, WI

**Erie Sand Steamship Co.**
**M/V J.S. St John**
Erie, PA

**Erie Sand Steamship Co.**
**M/V Richard Reiss**
Erie, PA

**Essroc Canada, Inc.**
Upper Lakes Group, Mgr
Downsville, ON

**Federal Terminals Ltd.**
Port Cartier, QC

**Ferriss Marine Contracting Inc.**
Detroit, MI

**Fraser Shipyards, Inc.**
Superior, WI

**Gaelic Tug Boat Co.**
Grosse Ile, MI

**Gananoque Boat Line**
Gananoque,ON

**Gardiner Marine**
Sault Ste. Marie, ON

**Geo, Gradel Co.**
Sandusky, OH

**Godench Elevators, Ltd.**
Goderich, ON

**Goodtime Transit Boats, Inc.**
Cleveland, OH

**Gravel & Lake Services, Ltd.**
**M/V Wolf River**
Thunder Bay, ON

**Gravel & Lake Services, Ltd.**
**Tug Peninsula**
Thunder Bay, ON

**Great Lakes Associates, Inc.**
Rocky River, OH

**Great Lakes Fleet, Inc.**
Duluth, MN

**Great Lakes International Towing & Salvage Ltd.**
Burlington, ON

**Great Lakes Maritime Academy**
Northwestern Michigan College
Traverse City, MI

**Great Lakes Towing Co.**
Cleveland, OH

**Great Lakes Transport Ltd.**
Halifax, NS

**HMC Ship Managment**
Lemont, IL

**Hamilton Harbor Commissioners**
Hamilton, ON

**Hamilton Marine & Engineering Ltd.**
Div. of ULS Corp.
Port Colborne, ON

**Hannah Marine Corp**
Lemont, IL

**Heritage Cruise Lines**
Parry Sound, ON

**Holly Marine Towing**
Chicago, IL

**Inland Bulk Transfer**
Cleveland, OH

**Inland Lakes Management, Inc.**
Alpena, MI

**The Interlake Steamship Co.**
Lakes Shipping Co.
Richfield, OH

**Jacobs Investments**
Cleveland, OH

**Kadinger Marine Service, Inc.**
Milwaukee, WI

**Kent Line Ltd**
St. John, NB

**Keystone Great Lakes, Inc.**
**Tug Michigan**
Bala Cynwyd, PA

**Kindra Lake Towing Co.**
Downer's Grove, IL

**King Company Inc.**
Holland, MI

**Lafarge Cement Corp.**
Toronto, ON

**Lafarge Cement Corp.**
Alpena, MI

**Lake Michigan Carferry Service, Inc.**
Ludington, MI

**Lake Michigan Contractors, Inc.**
Holland, MI

**Le Groupe C.T.M.A. Navigation Madeline Inc.**
Cap-Aux-Meules, QC

**Le Groupe Ocean Inc.**
Quebec, QC

**Lee Marine, Ltd.**
Sombra, ON

**Les Equipment Verreault, Inc.**
Les Mechins, QC

**Lock Tours Canada**
Sault Ste. Marie, ON

**Lower Lakes Towing, Ltd.**
**Lower Lakes Transportation Ltd.**
Port Dover, ON

**Luedtke Engineering Co.**
Frankfort, MI

**M.C.M. Marine Inc.**
Sault Ste Marie, MI

**MacDonald Marine Ltd.**
Goderich, ON

**Madeline Island Ferry Line, Inc.**
LaPointe, WI

**Maid of the Mist Steamboat Co., Ltd.**
Niagara Falls, ON

**Malcom Marine**
St. Clair, MI

**Marine Atlantic, Inc.**
Moncton, NB

**Marine Tech Inc.**
Duluth, MN

**Mariposa Cruise Line**
Toronto, ON

**McAllister Towing & Salvage, Inc.**
**Subsidiary of Le Groupe Ocean, Inc.**
Montreal, QC

**McAsphalt Marine Transportation**
Upper Lakes Group, Mgr.

**McKeil Marine Ltd.**
**M/V Capt. Ralph Tucker**
Hamilton, ON

**McKeil Marine Ltd.**
Hamilton, ON

**McNally Marine, Inc**
Toronto, ON

**Miller Boat Line, Inc.**
Put-In-Bay, OH

**Museum Ship CCGC Alexander Henry**
Scarborough, ON

**Museum Tug Edna G**
Two Harbors, MN

**Museum Ship HMCS Haida**
Hamilton, ON

**Museum Ship Keewatin**
Douglas, MI

**Museum Ships USS Little Rock USS The Sullivans**
Buffalo, NY

**Museum Ship Meteor**
Superior, WI

**Museum Ship City of Milwaukee**
Manistee, MI

**Museum Ship Milwaukee Clipper**
Muskegon, MI

**Museum Ships**
**Norgoma** (Sault Ste. Marie,ON)
**Norisle** (Manitowaning,ON)

**Museum Ship Valley Camp**
Sault Ste. Marie, MI

**Museum Ship William A. Irvin**
Duluth, MN

**Museum Ships**
**Willis B. Boyer** (Toledo,OH)
**William G. Mather** (Cleveland,OH)

**Muskoka Lakes Navigation & Hotel Co.**
Gravenhurst, ON

**Nadro Marine Services**
Port Dover, ON

**Neuman's Kelly's Island Ferry**
Sandusky, OH

**Oglebay Norton Marine Services Co.**
Cleveland, OH

**Ontario Ministry of Transportation & Communication**
Kingston, ON

**Osborne Materials Co.**
Mentor, OH

**Owen Sound Transportation Co. Ltd.**
Owen Sound, ON

**Pelee Island Transportation Services**
Pelee Island, ON

**Pere Marquette Shipping Co.**
Ludington, MI

**Provmar Fuels, Inc. Div. of ULS Corporation**
Toronto, ON

**Purvis Marine Ltd.**
Sault Ste. Marie, ON

**Purvis Marine Ltd. M/V Yankcanuck**
Sault Ste. Marie, ON

**Reinauer Transportation Companies, Inc.**
Staten Island, NY

**Rigel Shipping Canada, Inc. Rigel Shipping Co., Inc**
Shediac, NB

**Roen Salvage Co.**
Sturgeon Bay, WI

**Sea Fox Thousand Islands Tours**
Kingston, ON

**Selvick Marine Towing Corp.**
Sturgeon Bay, WI

**Shell Canadian Tankers Ltd.**
Montreal, QC

**Shoreline Sightseeing Co.**
Chicago, IL

**Sivertson's Grand Portage Isle Royale Transportation Lines**
Superior, WI

**Societe des Traversiers du Quebec**
Quebec, QC

**Society Quebecoise D'Exploration Miniere Algoma Central Corp.-Mgr.**
Sault Ste. Marie, ON

**Soo Locks Boat Tours**
Sault Ste. Marie, MI

**St. Lawrence Cruise Lines, Inc.**
Kingston, ON

**St. Lawrence Seaway Management Corp.**
Cornwall, ON

**St. Lawrence Seaway Development Corp.**
Massena, NY

**Three Rivers Boatmen, Inc.**
Trois Rivieres, QC

**Thunder Bay Marine Services Ltd.**
Thunder Bay, On

**Thunder Bay Tug Services**
Thunder Bay, ON

**Transport Desgagnes, Inc.**
Quebec, QC

**Transport Iglooik, Inc.**
Montreal, QC

**Upper Lakes Group Jackes Shipping, Inc.**
Ottawa, ON

**United States Army Corps of Engineers Great Lakes and Ohio River Division**
Chicago, IL

**United States Coast Guard 9th Coast Guard District**
Cleveland, OH

**United States Environmental Protection Agency**
Bay City, MI

**United States Department of the Interior**
Ann Arbor, MI

**United States National Park Service**
Houghton, MI

**University of Michigan Center for Great Lakes & Aquatic Sciences**
Ann Arbor, MI

**Upper Lakes Towing, Inc.**
Escanaba, MI

**Wendella Boat Tours Co.**
Chicago, IL

**Zenith Tugboat Co.**
Duluth, MN

# Colors of Saltwater Fleets

**Alba Shipping Ltd. A/S**
Aalborg, Denmark

**Albamar Shipping Co., S.A.**
Piraeus, Greece

**All-Trust Shipping Co. S.A.**
Piraeus, Greece

**Atlantis Management, Inc.**
Piraeus, Greece

**Atlantska Plovidba**
Dubrovnik, Croatia

**Arklow Shipping Ltd.**
Wicklow, Ireland

**Aurora Shipping, Inc.**
Manila, Philippines

**Azov Shipping Co.**
Mariupol, Ukraine

**B&N Bylok &
Nordsjofraktas**
Oslo, Norway

**B&N Bylok &
Nordsjofraktas**
Oslo, Norway

**Bay Ocean Management, Inc**
Englewood Cliffs, NJ

**Bison Shipmanagement
& Chartering Co. Pte. Ltd.**
Singapore

**Briese Schiffahrts
GMBH & Co. KG**
Leer, Germany

**Canadian Forest
Navigation Co. Ltd.**
Montreal, QC

**Canada Maritime Ltd.**
Hamilton, Bermuda

**Cape Shipping S.A.**
Piraeus, Greece

**Carisbrooke Shipping PLC**
Cowes, UK

**Catsambis Shipping Ltd.**
Piraeus, Greece

**Ceres Hellenic Shipping Enterprises**
Piraeus, Greece

**Chellaram Shipping Ltd.**
Hong Kong, PRC

**China Ocean Shipping Group**
Bejing, PRC

**Commercial Trading &
Discount Co., Ltd.**
Athens, Greece

**Compagnie des Iles
du Ponant
M/V LeLevant**
Nantes, France

**Corner Shipping Co. Ltd.**
Piraeus, Greece

**Dalex Shipping Co. S.A.**
Piraeus, Greece

**Densan Shipping Co. Ltd.**
Istanbul, Turkey

**Det Nordenfjeldske D/S AS**
Trondheim, Norway

**Diana Shipping Agencies S.A.**
Piraeus, Greece

**Dockendale Shipping Co. Ltd.**
Nassau, Bahamas

**Donnelly Shipmanagment Ltd.**
Limassol, Cyprus

**Dorval Kaiuan K.K.**
Tokyo, Japan

**Egon Oldendorff Ltd.**
Luebeck, Germany

**ER Denizcilik Sanayi Nakliyat
ve Ticaret A.S.**
Istanbul, Turkey

**Eidsiva Rederi ASA
Fednav Ltd. Mgr.**
Oslo, Norway

**Eidsiva Rederi ASA**
Oslo, Norway

**Elmira Shipping & Trading S.A.**
Athens, Greece

**Enzian Shipping AG**
Berne, Switzerland

**Fafalios Shipping S.A.**
Piraeus, Greece

**Fednav International Ltd.**
Montreal, QC

**Fednav International Ltd.**
Montreal, QC

**Flinter Groningen B.V.**
Groningen, Netherlands

**Fortum Oil & Gas**
Espoo, Finland

**Gourdomichalis Maritime S.A.**
Piraeus, Greece

**Great Circle Shipping Agency Ltd.**
Bangkok, Thailand

**Great Lakes European Shipping A.S.**
Ornskoldsvik, Sweden

**Hapag Lloyd Cruises M/V c. Columbus**
Hamburg, Germany

**Harbor Shipping & Trading Co. S.A.**
Chios, Greece

**Hilal Shipping, Trading & Industry Co.**
Istanbul, Turkey

**H.S.S. Holland Ship Service B.V.**
Rotterdam, Netherlands

**J.G. Goumas (Shipping) Co.**
Piraeus, Greece

**J.G. Roussos (Shipping) Co. S. A.**
Athens, Greece

**Jo Tankers, B.V.**
Spijkenisse, Netherlands

**Jugoslavenska Oceanska Plovidba**
Kotor, Yugoslavia

**Jumbo Shipping Co. S.A.**
Geneva, Switzerland

**Kil Shipping A/S**
Kristiansand, Norway

**Knutsen O.A.S. Shipping**
Haugesund, Norway

**Krey Schiffahrts GMBH & Co.**
Simonswolde, Germany

**Laurin Maritime, Inc**
Houston, TX

**Lisco Baltic Service**
Klaipeda, Lithuania

**Lykes Lines Ltd.**
Tampa, FL

**Malaysia International Shipping Corp.**
Selangor, Singapore

**Mammoet Shipping Ltd.**
Roosendaahl, Netherlands

**Marbulk Shipping Inc. CSL International Inc., Mgrs.**
Beverly, MS

**Metron Shipping & Agencies, Ltd.**
Piraeus, Greece

**Mikkal Myklebusthaug Rederi**
Fonnes, Norway

**Murmansk Shipping Co.**
Murmansk, Russia

**Navigation Maritime Bulgare Ltd.**
Varna, Bulgaria

**NB Maritime Management**
Limassol, Cyprus

**Nissen Kaiun K.K.**
Hakata, Japan

**Novoship (UK) Ltd.**
London, England

**Orient Overseas Container Line Ltd.**
Hong Kong, PRC

**Oceanbulk Maritime S.A.**
Athens, Greece

**Olympic Shipping and Management S.A.**
Athens, Greece

**Orion Schiffahrts-Gesellschaft**
Hamburg, Germany

**P&O Nedlloyd B.V.**
Rotterdam, Netherlands

**Pacific Ship Managers**
Singapore, Singapore

**Pacific Basin Agencies Ltd.**
**Fednav Ltd. Mgr.**
Hong Kong

**Pan Ocean Shipping Co., Ltd.**
Seoul, South Korea

**Polclip (Luxembourg) S.A.**
Luxembourg, Luxembourg

**Polish Steamship Co.**
Szczecin, Poland

**Primal Ship Management**
Athens, Greece

**Prime Orient Shipping S.A.**
Panama City, Panama

**Prisco (UK) Ltd.**
London, England

**Reederei Hans-Peter Eckhoff Co., H.G.**
Hollenstedt, Germany

**Scandia Shipping Hellas, Inc.**
Athens, Greece

**Scanscot Shipping Services GmbH**
Hamburg, Germany

**Seastar Navigation Co. Ltd.**
Athens, Greece

**Sherimar Management Co. Ltd.**
Athens, Greece

**Shih Wei Navigation Co. Ltd.**
Taipei, Taiwan

**Shipping Corp. of India Ltd.**
Mumbai, India

**Shunzan Kaiun Co., Ltd.**
Ehime, Japan

**Sidemar Servizi Accessori S.p.A.**
Genoa, Italy

**Societe Anonyme Monegasque d' Administration Maritime et Aerienne**
Monte Carlo, Monaco

**Sohtorik Denizcilik ve Ticaret A.S.**
Istanbul, Turkey

**Spar Shipping A.S.**
Bergen, Norway

**Spliethoff's Bevrachtingskantoor Ltd.**
Amsterdam, Netherlands

**Split Ship Management, Ltd.**
Split, Croatia

**Stolt Parcel Tankers**
Greenwich, CT

**Surrendra Overseas Ltd.**
Calcutta, India

**Teo Shipping Corp.**
Piraeus, Greece

**Thenamaris Ships Management, Inc.**
Athens, Greece

**Thoresen & Co. Ltd.**
Bangkok, Thailand

**Tomasos Brothers, Inc.**
Piraeus, Greece

**Torkel Alendal Rederi A.S.**
Karmsund, Norway

**Transman Shipping Enterprises S.A.**
Athens, Greece

**Triton Bereederungs GMBH & Co.**
Leer, Germany

**Union Marine Enterprises S.A.**
Piraeus, Greece

**Univan Ship Management Ltd.**
Hong Kong

**V. Ships (Cyprus) Ltd.**
Limassol, Cyprus

**Vergos Marine Management**
Piraeus, Greece

**Viken Shipping AS**
Bergen, Norway

**W. Bockstiegel Reederei KG**
Emden, Germany

**Wagenborg Shipping B.V.**
Delfzijl, Netherlands

**Yaoki Shipping S.A.**
Japan

**Z&G Halcoussis Co. Ltd.**
Piraeus, Greece

# House Flags of Great Lakes & Seaway Fleets

**Algoma Central
Marine Group**
Sault Ste. Marie, ON

**American Steamship Co.**
Williamsville, NY

**Atlantic Towing Ltd.**
St. John, NB

**Bethlehem Steel Corp.**
Chesterton, IN

**Canada Steamship
Lines, Inc.**
Montreal, QC

**Cleveland Tankers,
(1991) Inc.**
Cleveland, OH

**Erie Sand & Steamship Co.**
Erie, PA

**Fednav Ltd.**
Montreal, QC

**Gaelic Tug Boat Co.**
Grosse Ile, MI

**Great Lakes
Associates Inc.**
Rocky River, OH

**Great Lakes
Fleet, Inc.**
Duluth, MN

**Great Lakes Towing Co.**
Cleveland, OH

**Inland Lakes
Management, Inc.**
Alpena, MI

**Interlake Steamship Co.
Lakes Shipping Co.**
Richfield, OH

**J.W. Westcott Co.**
Detroit, MI

**LaFarge Cement
Corp.**
Montreal, QC

**Lake Michigan
Carferry Service, Inc.**
Ludington, MI

**Lower Lakes
Towing Ltd.**
Port Dover, ON

**McKeil Marine Ltd.**
Hamilton, ON

**McNally Marine, Inc.**
Toronto, ON

**Oglebay Norton
Marine Services Co.**
Cleveland, OH

**Owen Sound
Transportation Co. Ltd.**
Owen Sound, ON

**Purvis Marine Ltd.**
Sault Ste. Marie, ON

**Rigel Shipping Canada, Inc.**
Shediac, NB

**Seaway Marine Transport**
Toronto, ON

**Transport
Desgagnes, Inc.**
Quebec, QC

**Upper Lakes Group, Inc.**
Toronto, ON

**Wagenborg Shipping B.V.**
Delfzijl, Netherlands

# Flags of Major Nations in the Marine Trade

Afghanistan

Antigua & Barbuda

Argentina

Australia

Austria

Azerbaijan

Bahamas

Bahrain

Barbados

Belgium

Belize

Bermuda

Bosnia & Herzegovinia

Brazil

Canada

Cayman Islands

Chile

China

Cote D'Ivoire

Croatia

Cyprus

Czech Republic

Denmark

Dominican Republic

Ecuador

Egypt

Estonia

Ethiopia

Fiji

Finland

France

Germany

Ghana

Greece

Guinea

Haiti

Honduras

Hong Kong

Hungary

Iceland

India

Indonesia

Ireland

Isle of Man

Israel

Italy

Japan

Jordan

Korea-South

Latvia

Liberia

Lithuania

Luxembourg

Malaysia

Malta

Marshall Islands

Mexico

Monaco

Morocco

Mozambique

Myanmar

Netherlands

Netherlands Antilles

New Zealand

Nicaragua

Nigeria

N. Mariana Islands

Norway

Pakistan

Panama

Peru

Philippines

Poland

Portugal

Republic of South Africa

Romania

Russia

Saudi Arabia

Singapore

Solomon Islands

Spain

St. Kitts Nevis

St. Vincent & The Grenadines

Sweden

Switzerland

Syria

Taiwan

Thailand

Trinidad & Tobago

Tunisia

Turkey

Ukraine

United Kingdom

United States

Vanuatu

Venezuela

Vietnam

Yugoslavia

Dangerous Cargo
On Board

Pilot On Board

U.S. Coast Guard
Auxiliary Ensign

U.S. Coast
Guard Ensign

U.S. Army Corps
of Engineers

St. Lawrence Seaway
Development Corp.

St. Lawrence Seaway
Management Corp.

Capt. Henry Jackman fights Lake Erie ice in January, 2003. *(Neil Schultheiss)*